Warfare from
Waterloo to Mons

WARFARE FROM
WATERLOO TO MONS

Michael Glover

CASSELL
LONDON

CASSELL LTD.,
35 Red Lion Square, London WC1R 4SG
and at Sydney, Auckland, Toronto, Johannesburg,
an affiliate of
Macmillan Publishing Co., Inc.,
New York

First published in 1980 by Cassell Ltd.
Edited, designed, and produced by Guild
Publishing, the Original Publications Department
of Book Club Associates

ISBN 0 304 30483 2

Designed by Graham Keen
Picture research by Jonathan Moore

Set in 11 on 12 point Garamond
and printed by
Lowe & Brydone Printers Ltd.,
Thetford, Norfolk

ENDPAPERS: Soldiers
before the battle,
Petersburg 1865

FRONTISPIECE: The Scots
Guards raising the
colours at the Battle of
the Alma, 1855

PAGES 6–7: A section
of the Gettysburg
Panorama, showing
Confederate troops
almost breaking through
the Union line

Contents

INTRODUCTION

This volume of the *History of Warfare* covers the period between the end of the Napoleonic wars and the outbreak of the Great (or First World) War. Thus, in a strict interpretation, Waterloo and Mons lie outside its scope. Nevertheless I have included both as prologue and epilogue respectively. In neither have I attempted a comprehensive description. Instead I have given a deliberately one-sided account intended to illustrate the conditions under which land battles were fought at the beginning and end of the period.

The nineteenth century, if the period between 1815 and 1914 may be so described, saw a revolution in every department of both armies and navies. On land it opened with the battlefield dominated by the musket, a weapon which was scarcely accurate at 80 yards, and ended with the machine-gun and the aeroplane. In 1815 navies consisted of sailing ships which engaged each other at 'half pistol shot', about 30 feet. By 1914 battleships powered by oil turbines could throw missiles weighing a ton to a range of 10 miles. This book is about the ways in which soldiers and sailors learned to cope with the new weapons and other devices which technicians handed to them with bewildering rapidity.

As centuries go, the nineteenth century was not notably bellicose. There were longer periods of peace than occurred in, for example, the eighteenth century. Nevertheless it has not been possible, in a book of this size, to cover all the wars that were fought. The long struggle in which Spain tried to hold her American empire, the Carlist wars, the Sikh wars, the Indian Mutiny, and several of the recurrent Russo–Turkish wars have all had to be omitted. On the other hand I have included several wars which do not always find their way into history books but which, to me, seem to illustrate the advances in, or the limitations to, military or naval capabilities.

I have divided the century into four periods corresponding, roughly, to the main development in armaments. The first of these (1815–39) covers the end of the flintlock era on land and of purely sailing ships at sea. In the next (1840–65) came the percussion cap, the naval shell gun and steam-assisted warships. The third period (1866–91) was dominated by the breech-loading rifle and the ironclad while in the fourth (1892–1914) came the final and fastest developments while Europe prepared to plunge herself once more into an all-embracing struggle. This was the period which saw the arrival of the machine-gun, the magazine rifle, smokeless powder, the quick-firer, the super-heavy gun, the motor vehicle, the aeroplane, the *Dreadnought*, and the submarine.

To avoid distracting switches of attention from the land to the sea, I have grouped the naval chapters at the junctions between parts I and II and between parts III and IV.

Important though it was to every fighting man, I have not attempted to describe the advances made in medical science during the nineteenth century. Military and naval medicine is a vital part of all military history but it should not be attempted by a layman.

Waterloo

*In the name and on behalf of His Majesty,
George P.R.
George the Third, by the Grace of God, of the
United Kingdom of Great Britain and Ireland, King,
Defender of the Faith, to our right trusty and right
entirely well beloved Cousin and Counsillor, Arthur,
Duke of Wellington, Knight of the Most Noble
Order of the Garter, Knight Grand Cross of the
Most Honourable Order of the Bath, Field Marshal
of our Forces, Greeting. We, reposing especial trust
in your loyalty, courage and good conduct, do by
these presents constitute and appoint you to be
Commander of our Forces serving on the Continent
of Europe during our pleasure. You are therefore
carefully and diligently to discharge the said trust of
Commander of our Forces by doing and performing
all and all manner of things thereto belonging.
Given at our court at Carlton House, the twenty-
eighth day of March 1815, in the fifty-fifth year of
our reign.*

Wellington was in Vienna when this imposing document was drawn up, but on the morning of the following day he set out for the Netherlands accompanied by two aides-de-camp and 'proceeding without delay, we reached Frankfort on the 2nd and arrived at Brussels on the 5th of April'. Napoleon had returned from exile in Elba on 1 March 1815 and had been acclaimed Emperor again eighteen days later.

On arrival the Duke found a letter from the Horse Guards apologising for his army. 'It is to be wished that you had a more

efficient army, composed of British materials but I earnestly hope that . . . by degrees we shall be enabled to augment your force. Empty tonnage has been despatched to bring home the army from America and we may expect the troops that composed the Mississippi expedition to arrive very soon. The Guards will march for embarkation about Tuesday or Wednesday next. They were unfortunately but unavoidably delayed in their preparation, owing to a wish not to weaken London until every symptom of riot was at an end.' Ten days later another letter added to the tale of woe. 'The 2nd battalion 59th Foot, which sailed from Ireland full three weeks ago for Ostend, but had not since been heard of, I am happy to say have arrived in Wales, and have sailed again for Ostend.'

Wellington's army when he reached Brussels amounted to only 18,800 British troops (of whom 6,000 were Germans in British pay) and even they were heavily diluted by recruits to replace time-expired men. There were far too few of the men he had hoped to find, his veterans of the Peninsula, 'my old Spanish infantry'. It was understandable that, in his early days in Brussels, the Duke complained that he had 'an infamous army, very weak and ill-equipped, and a very inexperienced staff'. It was inevitable that the staff should be inexperienced. The men who had administered the army in Spain and Portugal were regimental officers who had been

ABOVE: The Coldstream Guards defending Wellington's forward bastion, the château at Hougoumont

PREVIOUS PAGE: The Scots Greys capturing the French eagle at Waterloo

returned to their regiments as soon as the Peninsular campaigns ended. The British army only possessed ten full-time staff officers below the rank of colonel. These were the Permanent Assistants in the Quartermaster General's Department, so called because they rarely served in the Quartermaster General's Department. Three of them eventually found their way to the Netherlands but, in April 1815 there 'are a good many here whom I must remove to make room for those more capable of doing the duty'.

Before mid-June the army had expanded to 88,000 men but only 33,000 of them were British and many of the remainder were more than suspect of Bonapartist sympathies. As the army grew in size so did the problem of feeding it. Each British soldier required each day 1lb. of meat, 1½lb. of bread or 1lb. of biscuit, and a quart of beer or a pint of wine or ⅓ pint of spirits. Each horse (and there were some 30,000 of them) required 10lb. of barley or oats, and 10lb. of hay or straw daily. While the army was in static quarters the provision of this quantity of rations from depots supplied from the sea was not an impossible task although the fact that the only British transport consisted of 306 officers and men of the Royal Waggon Train meant that most of the cartage had to be done by hired civilians. Once the army marched into action the situation changed. The commissariat officers attached to each division had to find and purchase the food they required. At the end of each day's march the commissary 'had to mount a fresh horse, scour the country in order to discover some concealed hoard of grain, accompany foraging parties, and proceed to organise the baking of bread and the slaughtering of cattle. Even after the wheat was found, a great deal remained to be done; for instance the banks of rivers to be explored in seeking mills, a spot determined on for a store to receive the flour when ground; and lastly the municipal authorities put into requisition and women appointed to bake the flour into bread.

Intelligence was another problem. The allies were not at war with France so that patrols could not be sent across the frontier. Wellington was forced to rely on accounts of varying reliability brought by travellers, accounts which prompted him to remark that 'there is a good deal of *charlatanism* in what is called procuring intelligence'. The best of his intelligence gatherers, Lieutenant-Colonel John Grant, had however been appointed to the newly created post of head of the Intelligence Department. Grant had moved across the frontier and set up a valuable network of agents in Paris and on the roads that led to the Belgian frontier.

As May gave way to June and Wellington cemented his alliance with Marshal Blücher who commanded the Prussian army which was quartered round Liège, rumours came in in growing quantities that Napoleon was massing his troops on the Belgian frontier. Most of these stories were premature but on 13 June, the day after Napoleon left Paris for the front, Grant received a note from a trusted agent saying that the roads leading towards Charleroi were '*encombrées de troupes et de matériel; les officers de toutes grades parlent hautes que la grande bataille sera livrée avant trois jours*'. This information was forwarded to Brussels post-haste but it had to go by way of Mons where the commandant, Major-General Dörnberg, a Brunswick officer in the British service, took it upon himself to discount the information it contained. He sent it back to Grant with a letter saying that 'so far from convincing him that the Emperor was advancing for battle, it assured him of the contrary'. By the time that Grant had ridden back to Wellington with the message the campaign was already under way.

Deprived of Grant's information it was after 3 pm on 15 June that Wellington first learned that the French had attacked the Prussians early that morning. This news was confirmed an hour later by a Prussian messenger who had taken six hours to ride 34 miles. The letter he brought said nothing about the scale of the attack and at no time was Wellington informed of the vast number of camp fires that the Prussians had seen on their front during the previous night. Thus Napoleon was reviewing his Guard in Belgian Charleroi, on the north bank of the Sambre, before Wellington heard that the campaign had started. It was 10 pm before he had enough information to enable him to judge where the weight of the attack was falling and after midnight before he heard that the French were threatening Quatre Bras.

Next day the Prussians were beaten but not crushed at Ligny and, because Napoleon and Ney were having their own communication problems, Wellington's advance guard were able to hold their ground at Quatre Bras. The Prussians fell back northward and Napoleon, misled by a mass of stragglers making for the Rhine, sent Grouchy with 40,000 men in pursuit to the east. Two Prussian aides-de-camp had been unhorsed between Ligny and Quatre Bras and it was 9 am on 17 June before Wellington learned where the Prussians were going. When he did he remarked, 'Old Blücher has had a damned good licking and gone back to Wavre, 18 miles. As he has gone back, we must go too.' It was not the least of his problems that he had no map which showed Wavre, a substantial town only 20 miles from Brussels.

His infantry retired in perfect safety but the rearguard of cavalry and horse artillery had their difficulties. One gunner officer described how:

about four o'clock (in the afternoon) the enemy discovered what we were about and pushed on some tremendous heavy columns of cuirassiers and lancers with three or four brigades of guns. (Major General) Vivian sent me in advance with a couple of guns and I blazed away at them furiously; the practice was good, but they dashed at me as if I had only been pointing my finger at them. Vivian then told me to get away as fast as I could and join the other four guns, when we received an order to make the best of our way to the rear, and we set off at a gallop and at that pace, with whip and spur, we were obliged to keep it up for ten miles, the rain coming down the whole time in bucketfuls, and the water up to the axle-trees in many parts of the road; to make my own situation more comfortable, my horse had cast a fore shoe.

The Gordon Highlanders charging with the Scots Greys

Despite such alarms and greatly helped by a torrential thunderstorm, the whole army was, that evening, in position at Mont St Jean, slightly to the south of Waterloo.

Napoleon's last battle was fought on a front of about 4,500 yards with each side taking up its position on low ridges on either side of a gently sloping valley. The action started at 11.40 am when eighty French guns, twenty-four of them 12-pounders, the largest field gun then in use, opened at a range of 1,300 yards, well within the effective range. This imposing battery achieved very little. Unlike Napoleon and Blücher, Wellington habitually formed his infantry on a reverse slope where solid shot could not reach them. The French guns had no targets except a few scattered skirmishers, some field guns, and a Netherlands brigade which its commander, used to fighting under Napoleon's command, had drawn up on the forward slope. Soon afterwards the French left started attacking Wellington's forward bastion, the château of Hougoumont.

The main French attack was made in the centre and was described by an officer of the Gordon Highlanders:

About two o'clock in the afternoon a column of between 3 and 4,000 men advanced to the hedge at the roadside (which ran across the front of our position). Previous to this the 92nd had been lying down under cover of the position when we were immediately ordered to stand to our arms, Major General Sir Denis Pack calling out at the time, '92nd, everything has given way on your right and left and you must charge this column,' upon which he ordered four deep to be formed and closed in upon the centre. The regiment, which was within about 20 yards of the column, fired a volley into them. The enemy on reaching the hedge at the side of the road had ordered arms, and were in the act of shouldering them when they received a volley from the 92nd. The Scots Greys came up at that moment and, doubling round our flanks and through our centre where openings were made for them, both regiments charged together, calling out 'Scotland for ever!' and the Scots Greys actually walked over this column and in less than three minutes it was totally destroyed. The grass field in which the enemy was formed, which was only an instant before as green and smooth as the 15 acres of Phoenix Park, was in a few minutes covered with killed and wounded, knapsacks and their contents, arms, accoutrements, etc. literally strewed all over, that to avoid stepping on either one or the other was quite impossible. The regiment was then recalled and formed on its former ground.

The Greys and the other British cavalry destroyed the French attack but were themselves driven back with heavy loss. Then the French threw brigade after brigade of cavalry, sixty-one squadrons in all, against Wellington's infantry:

No man present could have forgotten in after life the awful grandeur of that charge. You perceived at a distance what appeared to be an overwhelming, long moving line which, ever advancing, glittered like a stormy wave of the sea when it catches the sunlight. On came

Napoleon sending forward the Imperial Guard at the climax of the battle

the mounted host until they got near enough, while the earth seemed to vibrate beneath their thundering tramp. One might suppose that nothing could have resisted the shock of that terrible moving mass. Just before this charge the Duke entered by one of the angles of our square, accompanied by only one aide-de-camp. As far as I could judge, he appeared perfectly composed; but looked very thoughtful and pale. The word of command 'Prepare to receive cavalry' had been given, every man in the front rank knelt, and a wall bristling with steel, held by steady hands, presented itself to the infuriated cuirassiers.

The French horsemen could not break through. No cavalry could overcome unshaken infantry formed in square and especially, as was now the case, they were supported by an excellent artillery, which:

waited until the head of the column might have been 50 or 60 yards from us, and then gave the word 'Fire!' The effect was terrible. Nearly the whole leading rank fell at once; and the round shot penetrating the column carried confusion throughout its length. The discharge of each gun (loaded with roundshot over case) was followed by a fall of men and horses like that of grass before a mower's scythe.

The guns and the infantry had no difficulty in driving off the French cavalry but their repeated assaults forced the battalions to remain in square where they were an easy target for the French guns which had advanced behind the squadrons. A Guards officer described the inside of one square as:

15

a perfect hospital, being full of dead, dying and mutilated soldiers. Inside we were nearly suffocated by the smoke and smell of burned cartridges. It was impossible to move a yard without treading on a wounded comrade or upon the bodies of the dead.

Through this scene rode the Duke of Wellington with his uncanny knack of being always where the danger was greatest. Appearing completely unruffled, he occasionally threw a glance to the east in the hope of seeing the arrival of Prussian help, promised but long overdue. A surgeon working in one of the squares wrote, 'The sight of him put heart into us all, and I am sure that had he been killed or wounded that shot would have decided the battle and the allied troops would have lost heart.'

A private Rifleman wrote that:

seeing that we had lost so many men and all our commanding officers, my heart began to fail but the Duke of Wellington came up to us in all the fire. He, himself, gave the word of command; the words he said to our regiment were these: '95th, unfix your swords, left face and extend yourselves once more. We shall soon have them over the hill.' Then he rode away on our right, and how he escaped being shot God alone knows, for all the time the shot was flying like hailstones.

At about 7 pm with the Prussians pressing in on his right, Napoleon made his last throw. He launched five battalions of the Imperial Guard up the slope. Blasted in front by the British Foot Guards and taken in flank by the 52nd Light Infantry, even Napoleon's incomparable Guard could not stand:

Presently a cheer, which we knew to be British, commenced far off to the right, and made everyone prick up his ears. It was Lord Wellington's long-wished-for order to advance. It approached gradually as it grew near. We took it up by instinct, charged through the hedge, sending our adversaries flying at the point of the bayonet. Lord Wellington galloped up to us at the instant, and our men began to cheer him; but he called out, 'No cheering, my lads, but forward and complete your victory!'

In the valley between the armies lay 52,000 dead and wounded. To the south the French army was streaming away in rout covered by two indomitable battalions of the Old Guard. Napoleon was faced with the irrevocable collapse of his empire and the world had, for once, seen a decisive battle. It had also seen the end of an era in the methods of making war.

PART ONE

Flintlock and Sail

CHAPTER ONE

The Legacy

LIKE ALMOST EVERY GREAT BATTLE since the ring bayonet had been introduced in the last half of the seventeenth century, Waterloo was decided by the muskets of the infantry. By later standards the musket was an astonishingly ineffective weapon. The best that could be said of it was that, in competent hands, it would throw a ball of lead weighing about an ounce with some degree of accuracy to a range of 80 yards. A British writer in 1814 declared that 'A soldier's musket, if not exceedingly ill-bored (as many are), will strike a figure of a man at 80 yards; it may even at a hundred; but a soldier must be very unfortunate indeed who shall be wounded by a common musket at 150 yards, provided that his opponent aims at him.' The musket used by Napoleon's army was subject to an error of 9 feet at 200 yards. When the Prussians adopted the new Potsdam musket after their disastrous defeat at Jena in 1806, tests showed that at 80 yards 75 per cent of shots would hit a 6 foot target. This was regarded as a great advance as, with their previous weapon, only 46 per cent of hits could be expected.

All this supposed that the musket would fire at all. It was set off by a hammer holding a piece of flint which, when the trigger was pressed, struck a pivoted piece of steel thus making a spark which ignited a pinch of powder in a 'flash pan' below. The flash of this priming powder communicated itself through a touch hole to the propellant charge in the barrel. Rain wetting the priming powder would cause a misfire; high humidity would cause either misfires or hangfires when the musket would only fire after a pause during which the aim would be lost. A French authority conceded that 'The locks of the British musquets are of better workmanship than those hitherto manufactured by any other nation in Europe. They will less frequently misfire upon a given number of rounds than all the rest.' Despite this testimonial, tests carried out in England under range conditions showed that the British musket would misfire twice in every thirteen rounds.

The business of loading and firing a musket, which could only be carried out while standing, was a complicated business requiring

Riflemen skirmishing, from an Ackermann print of 1841. They are still using the Baker rifle, shown in a very shortened form

twenty drill movements. Nevertheless it was possible for highly-trained men to discharge five or six shots a minute. This was the rate of fire insisted upon by Frederick the Great but it was achieved only by abandoning any pretence of accuracy. Frederick went so far as to forbid his soldiers to aim and merely to level their weapons from the hip. Later commanders regarded two or three rounds a minute as the highest practicable rate but accuracy was still not highly regarded. The French admitted that in the British infantry 'the firing was far more accurate than that of any other army', but, except in the light infantry, British muskets had no backsight and the soldier could only aim with the line of the barrel and a vestigial foresight.

Since muskets could only fire every twenty to thirty seconds and that they were accurate only up to 80 yards, fire effect could only be obtained by employing them *en masse*. If a battalion 1,000 strong fired a volley some of the balls would be sure to find their mark, the

The manual and platoon exercises of the British army at the end of the eighteenth century, showing basic arms drill and the procedure for loading and firing a musket

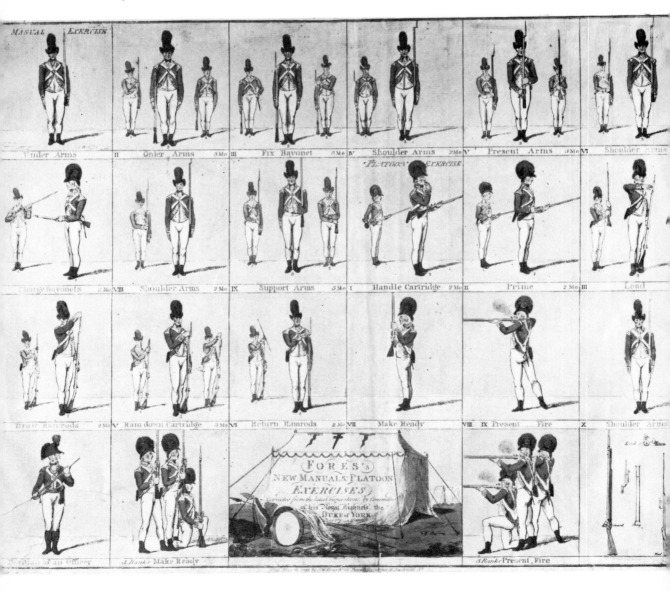

more so since the enemy, who were also anxious to produce fire effect, would certainly be in close formation. The answer to the inaccuracy of the musket was to fire as many as possible on as short a front as was possible. In the British army the space allotted to each man in his rank was only 22 inches and the space between the ranks 30 inches. Thus, with a two-rank formation, there would be one musket for every 11 inches of the front and with a battalion at its full strength of 1,000 muskets (an unusual event), they would all be deployed on a front of little more than 300 yards.

As long as such a formation was stationary no serious problems were encountered but it was a matter of extreme difficulty to manoeuvre with a line of two ranks 300 yards long with 30 inches between the ranks and the files 'lightly touching, but without crouding [sic]'. Even on perfectly smooth ground, a terrain seldom found on a battlefield, to move a battalion, to say nothing of a brigade, in line called for an exceptionally high standard of foot drill. It was not a formation to be adopted an instant before it was necessary and troops would move to the attack in columns, deploying only just before they reached the effective range of the enemy's musketry. Here again precise foot drill was essential and it had to be seconded by great accuracy in the placing of the columns at 'deploying distance' and by split-second timing by the officers giving orders to form line from column. Any mistakes in the placing of the columns or the giving of the orders would result in the line being formed with gaps and no straighter than a saw's edge, both faults fatal to the efficiency and safety of the line.

Only armies composed of highly-trained professionals full of confidence in themselves and their officers could employ such tactics. In the early years after the revolution France could not field such infantry and they found themselves faced with many enemies. She had to rely firstly on enthusiastic volunteering and later on the conscription to supply her with an apparently inexhaustible reservoir of recruits. These she employed all but untrained and with a total disregard for casualties. France could replace her losses while her enemies, still thinking in eighteenth-century terms, were busily trying to bribe or coerce recruits into their armies and then spending months in training them.

France had other advantages. Although the revolution had ruined her infantry and cavalry, her artillery was almost unaffected and remained as good as any in Europe. Her strategy was expansionist and, after 1793, she could wage her campaigns on foreign soil where supplies could be requisitioned, thus doing away with the lumbering supply trains which hobbled her opponents. Most importantly the French had always excelled in the attack and revolutionary fervour reinforced a natural *élan*.

FRENCH COLUMN AGAINST BRITISH LINE
From a distillation of all these factors the early revolutionary generals evolved a technique for overcoming their enemies. First the opposing line was bombarded by the French artillery which was

ABOVE AND LEFT:
Contemporary prints of
French columns in the
attack. Both illustrations
show how tightly packed
the men were, and how
good a target they made
for enemy fire

handled in an unusually thrusting fashion, then it was harassed by a swarm of skirmishers who made up for their lack of formal training by natural cunning and effrontery. Lacking adequate light troops of their own there was nothing that the enemy could do against this form of preparation. Volley firing was an ineffective reply to the small and shifting target presented by skirmishers while limited counterattacks, which might drive the tormentors away, disordered the line and limited its effectiveness. Finally, when artillery and *tirailleurs* were judged sufficiently to have galled the enemy, the French would launch masses of men formed in heavy columns, each formed of up to a division, in the hope, frequently fulfilled, of rupturing the line. Against the cumbersome armies, stolid men led by pedantic generals, of Austria and Prussia the new French tactics worked with predictable success and heavy cost.

Before Bonaparte set out on his brilliant Italian campaign of 1796 these expensive improvisations were scarcely necessary. The French army was, by that time, as well trained as its opponents and capable of fighting in line. Nevertheless French generals clung to the idea of rupturing their enemy's line by hurling heavy columns at it. Their drill books enjoined the use of the three-deep line and Bonaparte, in theory, deprecated the use of columnar attacks, advocating rather the *ordre mixte*, a hybrid intended to combine the fire power of the line with the solidity of the column. Nevertheless, despite Napoleon's presence at Waterloo, the first great French attack was launched by four divisions in column and, under Napoleon's close supervision, the final assault was made by five battalions of the *Moyenne Garde*, four of which were in battalion columns and the fifth, for some inscrutable reason, in square. The result was predictably disastrous but it may have been in the Emperor's mind that six years earlier at Wagram, Marshal Macdonald had broken the centre of the hard-fighting Austrians with a single column of twenty-one battalions, 8,000 men.

Macdonald's success, the apotheosis of the attack in column, was bought at heavy cost, three men out of four of his men being killed or wounded. Nevertheless victory had been achieved and the armies of eastern Europe – Austrian, Prussian, and Russian, followed the French example and became converts to the columnar heresy.

Britain remained unconvinced. As Sir Arthur Wellesley remarked before he sailed to win the dukedom of Wellington in the Peninsula: 'If what I hear of (the French) system of manoeuvres be true, I think it is a false one against steady troops.' Mathematics were certainly on his side. By devoting their efforts to obtaining momentum and shock effect, the French had sacrificed firepower. A French division, 5,000 strong, would advance on a front of 170 men, the rest following rank on rank behind them. Since only the front two ranks could fire with safety, only 340 muskets could bear on the enemy. A British division of the same strength would be formed two-deep with every musket able to fire. Since their front would be that occupied by 2,500 men it was possible for them to wheel forward the wings and fire into the flanks of the column attacking them. A future Marshal of

France, Thomas Robert Bugeaud, described what it was like to attack a British position:

About a thousand yards from the English line our men became excited, they started talking and quickened the pace; our column becomes somewhat disordered. The English, firm as a long red wall, are motionless with their arms at the port. Inevitably their steadiness has an effect on our young soldiers. As we get nearer there are shouts of Vive l'Empereur! En avant avec la Bayonette!, shakos are hoisted on the muzzles of muskets, we break into a double, the ranks become ragged, there is a tumult of shouting, scattered shots are fired. The English line is still silent and immovable. They appear to ignore the storm about to break over them although we are now less than three hundred paces from them. This is unnerving. Each of us begins to feel that it will not be pleasant when the enemy, having waited so long, decides to fire. Our ardour begins to cool. We keep up our spirits by shouting all the louder. At last the English muskets come down – they are making ready. Appalled, many of our men halt and open a scattering fire. Then comes the English volley, precise, deadly thunderous. Decimated, our column staggers, checks, tries to recover itself. The enemy break their long silence with a cheer. Then a second volley, perhaps a third. Then they are upon us, chasing us into a disorderly retreat.

The simple counting of muskets was not the only factor in the repeated victories of the British line over the French column. The British army, which with its Hanoverian and Portuguese allies remained the only European army to cling to fighting in line, was a very small force. At its largest it never, apart from colonial auxiliaries, exceeded 207,000 men, only two-thirds of the size of the allied army actually engaged at the battle of Leipzig. The largest number of British troops actually employed in a single expeditionary force was only 58,000. From an army on this small scale and composed of long-term volunteers it was possible to exact a level of training and discipline that few continental armies could match. To this advantage should be added the traditional steadiness of British infantry, a supply service which, eventually, was able to provide rations with a regularity unknown in any other service, and a commander who, if he lacked some of Napoleon's brilliance, had an unrivalled eye for ground and an impeccable sense of timing. By 1812 the Anglo–Portuguese army in the Peninsula had become confident they were going to win any battle they joined and the French developed an equal certainty that, where Wellington commanded, defeat was inevitable. More than half the regiments in D'Erlon's corps at Waterloo had fought in Spain and, as they marched up towards the British in the first great attack, the older soldiers must have felt that their Emperor had committed them to the kind of frontal attack which had proved ineffective against the redcoats.

The musket was a smoothbore, hence its remarkable inaccuracy. All European armies, except the French, armed some of their

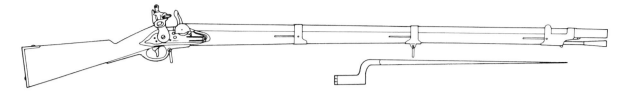

ABOVE: The Prussian
musket of 1809. It
weighed 10 lb.; had a
43-inch barrel; and was
accurate up to 80 yards

infantry with rifles. The best rifles at Waterloo, the British model designed by Ezekiel Baker, was accurate up to 200 yards and, in the hands of a marksman, could count on hitting a man's torso at 300. To compensate for this it had a very slow rate of fire. Being a muzzle-loader the need to ram the ball down the barrel through the twists of the rifling meant that few riflemen could manage more than four aimed rounds in three minutes. Being a flintlock it was as likely to misfire as a common musket and it suffered from the additional hazard that, with the coarse powder of the day, fouling built up in the rifling making it difficult, in extreme cases impossible, to load. It was because of these failings that Napoleon had, in 1807, ordered the withdrawal of all rifles from the French army. Other armies had continued to employ a number of riflemen as specialists. At Waterloo one British infantryman in fourteen was so armed.

THE ROLE OF CAVALRY

Cavalry had long since lost its supremacy on the battlefield. As early as the sixteenth century Machiavelli had written that 'they are fitter to pursue an enemy that is routed and flying than anything else . . . (but) they are highly necessary to reconnoitre, to scour roads, to make raids and lay waste the enemy's territory, to beat up their quarters, to keep them in continual alarm and to intercept their supply trains'. In 1815 that was still a fair statement of cavalry's useful functions. Light cavalry – hussars, light dragoons, and *chasseurs à cheval* – still had a definite function to fulfil. Their task

BELOW: The Baker rifle
used by the British army
from 1800–38. It allowed
prone firing and was
accurate to more than
200 yards

The post-Waterloo armies

Uniforms of the Napoleonic era were designed so as to enable friends to be distinguished from enemies and to appear as imposing as possible. The trooper of 1er Cuirassiers (France 1815) (RIGHT) and the Scots Greys shown charging at Waterloo (BELOW) are all dressed to impress rather than for utility or comfort. Their headdress is designed to increase the apparent height of the wearer and serve little practical purpose. The cuirassier's body armour was barely proof against musketry at 80 yards. The infantrymen had to carry all their own belongings. The cross belts of the private 44th Foot (British 1815) (OPPOSITE BELOW RIGHT) constrict the wearer's breathing and make a good aiming mark but increase the apparent width of his chest. Thirteen years later the private 3rd Guards (Britain 1828) (OPPOSITE BELOW LEFT) wears much the same uniform and equipment but has been given a more impressive, less comfortable, shako. Divisional organisation (OPPOSITE ABOVE) was simple with few services. This can be compared with the complex structure of a century later (see page 235)

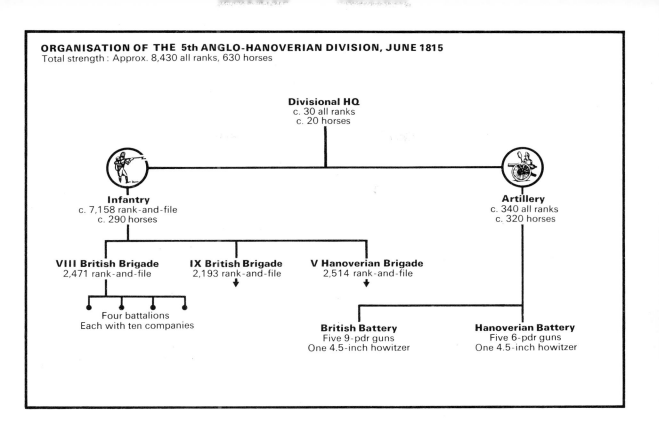

ORGANISATION OF THE 5th ANGLO-HANOVERIAN DIVISION, JUNE 1815
Total strength : Approx. 8,430 all ranks, 630 horses

Divisional HQ
c. 30 all ranks
c. 20 horses

Infantry
c. 7,158 rank-and-file
c. 290 horses

Artillery
c. 340 all ranks
c. 320 horses

VIII British Brigade
2,471 rank-and-file

IX British Brigade
2,193 rank-and-file

V Hanoverian Brigade
2,514 rank-and-file

Four battalions
Each with ten companies

British Battery
Five 9-pdr guns
One 4.5-inch howitzer

Hanoverian Battery
Five 6-pdr guns
One 4.5-inch howitzer

was to man the outposts, to make deep penetration patrols, and to act as the eyes of the general. This reconnaissance function was one that no other arm of the service could fulfil and one in which they were irreplaceable until the coming of the aircraft and the light armoured vehicle.

By contrast heavy cavalry – horse grenadiers, cuirassiers, carabineers, and, in Britain the Life and Horse Guards – had a steadily declining value. Waterloo had shown that even the most imposing charge of heavy horsemen could do nothing against steady infantry formed into square. They could wreak havoc on scattered infantry but this was a function that light cavalry could perform equally well at a very much lower cost. Nevertheless every European army continued to maintain regiments of heavy horse in the hope that there might be an occasion to use them. More than that, lighter regiments were converted into heavy cavalry with the reintroduction into warfare of the lance which had suffered a century of neglect. It had last been seen in Britain in the hands of the Scots at the battle of Dunbar. Lancers, as reintroduced into battle by Napoleon, were essentially units to be used in the set-piece, stirrup to stirrup charge. Isolated lancers were very vulnerable to swordsmen and even, as Marshal Beresford had demonstrated at Albuera, to a powerful unarmed horseman. The one advantage of the lance was that it could outreach the muskets and bayonets of infantry formed to receive cavalry, and on two occasions, at Dresden and on the Katzbach, Napoleon's lancers had broken squares of infantry. These successes were sufficient to purchase for heavy cavalry a further century of expensive life. Indeed it is noticeable that in 1914 all German cavalry carried the lance.

There was one further cavalry function which needed to be fulfilled. This was the role of the dragoon (and in Britain the dragoon guard) which was that of mounted infantry. There was and, until the advent of the internal combustion engine, continued to be, a need for mounted men who could head an advance at something more than the marching pace of the infantry and then dismount to secure key points. A similar function was also necessary during retreats, although in all dragoon operations one man in six had to be left out of the firing line while he held the horses of his comrades. All European armies had dragoon regiments but all of them regarded themselves as heavy cavalry *manqué*. Even Napoleon had been unable to persuade his dragoons to fight dismounted. His only defeat in his brilliant Ulm campaign had been when 5,000 dragoons whom he had forced to go to war without their horses were routed by the Archduke Ferdinand. Only in the United States during the Civil War were dragoons successfully used as mounted infantry during the nineteenth century. It was a lesson the British learned with enormous loss in South Africa in 1900–1.

DEVELOPMENTS IN ARTILLERY
The role of artillery had increased during the eighteenth century. The design of guns had improved little but advances had been made

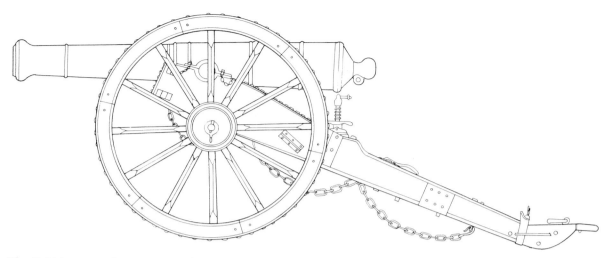

The British 9-pounder
fieldgun

in their mobility and, thanks partly to the needs of the revolutionary
French armies and to the fact that Napoleon was himself a gunner,
the deployment of artillery had become more effective. Improved
mobility and the construction of better roads in western Europe had
also allowed considerable increase in the size of guns. In
Marlborough's wars the 4-pounder was the standard field-piece; by
Waterloo the 9-pounder was the more commonly used size and, as
has been seen, Napoleon favoured the use of 12-pounders as field
guns. The 9-pounder had an effective range, calculated to the point
where the shot first pitched, of 1,400 yards and a normal rate of fire
of two rounds a minute.

The most usual missile for guns was a solid ball, roundshot, and
this would do no harm to anyone not standing in its direct line of
flight. This again favoured troops deployed in line where a shot fired
from front or rear could at most strike two men. The column was far
more vulnerable and an officer of the 40th Foot at Waterloo wrote
that 'towards evening, whilst the regiment was in open column, a
round shot from the enemy took off the head of a captain near me,
and striking his company put *hors de combat* more than twenty-five
men'. Even more damage could be done by case-shot, a development
of grape, consisting of a tin canister which sprayed out small lead
balls (34 x 3½-ounce balls in one British model) as soon as it left the
muzzle. Unfortunately the effective range of canister was only 300
yards. Both roundshot and canister suffered from the extremely flat
trajectory of guns which meant that soldiers on the reverse slope of a
hill or even behind a stout bank were safe from gunfire. In most
armies batteries (then called brigades) of guns included one howitzer
which would principally fire shells. These consisted of an iron sphere
containing a small charge of powder which was activated by a fuse
cut to length and lit before firing. The inaccuracy of fuses meant that
most shells exploded harmlessly and many did not explode at all. In
wet weather a shell was likely to bury itself in soft ground and do no
harm. The 5½-inch howitzer, a widely used type, had a range of
1,350 yards.

Three facets of warfare which saw particularly rapid change during the nineteenth century were weaponry, communications, and mobility. Portents of change appeared within twenty years of Waterloo: the vulnerable despatch rider (RIGHT) was being supplemented with a primitive telegraph; the Congreve rocket (LEFT) was being fired by the Royal Horse Artillery in 1835; and the first long-distance railways, such as the Liverpool to Manchester line in 1831 (BELOW), were being built

The only advances made in artillery missiles during the Napoleonic wars were both British. The most successful was the invention of Colonel Henry Shrapnell and was known as spherical case-shot. It was a combination of case-shot and shell and was supplied with alternative fuses of different lengths built into the ball. This was the first missile to give a reliable air-burst and, filled with musket balls, was to be a British monopoly for a quarter of a century after Waterloo. The other British device was less favourably received. This was the explosive rocket devised, from Indian models, by Colonel William Congreve. His contraptions were produced with warheads of between 6 and 42 pounds and not only far-outranged conventional artillery but were much easier to transport. Although a British rocket troop greatly impressed the allied sovereigns at the battle of Leipzig, Congreve never produced a rocket that could be relied upon to go in the direction in which it was aimed.

Every army possessed, in addition to its field guns, heavier pieces for use in sieges. The largest type in common use were 24-pounders capable of firing a round every two minutes to an effective range of 2,400 yards. Such guns which, with their limber, weighed 4 tons and were extremely cumbersome to move about the country. Five pairs of oxen were needed to move a 24-pounder on its travelling carriage on good roads in fine weather and it would be unlikely to achieve more than 7 or 8 miles a day, about half the normal marching average of infantry.

MOBILITY AND COMMUNICATIONS

It will be clear from this summary of weapons and tactics that no commander could rely on winning a battle by fire power alone. Battles of attrition did sometimes occur, Albuera and Borodino are notable examples, but they were unlikely to prove decisive since the winning army would be too exhausted to pursue. Waterloo was such a battle of attrition, 'I never saw such a pounding match' was Wellington's comment, but at Waterloo the weight of the pounding match was borne by the Anglo-Netherlands army and the arrival of the Prussians, tired but still fresh enough to pursue, made it decisive. Nor was the inadequacy of arms the only handicap under which commanders suffered. One was the extreme slowness with which troops could move. About 15 miles a day was a good average speed for tactical movement. Forced marches could achieve more, going to Talavera, Craufurd's Light Brigade had achieved 42 miles in twenty-six hours but such feats could not be done day after day and left the troops exhausted. Cavalry could, of course, achieve longer distances but again only for limited periods. Troop horses became exhausted more quickly and needed longer to recover than infantrymen. The only alternative to moving at a foot pace was transport by water. In 1806 The Times reported the movement of a battalion by barge from London to Liverpool, remarking that 'by this mode of conveyance the men will be only seven days in reaching their destination and with comparatively little fatigue, as it would take them fourteen days to march that distance'. It was, however, a fortunate commander who could find a convenient waterway on which to transport his reinforcements and supplies.

On the battlefield troops could move at a steady 2.14 m.p.h. This was known as 'ordinary time' and was the fastest that men in line could march. In column the speed could be put up to just over 3 m.p.h., 'quick time' which was 100 paces of 25.6 inches in the French army and 108, 30-inch paces in the British. 'Double quick' time gave 3.41 m.p.h. but the Drill Book laid down that it was 'applied chiefly to the purpose of wheeling'. Light infantry moved somewhat faster than others but it was enjoined that 'They are never to run unless particularly directed, and in that case, they are only to run at that pace in which they can preserve their order'.

Communications presented another problem. Over short distances, 100 or 200 yards, simple orders could be passed by drum, trumpet, or bugle horn. Beyond that no message could be passed at a rate faster than a horse could travel. At Waterloo the Prussian liaison officer was astonished at the speed at which Wellington's aides-de-camp went about their business. 'Mounting the best horses of England's famous breeds, they make it a point of honour, whenever the Duke adds *Quick* to a message, to ride 12 miles in the hour, or 4 miles in eighteen minutes.' This, of course, was the rate for short distances in daylight over open country. Any aide-de-camp was liable to be delayed by his horse casting a shoe and he was always at the mercy of a stray cannon ball or of marauding cavalry.

The Waterloo campaign has examples of the speed of messages over longer distances. It has been seen that Wellington's first message from the Prussians took six hours to cover the 34 miles from Charleroi to Brussels. Wellington ascribed the reason that this message, carried over good roads in daylight, averaged only 5.66 m.p.h. to the fact that the bearer was the fattest officer in the Prussian army. Later that day his first definite information of the French whereabouts was carried by a British officer in darkness from Braine-le-Comte, 23 miles, in two and a half hours, 9.1 m.p.h. Against that the promise that Blücher would move to Wellington's support left Wavre half an hour after midnight and reached Waterloo at 6.30 am. The distance, as the crow flies, is only 10 miles but the fact that the aide-de-camp averaged only 1.66 m.p.h. can reasonably be blamed on winding lanes in total darkness and deep mud made worse by torrential rains.

Over very long distances letters travelled overland at about 60 miles a day. If a stretch of sea had to be crossed, the time could vary almost indefinitely according to the direction and strength of the wind. This is best illustrated by the progress of the Waterloo despatch which Major Henry Percy was determined to carry with all possible speed. He left Brussels in a post-chaise with four horses at noon on 19 June and covered the 72 miles to Ostend in twenty-five hours. It was five and a half hours before HMS *Peruvian* could set sail and, given a fair wind, the Straits could have been crossed in little more than six hours (c. 10 m.p.h.). Unfortunately the wind failed and it was 3 pm on 21 June before Percy could be put ashore near Broadstairs, having been rowed in a gig for the last part of the voyage. For the last 77 miles to London he hired another post-chaise and, having changed horses at Canterbury, Sittingbourne, and Rochester, he crossed Westminster Bridge at 10 pm. For the whole journey of 220 miles he had averaged 3½ m.p.h.

Any kind of advanced planning for campaigns was hampered by a lack of adequate maps. In their own country the French had a clear advantage since their long-established *Bureau Topographique*, of which both Carnot and Berthier were former members, had mapped all of France and Belgium. Napoleon, therefore, started the Waterloo campaign with a full set of detailed maps. Wellington had no such advantage. Although he had ordered the Royal Engineers to make a plan of the area between Brussels and the frontier a year earlier, no map could be found for him except a collection of sketches which were brought to him towards the end of the action at Quatre Bras.

Visibility in battle also made the commander's task difficult. Every weapon fired used black powder and their volleys covered the field with a pall of white smoke. This was particularly the case at Waterloo where the humid atmosphere after the thunderstorm caused the smoke to hang over the valley on a windless day. After the Imperial Guard had been repulsed and Wellington ordered his remaining cavalry forward, a cavalry officer still did not know that the battle had swung against the French. He wrote that, as they advanced, 'We every instant were expecting through the smoke to see the enemy appearing under our noses, for the smoke was literally so thick that we could not see ten yards off'. In these circumstances it was important that the colour and style of the soldier's uniform should be as distinctive as possible if friend and foe alike were not to take him for an enemy. 'I only beg,' Wellington had written to London, 'that we may be as different from the French in everything.' This plea would have been feelingly echoed by the Nassauers who held the farm of Papelotte on the left flank. They were wearing French uniforms which had been dyed dark green. All day they had kept the French out of this important outpost of the allied line but when, towards evening, the Prussians arrived they saw only the silhouette of the Nassauers' uniforms and took them for enemies, routing them before the mistake could be rectified.

The difficulty experienced in seeing troops at any distance made the business of command intensely personal. Not the least of the reasons for Napoleon's defeat at Waterloo was that, physically exhausted and suffering the agonies of piles, he established himself on a chair outside La Belle Alliance and left the control to Marshal Ney, of whose tactical ability he had a low opinion. Wellington, by contrast, was always at the point of crisis, ordering up reinforcements, steadying the waverers, rallying broken units, and inspiring his men. 'Three times,' he remarked, 'I have saved this day by perseverance.'

This close personal supervision by senior commanders meant that there was little point in developing a staff system capable of doing more than day to day administration. There was a post of chief of staff (*major général*) in Napoleon's headquarters but the officer who held it was little more than a skilled administrator at the head of the Emperor's military office. In the British army there was no chief of staff and his functions were divided, according to the whim of the General, between the Quartermaster General and the Adjutant General. In neither the French nor the British army would the senior staff officer expect to put forward his views on how the troops should be deployed or manoeuvred. This was the absolute prerogative of the general in command. The beginning of a staff system as it later came to be understood arose in the armies of Austria and Prussia. In these the command tended to be entrusted to some prince, whose experience might be slight, or to a veteran, whose seniority and prestige might outweigh his failing abilities. To such it was essential to attach a competent professional with power to influence his decisions. Prussia learned this lesson at Jena when her armies, entrusted to the 71-year-old Duke of Brunswick and to Prince Frederick of Hohenlohe-Ingelfingen, went to disaster at Jena and Auerstadt. Henceforward all Prussian commanders had at their side an influential staff officer trained to a recognised tactical doctrine.

In any case the day of personal command by generals in the field was passing. The size of armies was increasing at a rate that would make close supervision impossible. In 1704 the combined army of Marlborough and Prince Eugen had been only 52,000 strong and their Franco–Bavarian opponents only slightly more numerous. At Waterloo, Napoleon had 70,000 men actually on the field against Wellington's 60,000 and Blücher's 70,000 and these figures shrank into insignificance beside the half million men who had been engaged at Leipzig two years earlier. One of the lessons which emerged from the Russian campaign of 1812 was that even Napoleon's genius was unequal to the task of controlling an army of 600,000.

The size of armies was, indeed, reaching the stage when it might be impossible for them to fight at all for the problems of feeding them were becoming insuperable. In the Peninsula, Wellington had calculated that an infantry division, 7,500 men with their attached battery, required 700 mules for its forward echelon transport. A cavalry brigade of 1,290 men and 1,350 horses needed 790 mules, and a troop of horse artillery 205 mules. When such numbers were multiplied to give armies of the size that fought at Leipzig it became clear that the number of draught animals required to feed them did not exist. Armies had to scatter to live and could only come together briefly, to fight. If no better transport system than the horse, the mule, and the ox could be invented, the time could not be far off when it would be impossible to bring armies together for even the briefest battle.

CHAPTER TWO

*Africa, Asia,
and Progress*

WATERLOO USHERED IN A PERIOD marked by a lack of international wars in Europe, and nations, with relief, set about reducing their armies and navies. There were, however, outstanding problems which required forceful solutions and to the trading nations none was more urgent than that of piracy in the Mediterranean. When Napoleon was induced to settle in Elba, clause five of the treaty he concluded with the allied powers contained an undertaking that they would protect his new island realm and its merchant ships from the Barbary pirates. The reports from the British commissioner on Elba show that the Emperor took the menace of the 'Algerines' very seriously.

The depredations of the north African pirates had been a menace to sea-borne trade for centuries. At times they had plundered not only in the Mediterranean but in the Atlantic and, on occasions, even so far afield as the North Sea. The larger powers had frequently made treaties with the various beys (or the Dey of Algiers) but these had seldom been effective for long. Small countries either sought the protection of the flags of the larger naval powers or suffered a proportion of their trade to be preyed upon and their seamen taken into slavery. The long wars which had followed the French revolution had greatly exacerbated the problem, for none of the European states had been able to spare forces to deal with African pirates and only the United States had acted when, in 1804, the Marines had made their famous foray against 'the shores of Tripoli'. For Britain the war years had been a time for conciliating the beys. The British fleet had constantly supplied itself with food and water along the Algerian coast and during the Peninsular War the population of Portugal had largely been fed on corn from the Barbary Coast. The little port of Arzew alone had sent 300 cargoes annually to Lisbon between 1809 and 1813. The French, when they had the opportunity, behaved similarly. It was in Algiers that Bonaparte placed contracts for supplying his army in Malta and Egypt. Even after the war the government of the restored Louis XVIII believed that it was so important to conciliate the Dey of Algiers that in 1819 they paid a debt of £280,000 left by Napoleon.

Before that time the British had already acted against the Dey. Since they were pressing the powers of Europe to follow their example in abolishing the slave trade they felt it incumbent on them to take some steps to free the Christian slaves on the Barbary Coast. They entrusted this task to Vice-Admiral Lord Exmouth, better known as the distinguished frigate captain, Sir Edward Pellew. He was given a squadron consisting of five ships of the line and seven smaller ships and with it he visited Algiers, Tunis, and Tripoli. He ransomed 1,792 slaves, mostly Italians, and from the last two ports extracted treaties ensuring that Christian captives would not be enslaved. From Algiers no such undertaking could be obtained, the Dey knowing that it was more than his life was worth to pledge his unruly subjects in this way. There was a sharp quarrel between Dey and Admiral and, had the wind been favourable, Exmouth might well have attacked the city immediately. Instead there was an uneasy pause lasting two days after which the Dey sent the Admiral an ostrich and a promise that he would refer the question to his nominal overlord, the Sultan of Turkey. This was a meaningless concession since it was many years since the rulings of the Sublime Porte had been received in Algiers with anything more than respectful derision. Exmouth, who was uncertain of the political support he might receive from London, decided to accept the Dey's gesture and sailed for home.

As he reached the Channel, news arrived that Algerian troops had massacred 2,000 Sardinian fishermen at Bône and the squadron was immediately ordered back to the Mediterranean with instructions to secure the abolition of Christian slavery in Algiers, together with the repayment of the ransom money recently given to the Dey. No land force was offered to him, nor did Exmouth, as far as can be ascertained, ask for one but on reaching Gibraltar he embarked a company of the Royal Sappers and Miners. He also strengthened his fleet with a few small auxiliary vessels and accepted the support of a Dutch frigate squadron which offered to serve under his orders. He thus had a combined force of thirty-four sail and as they made their way eastward he learned that the Algerians had arrested eighteen British sailors, the crews of two boats from HMS *Prometheus*, and that as a final insult the British Consul in the city had been confined in irons.

Exmouth's problem was one of extreme difficulty. The city of Algiers was stone-built and it was unlikely that bombardment would have any significant effect on it. All he could do was to destroy the shipping in the harbour which was very heavily defended. The seaward side was protected by a long narrow island which, near its northern end, was linked to the mainland by a breakwater 250 yards long. Both island and breakwater were intensively fortified. The northern tip of the island carried a semi-circular battery mounting forty-four guns in two tiers. At the junction of island and breakwater was the lighthouse battery, another forty-four gun work but in three tiers and on the southern stretch of the island was a sixty-six gun three-tier battery flanked by four smaller works mounting,

PREVIOUS PAGE: A painting by Horace Vernet of French troops repulsing an attack by the defenders during the siege of Constantine

between them, sixty more guns. A mole projected from the shore to narrow the entrance to the harbour and this was protected by batteries on the shore which, like those on the island, were built of masonry five feet thick. In all 1,000 guns were mounted to protect the harbour and most of them were 18-, 24-, or 32-pounders except at the southern tip of the island where there were two 68-pounders each 20 feet long. In the harbour were 4, 44-gun frigates, 5 large corvettes, and 35 bomb and mortar vessels. The city's garrison amounted to 40,000 more or less disciplined troops and the population was large, hostile, and armed.

To pit 'wooden walls against stone' was traditionally an unprofitable naval operation and the prospects for a successful attack would have been small had not Lord Exmouth been a master tactician. Fortunately he knew the harbour well and, on his earlier visits, had had the approaches carefully sounded and charted. He had realised that there was a position off the south-eastern side of the island where four battleships could lie out of the worst of the defensive fire while having the flanks of the batteries within range.

An ultimatum was sent to the Dey on 27 August 1816 and, no answer being returned, the fleet went into action. The Dutch frigates and some of the smaller British ships engaged the mainland batteries while four ships of the line made for the 'dead ground'. Exmouth's flagship *Queen Charlotte* (100) pushed on to within 50 yards of the mole and engaged an Algerian frigate which was moored across the entrance to the harbour. A counterattack by gunboats was frustrated by the frigate *Leander* which sank thirty of the attacking craft. A boat from the *Queen Charlotte* then boarded and fired the frigate at the harbour mouth and an explosion vessel loaded with 143 barrels of powder was sailed to the foot of the most northerly battery and when it was fired the battery all but disappeared. From a range of 2,000 yards bomb vessels and others mounting Congreve rockets set about destroying the shipping inside the harbour while three ships of the line hammered the southern island batteries from the relative security of the 'dead ground'. Unfortunately one battleship, *Impregnable* (98) dropped her anchor too soon and for some time lay under the fire of the main batteries, suffering 200 casualties.

By 10 pm the fire from the batteries was almost silent, the shipping in the harbour had all been destroyed and the warehouses at the dockside were in flames. Some 7,000 Algerians had been killed and wounded, the British and Dutch ships having lost 141 killed and 742 wounded. There was scarcely a round of shot left in the fleet and they had fired away 118 tons of powder.

On the following morning the Dey agreed to all Exmouth's demands. He released a further 1,200 slaves, repaid 382,500 dollars of ransom money, and gave 30,000 dollars as compensation to the imprisoned consul. He also undertook to abolish slavery, a pledge which resulted in his murder by his subjects who also killed his two successors within thirteen months. Meanwhile the fortifications were rebuilt and, before the end of 1816, a Barbary pirate captured a prize within sight of Dover.

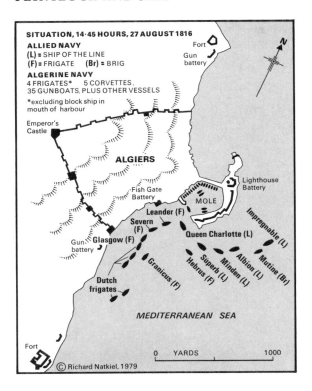

SITUATION, 14·45 HOURS, 27 AUGUST 1816
ALLIED NAVY
(L) = SHIP OF THE LINE
(F) = FRIGATE   (Br) = BRIG
ALGERINE NAVY
4 FRIGATES*   5 CORVETTES,
35 GUNBOATS, PLUS OTHER VESSELS
*excluding block ship in
mouth of harbour

ABOVE LEFT: The
bombardment of Algiers

Another consequence of the bombardment of Algiers was that the lease of the Bône fisheries, largely worked by Sardinians, was given to France. Minor frictions arising from this lease decided the French to blockade Algeria in 1827 and this led to war. In fact neither side was anxious to avoid fighting. In Paris, Charles X looked for an easy victory to support his tottering prestige; in Algiers, Hussein Dey, a stronger man than his immediate and ill-fated predecessors, was glad of a war to unite his troublesome subjects against an infidel enemy. In 1829 a French ship leaving Algiers harbour under a flag of truce was fired upon by the batteries and the French decided to use this unfortunate incident as a pretext for a campaign of conquest, despite vehement protests from Britain whose trade with Algeria was running at £7,000,000 annually.

THE FRENCH CONQUEST OF ALGERIA

There was a long record, stretching back to the fourteenth century, of European attempts to subdue Algeria. All of them had ended in failure, many in disaster with disease as a worse enemy than the brave and resolute native population. The French set out to undertake the conquest of this huge territory – it was 600 miles long and 200 miles deep – with an army of only 40,000 men of all arms. Nor, for a country devoid of navigable waterways, had much attention been paid to transport since only 630 pack mules and 256 waggons, half of them two-wheelers, were embarked. The command was entrusted to General Louis de Bourmont, a highly competent

ABOVE: A contemporary
French print of the
capture of Algiers in
1830

soldier who is chiefly remembered for his desertion of Napoleon during the Waterloo campaign. The fleet which escorted the army across the Mediterranean included some armed steamships with British-built engines.

To oppose the invasion the Dey assembled 60,000 soldiers and he could supplement these without difficulty since, especially among the Kabyle (Berber) tribesmen in the hills, every man was a warrior and armed with muskets comparable (and in many cases identical) to those carried by the French infantry.

On 14 June 1829 de Bourmont started to disembark a few miles west of Algiers at Sidi Ferruch, a small promontory on which, 113 years later, 1st Commando was to make an assault landing during the Allied 'Operation Torch'. Flat-bottomed boats, each holding 150 men, were available and the leading troops were firmly ashore before the Algerians attempted some desultory opposition with irregular cavalry and artillery firing at its extreme range of 1,400 yards. These guns were immediately attacked by infantry, supported by field guns which were manhandled forward, and taken with only thirty-two casualties. It was not until 19 June that the Dey's troops attacked in any strength and, in a series of assaults, were repulsed, the French suffering substantial casualties only when the Algerians managed to close for hand-to-hand fighting.

By 29 June, de Bourmont was able to start the siege of the Emperor's castle, a sixteenth-century legacy of Charles V who had made an unsuccessful attack on Algiers, and which dominated the city on its landward side. With much trouble the battering guns were dragged up and, after a seven-hour bombardment, the garrison evacuated the castle on 4 July. The city surrendered on the same day and Hussein Dey was exiled to Naples from where he made his way to Egypt. He was received with every honour by Mehemet Ali who lost no time in poisoning him. About 2,500 regular soldiers who could make some claim to be Turks were repatriated and Algiers settled down to more than a century of French rule.

The French were soon to learn that the capture of the city did not mean the capture of Algeria. That took a further twenty-seven years of fighting, and rebellion remained endemic into the twentieth century. Hussein Dey's soldiers had not been inferior to the French in weapons or courage. They had, however, been short of training. Their gunners had fought their pieces until they were overrun but their shot had been so badly aimed that they did little harm. Hussein's successors, though unrecognised by the French, set about building an army that could compete with the invaders on equal terms including a number of infantry battalions founded on a cadre of soldiers of fortune and deserters from the French, Spanish, and Italian armies. These were to fight admirably but the main strength of the Algerian resistance was a matter of irregular warfare, the ambushing of columns, and the investment of isolated garrisons.

The reign of Charles X ended abruptly with the revolution of 1830, but his successor, Louis Philippe, continued the conquest of Algeria merely replacing de Bourmont with Marshal Clausel, who

had been Soult's chief of staff in the Peninsula. It was under Clausel that the French started raising indigenous regiments in Africa. First came the Zouaves, drawn originally from all the racial groups in Algeria but later becoming entirely composed of Frenchmen. Then, in 1835, came the *Chasseurs d'Afrique*, a body of cavalry composed equally of Frenchmen and the Algerians. In the same year the Foreign Legion was raised. In the years that followed the French came to rely increasingly on locally recruited regiments who served them with a faithfulness and staunchness similar to the Punjab Frontier Force which Britain was to raise in India.

Militarily the chief event of Clausel's command was his attempt to capture Constantine, the main inland town of Algeria. Basing himself on Bône, then the nearest port, Clausel started out in November 1835 with only 9,000 men and 1,500 pack mules. The roads were worse than had been reported and, before half the distance had been covered, all the engineering stores and most of the reserve of rations had to be jettisoned. To make matters worse the weather broke earlier than had been expected. Soon after they sighted their goal twenty men froze to death in a single night.

There can be few more formidable natural positions than the fortified city of Constantine. The Rummel river, which was flowing fast and was shoulder deep, surrounds the place on three sides and runs in a ravine 1,000 feet deep and nowhere less than 200 feet wide.

ABOVE: Fresh assault columns being brought up during the taking of Constantine

RIGHT: The assault landing before the capture of Algiers

42

On the fourth side the city can be approached up a rocky spur covered by fortifications. This approach could only be reached by fording the turbulent Rummel. Clausel had expected to find the place evacuated when his little force arrived. He brought with him only six light field guns and ten mountain pieces which were greatly out-ranged by the many guns behind the walls.

Without tools or a siege train and with the troops having been without rations for three days, Clausel should have ordered an immediate retreat. Instead he ordered the place to be taken by escalade. Two attacks were launched. One attempted the rocky spur with the intention of blowing in two of the gates in the wall. The other force was to dash across the Roman bridge which spanned the ravine, an astonishing construction based on a series of natural arches above which the Romans had constructed a bridge with two tiers of arches. Both attacks, not unnaturally, failed and Clausel had to undertake a difficult retreat under constant harassment from the Kabyles. He was lucky that he lost only one man in nine from the army.

A painting by Horace Vernet of French troops skirmishing with Kabyles

44

The following year another expedition set out from Bône commanded by General Charles Marie de Damrémont. Once more there were 9,000 infantry but in addition there were a force of cavalry, 1,000 engineers, and sufficient gunners to man not only field guns but a siege train with four 24-pounders, four 16-pounders, and some heavy howitzers. Rations for fourteen days were carried by 2,500 horses and mules and each soldier carried food for eight days. The expedition set out in October and, while it encountered much torrential rain, there was no snow and the Rummel was both lower and less fast running.

Damrémont decided to make a single assault up the rocky spur which could be taken in enfilade by heavy batteries firing across the ravine. The garrison, which greatly outnumbered the attackers, made several sorties but the breaching batteries were in place by 9 October. Unfortunately the stretch of wall selected for breaching turned out to be stronger than had been expected and the gunners' task was made no easier because every one of the 24-pounder balls had to be carried forward by an infantryman running across 300 yards of bare rock. To obviate these problems four heavy guns were transported across the ravine and put into battery within 130 yards of the wall. During these preliminary operations both Damrémont and his chief of staff were killed by snipers.

The command passed to General Sylvain Valée, the senior gunner officer, and by 12 October a breach 33 feet wide was blown in the wall. At 7 am the following morning 1,600 men, in three storming parties, dashed up the spur to the breach. For covering fire the artillery loosed off their last five cannon balls. The stormers reached the crest of the breach without difficulty and bayonetted the defending gunners who fought their pieces to the end. Beyond that they were in danger of being fought to a standstill in street fighting against greatly superior numbers. Fortunately the explosion of a powder magazine allowed them to break out from the immediate neighbourhood of the wall and, before the full strength of the defence could come into action, the city was surrendered by the civil magistrates. The cost of taking Constantine was never revealed in full. It is known that 500 wounded were removed from the breach and the area behind it and that 23 officers were killed and 57 wounded. It was probable that almost 1,000 out of the 1,600 stormers were casualties.

The taking of Constantine was a feat remarkable even for the French army but it was far from being the end of the conquest of Algeria. Resistance from regular troops went on until 14 August 1844 when Marshal Bugeaud defeated a combined Algerian and Moroccan army on the Isly river and guerrilla operations dragged on for many more years. The whole protracted operation was a great school of war for the French army but it was very much a matter of minor tactics. Divisional strength actions, such as Constantine and Isly, were very rare and it was seldom that even a brigade was engaged at any one time. For the most part it was a matter of battalions or companies fighting small, desperate actions against a

swarm of tough mountaineers as well armed as themselves. It also taught the French commissariat, a branch much neglected by Napoleon, some much-needed lessons; but although the fighting in Algeria was invaluable for junior officers and soldiers, it did little to produce generals. Worse, it taught the lesson that the British learned in India, that brave but ill-disciplined opponents will give way if attacked with sufficient confidence. This was a dangerous approach to use against a powerful and disciplined European army.

THE SIEGE OF BHURTPORE

The British also conducted a notable siege during the period after Waterloo. The great fortress city of Bhurtpore (Bharattpur), 100 miles south of Delhi and 32 west of Agra, had been a thorn in the British side since the opening of the nineteenth century when Lord Lake had made four separate and unsuccessful attempts to storm it. At that time the problem of its resistance had been solved by a treaty with the Rajah of the Jats, whose capital it was, but the Rajah died in 1824 and his son, whose succession was guaranteed by the British, was supplanted by his cousin. The Resident at Delhi at once marched against the city but was recalled by the Governor-General. This was doubly unfortunate since its earlier resistance had given it a mystical significance as the town which the otherwise all-conquering British could not take. In 1825 this myth was reinforced when a British army marched up to it and immediately retired. As a result it became the resort of mercenaries and plunderers from all over India. By 1826

ABOVE: French troops occupying an Algerian town in 1841

RIGHT: An aquatint of the 16th (Queen's Own) Lancers in action during the Sikh wars

46

even the Governor-General agreed that it must be subdued.

The task fell to the newly arrived Commander-in-Chief, India, Lord Combermere, better known as Sir Stapleton Cotton, Wellington's dandified but highly-competent cavalry commander. Troops were short since Britain was already involved in a long and so far inconclusive campaign in Burma. Combermere, however, managed to scrape together two British and six Bengal cavalry regiments with two British and sixteen Bengal battalions of infantry. These were later joined by a Bengal European battalion and two companies of Gurkhas, the first time these splendid soldiers were actively employed in the British service. He also assembled something that Lake had lacked, an adequate siege train, which included sixteen 24-pounders, twelve 8-inch howitzers, and sixty mortars, two of which had a 13-inch bore.

Bhurtpore was a very large town with a circuit of walls 8 miles long and punctuated by thirty-five bastions, the whole being surrounded by a wet ditch. It was surrounded by a belt of open country a mile wide so that the circumference of the siege lines was little less than 24 miles, far more than could normally be guarded by the troops available. When he invested the place on 12 December 1825, Combermere disposed his native infantry at the most vulnerable points, protecting them with abattis constructed of fallen trees, while the rest of the perimeter was covered by piquets of

cavalry and horse artillery. He then brought up his heavy guns and, on 23 December, started to build batteries against the north-east sector of the wall.

There were peculiar problems in bombarding Bhurtpore. European fortresses were built of masonry but here the walls were composed of dried mud bound with straw and reinforced with tree trunks placed vertically. The technique employed in European sieges was to concentrate the battering shot on a single stretch of the base of the wall until the sector of wall fell forward into the ditch. At Bhurtpore this did not happen. 24-pounder shot went straight through, leaving a clean hole and a cloud of dust. Even when, as happened on 4 January, the honeycombed wall, battered from a range of only 40 yards, fell, there remained a jagged row of upright tree trunks surrounded by a mass of powdered mud in which a man could sink to his waist. Combermere therefore ordered four mines to be sunk under the wall and postponed the assault until they were ready to be fired.

The attack was ordered for 18 January and was entrusted to the three white battalions and the Gurkhas. Unfortunately, in their eagerness, they edged too far forward and, when the largest of the mines, which contained a ton of gunpowder, was sprung, two dozen of them including their divisional commander were killed or wounded by falling debris. Combermere dashed forward to lead the assault but was physically restrained from mounting the breach by his aide-de-camp. Despite a desperate resistance the disordered stormers burst into the city which surrendered that night. The Jat casualties were estimated at 14,000 apart from 7,000 who were captured by the investing cordon as they tried to escape. Combermere's casualties were only 563 of whom 308 were Europeans. The survivors divided £480,000 among themselves in

prize money. Combermere's share was £60,000 which, by his careful arrangements, he richly deserved, but he was defrauded of the whole of it by his Calcutta banker.

REVOLUTIONARY DEVELOPMENTS IN EQUIPMENT

Bhurtpore was stormed by an army which relied wholly on smoothbore flintlock weapons and, on the face of it, there was little advance in arms in the quarter-century which followed Waterloo. Beneath the surface, however, inventions were maturing which would change the whole face of land warfare. Since the early years of the eighteenth century it had been known that certain forms of explosive could be detonated by percussion, by striking it a sharp blow. No military use of this principle was made until 1805 when the Reverend Alexander Forsythe, the minister of Belhelvie and a keen wild-fowler, devised a compound of fulminate of mercury and chloride of potash, which he enclosed in a metal tube provided with a touchhole just large enough to admit the point of a cambric needle, which was, in turn, struck by a hammer. He found this device far more efficient for setting off the propellant charge of his fowling piece than a flintlock which was much affected by the mists of his native Aberdeenshire. He took his invention to London where friends introduced him to Lord Moira, Master General of the Ordnance. Moira was impressed and installed him in a laboratory in the Tower of London where considerable progress was made until, on a change of government, the indolent Lord Chatham became Master General and turned Forsythe and 'all his rubbish' out of the Tower. That was in 1807, the year in which Forsythe patented a percussion lock which soon became popular with sportsmen. No military use was made of the invention for the next twenty-seven years, by which time similar devices had been made in Britain,

France, and the United States.

In 1834, at last, the Board of Ordnance again took an interest. Trials were held at Woolwich at which six percussion muskets were tried against six standard flintlocks. The result was overwhelming. The percussion type was found to be twenty-six times more reliable and, after the Duke of Wellington had made his own exhaustive tests with his own sporting guns, orders were given for all British muskets to be converted to percussion, a change completed in 1842. Forsythe was given a grant of £200 but the extraordinary meanness of this award raised a public outcry and a pension of £1,000 was added. The first instalment of this was paid on 11 June 1843, the day on which he died.

The introduction of the percussion cap greatly increased the reliability of the musket, reducing the number of misfires from two in thirteen to almost nil. It did nothing to increase the rate of fire, indeed it may have slowed it down while the soldier fumbled for the little cap in his pouch. Nor did it do anything to increase the range of the musket. This could only be done by introducing rifling and, as long as muzzle-loading weapons remained standard, the problem remained of how to force the ball down the barrel. In France, Captain Delvigne in 1826 had designed a musket which, at the rear end of the barrel, had a chamber of smaller calibre which was filled with powder. The ball was rolled down the barrel until it rested on the shoulders of this chamber and then tapped sharply with the ramrod. Being of lead it was expanded by the tapping so that it now fitted into the rifling grooves. Delvigne rifles were issued to a battalion of *Chasseurs d'Afrique* in 1838. At about the same time the British were also issuing a new weapon to the Rifle Brigade. This was the Brunswick rifle which had only two rifling grooves which made one turn in the length of the barrel (30 inches). The ball was equipped with a belt which fitted into the grooves, enabling it to be spun down the barrel. The Brunswick was as accurate at 300 yards as its predecessor, the Baker, was at 200 but it was unpopular with the Riflemen. It was two pounds heavier than the Baker and fouling in the grooves soon made it very difficult to load especially as the belt on the ball was often damaged in the pouch. It was, however, the first percussion weapon issued to any army.

As armies began to struggle free from the limitations imposed by the flintlock musket, they were beginning to break out of the stranglehold on mobility imposed by the pace of the marching infantry and the plodding pace of the supply waggon. In 1829 the railway from Stockton to Darlington was opened and in the following year a battalion was moved from Liverpool to Manchester on a newly-opened line. The journey took two hours compared to the two days by marching.

Britain pioneered the railway but, being an island, she gave little thought to strategic lines. It was Prussia, exposed to attack from France on the west, Austria on the south, and Russia to the east, to whom strategic railways made the strongest appeal. Early in the thirties Dr F. W. Harkort, a Westphalian business man, was urging that lines should be built with war in mind. 'Let us suppose that we had a railway and a telegraph line on the right bank of the Rhine from Mainz to Wesel. Any crossing of the Rhine would then scarcely be possible since we would be able to bring a strong defensive force to the spot before an attack could develop.' Despite strong military opposition which, as late as 1847, contended that horses and guns could not be moved by train, Prussia did develop an unrivalled network of strategic railways.

France also saw the importance of railways but regarded them principally as a way of saving money. In 1833 M. de Berigny told the Chamber of Deputies, 'An army could, in a few days, be transported from the north to the south, from the east to the west. If a country could thus speedily carry considerable masses of troops to any given point, would it not be in a position to effect great economies in its military expenditure?'

Meanwhile military thought was being stirred by two men who attempted to distil their experience as staff officers in the Napoleonic wars. Karl von Clausewitz, a Prussian who had joined the Russian army when his own country became Napoleon's ally, died before his great work *On War* was completed, but it was issued, as far as it was written, by his widow in 1832. Clausewitz put his main stress on the psychological factors in war and was best remembered for his dictum: 'To introduce into the philosophy of war a principle of moderation would be an absurdity . . . War is an act of violence pushed to its utmost bounds.' Had he lived it seems probable that he might have modified this advocacy of total war and it is certain that strategists would have done better to lay more stress on another of his sayings: 'There is no more imperative and no simpler law of strategy than to keep the army concentrated'. This maxim was made much more feasible by the coming of the railways, which Clausewitz did not live to see.

Henri Jomini, a Swiss, had also served with the Russian army but his previous experience had been on the other side, as chief of staff to Marshal Ney. His *Précis de l'Art de la Guerre* was published in 1838 and, like Clausewitz, he laid great stress on concentration. His most memorable passages are those in which he advocates 'manoeuvring in such a manner as to engage the mass of one's own force against only fractions of the enemy's armies . . . directing this mass successively on the decisive points of a theatre of war and, as far as possible, on the enemy's communications without endangering one's own'. Here Jomini formulated what came to be known as the 'strategy of the indirect approach' but, even with the coming of the railway, tactical mobility was still controlled by the pace of the man and the horse. It is doubtful whether Jomini's teaching, which tended to reduce war to a series of geometrical manoeuvres, was of much practical value until, in the twentieth century, the internal combustion engine brought tactical mobility to the battlefield.

CHAPTER THREE

The End of Sail

$\underset{\text{N}}{\text{A}}$N ERA OF NAVAL HISTORY came to an end on 20 October 1827 when the last great battle was fought entirely under sail. It was fought out at Navarino, a bay on the west coast of Greece only about 100 miles from Lepanto where, in 1571, a great battle had marked the supremacy of sailing ships over oared galleys. Navarino was fought between two fleets, each composed of allies, at a time when none of the nations whose ships took part was at war with any other.

This 'untoward incident', as the Duke of Wellington described it in the House of Lords, arose from the Greek War of Independence which had broken out in Romania in 1821 and sharply divided public opinion in Europe. The Austrians were firmly pro-Turk; the Russians strongly supported their co-religionists, the Greeks. French and British support for the Greeks was tempered by a reluctance to see Greece dominated by Russia. The horror aroused by reports of atrocities committed by Turkish and Egyptian troops in Greece was diminished by the dislike caused by the unashamed piracy against merchant ships of all nations practised by the Greek 'navy', which was commanded by a cashiered Royal Navy officer, Lord Cochrane.

Britain, France, and Russia found that they could agree to go as far as to try to obtain a cease-fire during which they could mediate between the two sides. To obtain this cease-fire they did not deploy a single soldier. Instead they sent a naval squadron composed of ships of all three nations, and comprising ten ships of the line, nine frigates, and seven smaller vessels. The chief command was entrusted to a British sailor, Vice-Admiral Sir Edward Codrington, who had been one of Nelson's captains at Trafalgar, and who, on the whole, managed to maintain friendly relations with his two colleagues, Rear-Admiral de Rigny of France, and Rear-Admiral Heiden, a Dutchman who had served in the Royal Navy and now commanded the Russian squadron.

There is no way of putting down a land war by the use of a naval squadron and Codrington's task was made no easier by the issue of ambiguous instructions from London, Paris, and St Petersburg. These were filtered through the Ambassadors of the three powers at Constantinople who added their own 'elucidations'. When

Donegal, Conqueror, Mars, and *Diadem* of the British channel squadron photographed in about 1850. These were among the last of the purely sail third rate ships of the line

53

Codrington asked what the instructions and elucidations meant he was told by the British Ambassador to the Porte: 'You are not to take part with either of the belligerents, but you are to interpose your forces between them, and keep the peace with your speaking trumpet if possible; but in case of necessity, with that which is used for the maintenance of a blockade against friends as well as foes; – I mean *force.*'

There were endless and inconclusive negotiations and, during the summer of 1827, the combined squadron kept the Sultan's fleet bottled up in the Bay of Navarino and thus prevented it from escorting troops to deal with outbreaks of Greek revolt. Such a blockade could not be maintained by sailing ships during the winter and, on 20 October, the three admirals decided that the only way of carrying out their orders would be to take the squadron into the bay and establish a close blockade, one within range of the Turkish cannon. The risks were obvious. The Sultan's fleet, apart from the shore batteries, had 2,000 guns against the 1,300 mounted in the broadsides of the blockaders and, in the confined waters of the bay, the Turks would have every opportunity of employing fireships with devastating effect. On the other hand, it was indisputable that the crews of the British, French, and Russian ships were far better trained than their opponents although in some Egyptian ships there were French advisers who arranged the defensive deployment of the Sultan's ships before the allies entered the bay, whereupon they sought shelter in the French ships. Moreover although all the commanders of the fleet inside the bay owed a nominal allegiance to the Sultan, they comprised three separate squadrons, Turkish, Egyptian, and Tunisian, and the aims of the three were far from being identical.

In his orders Codrington laid down that 'No gun is to be fired from the combined fleet without a signal made for that purpose, unless shot be fired from any of the Turkish [i.e. Turkish, Egyptian, or Tunisian] ships; in which case the ships so firing are to be destroyed immediately . . . In case of a regular battle . . . it is to be observed that, in the words of Lord Nelson, "No captain can do very wrong who places his ship alongside that of an enemy."'

There is no record of how the French, now Britain's allies, reacted to this last, somewhat tactless, injunction but, when the need arose, they did not hesitate to obey it. Firing started at the extreme right of the line when a British boat tried, in accordance with Codrington's instructions, to disarm a Turkish fireship whose crew were seen to be 'occupied in preparing their train'. Even then the outbreak might have been contained and a British officer had boarded the Turkish flagship under a flag of truce but, as he was leaving, his Greek interpreter was shot with a pistol through a gun-port. The firing then became general except on the allied left where the Tunisians declined to have any part of the battle.

By the end of the day sixty Turkish and Egyptian ships had been burned or driven ashore, including three ships of the line and five, sixty-eight gun frigates. Some 10,000 of their sailors were killed or

A contemporary engraving of the Battle of Navarino, showing how closely the ships were engaged

wounded. No allied ships were lost and their casualties were only 174 killed and 475 wounded. Admiral Codrington was advanced to a KCB and relieved of his command.

No steam-assisted vessel was present at Navarino although the Greeks had a steam warship in commission and the British had employed one in the Burma War of three years earlier. The ships that were used were almost identical with those Nelson had commanded at Trafalgar. In both propulsion and armament there was little significant difference between them and the ships which had disputed the Anglo-Dutch War which had followed the Restoration of Charles II. Built largely of oak they were, despite the skill of their officers and men, entirely dependent on the whims of the wind. They were also highly inflammable. In the wars between 1793 and 1814 the British had lost eight of their battleships to accidental fire compared to five to enemy action. Nineteen more had been lost to the perils of the sea.

By the standard of the guns used by the armies, warships carried an enormous armament. A single broadside from a seventy-four-gun ship, the standard ship of the line, threw a greater weight of metal than the whole of Wellington's artillery could fire at one discharge at the Battle of Vitoria. It threw it, however, with great inaccuracy. The only aiming device consisted of a few notches along the barrel of a gun which could be aligned with a piece of string which was held taut above it and secured to a ring screwed into the top of the gun-port. A traverse of more than ten degrees to either side required the ship to be moved, hence Nelson's advice that a captain should place his ship alongside his enemy. As he remarked on another occasion, 'I hope we shall be able, as usual, to get so close to our enemies that our shot cannot miss the object.' Naval actions were fought at very close range, frequently with the opposing ships touching each other. Even then it was very rare for a ship to sink in battle, its oak timbers would keep it afloat under almost any circumstances. Of the eighty battle-ships which the French lost in battle during the long wars, many caught fire in action, many were driven ashore, many were so shattered that their crews were no longer able to defend them, but only one sank in action – *L'Orient* whose powder magazine blew up during the battle of the Nile. The largest guns employed were 32-pounders, it having been found that larger guns, 42-pounders, imposed too great a strain on the fabric of the ship and, thanks to the weight of the shot, were slow to load. Even with the normal guns, an immense quantity of powder and shot was required. At Navarino the three British two-deckers, which had a combined broadside of 232 guns (not all of which were fired), consumed 27,470lb. of powder and 122 tons of shot in about four hours firing. Steps were, at long last, being taken to improve the standard of gunnery at least in the Royal Navy and in 1832 the training establishment HMS *Excellent* was set up at Portsmouth.

THE COMING OF STEAM

The changes in ship design were almost imperceptible. Codrington's flagship *Asia*, built in 1824, had been designed on the lines of the French battleship *Franklin* which had been captured at the Nile in 1798 and taken into the Royal Navy as HMS *Canopus*. Exmouth's flagship at the bombardment of Algiers, HMS *London*, had been built in 1810 to the designs used for *Victory* in 1765. A step forward had been made by Sir Robert Sepping in his design for *Tremendous*, launched in 1811. By introducing additional diagonal frames between the parallel frames of the hull, Sepping found that ships could be built considerably longer, and thus with a bigger broadside armament, without a loss in rigidity. *Victory* is only 186 feet on the gun deck but by 1830 British battleships with a 200-foot gun deck were being built and the French were using even longer ships. Before the sailing battleship finally disappeared both countries had ships 250 feet long.

Change, however, was on the way. The first steam warship, USS *Demologos* had been completed in 1815 by Robert Fulton for the defence of New York harbour. She had two hulls, one containing the engine (which was British built) and one the boiler. A paddle wheel was mounted between them and thus partially protected from gun-fire. She could steam into a modest breeze at 5½ knots and carried an armament of thirty long 30-pounders and had two experimental 100-pounders mounted below the waterline. *Demologos* never saw action but, in her harbour protection role, she would have been a formidable opponent. It was doubtful how long she could have survived in the open sea.

The Royal Navy acquired its first steamship, the *Monkey*, a tug, in 1821. The first British armed steamers, used in Burma, belonged to

French sailing warships in Toulon harbour. The front three ships are a second rate, a frigate, and a third rate

the East India Company but in 1828 the Admiralty, then in the charge of the Duke of Clarence (later William IV), not usually regarded as a forward-looking prince, ordered two armed steamers, *Active* and *Lightning*. These were primarily intended as tugs and there was no intention of making wide use of steam. As the First Lord of the Admiralty announced, also in 1828, 'Their Lordships feel it their bounden duty to discourage to the utmost of their ability the employment of steam vessels, as they consider the introduction of steam is calculated to strike a fatal blow at the naval supremacy of the empire.'

It was not only from motives of conservatism and economy that this was a tenable view. What passed for an efficient maritime steam engine at that date (and no country outside Britain was then capable of manufacturing one) produced only one horse power for every ton of its weight and consumed coal at such a rate that it must have a coaling station every 500 miles. It was not until 1838, when the first direct crossing of the Atlantic was made under steam, that the idea of a steam battle fleet became practicable. Even that crossing was made by a paddle steamer and the huge paddlewheels necessary to propel a heavy gun ship represented a target that would be every gunnery officer's dream.

The revolution in warship design started in France and was, initially, more concerned with armament than propulsion. In 1822 a French artillery officer, H. J. Paixhan, published a pamphlet entitled *La Nouvelle Force Maritime* which advocated a navy of small, steam-driven, iron-built ships. At the time such a proposal was beyond French capabilities since France could manufacture neither the steam engines nor the iron for the hulls but Paixhan put forward another, more significant proposal. His iron-built fleet would be armed with large, long guns which would fire only explosive shells. It was 1837 before the French Admiralty, always intent on shaking Britain's naval supremacy, could be persuaded to adopt this proposal and, although Paixhan's shells were no more than hollowed-out roundshot with unreliable fuses, the 'wooden walls', with their high fire risk, were doomed from the day on which the French navy adopted explosive missiles.

PART TWO

Steam and the Percussion Cap

CHAPTER FOUR

Steam and Iron

W̲HILE THE FRENCH introduction of the Paixhan explosive shell meant that wood was no longer a safe building material for warships, it was not immediately clear what should take its place. Iron seemed to be the obvious answer and the major naval powers launched themselves, cautiously, into iron construction. Once more the East India Company led the way when, in 1839, they ordered two iron gunboats from Lairds of Birkenhead. Paddle driven and armed with 32-pounder solid shot guns these saw effective service in the China War of 1842 where the naval opposition was negligible. Meanwhile the French were beginning to build an all-iron navy and in 1840 Britain ordered an all-iron packet, the *Dover*. Three years later the United States launched the world's first iron-built frigate, the *Princeton*, an example quickly followed by Britain and France. Britain also adopted shell guns, choosing an 8-inch model for larger warships. They did not, however, abandon the old fashioned type of cannon, believing that roundshot still had a role to play. Indeed, counting on the stronger build of their newer ships, they installed on each ship of the line a 68-pounder, mounted at the bows to act as a chase gun. These monsters each weighed 95 cwt. compared to the 56 cwt. of the standard 32-pounder.

Simultaneously tests carried out at Woolwich produced disturbing results. Iron ships at that time were usually built with plating ⅝th inch thick and it was demonstrated that at a range of 40 yards 32-pounder shot would penetrate this even if fired with a greatly reduced charge. Moreover, there was great splinter effect from the plating and the hole produced could not be immediately plugged as it usually could be in a wooden ship. The publication of this report caused both Britain and France to suspend all iron construction for major ships. Britain had, in fact, already built four iron frigates and these were relegated to transport status. The earliest of them, launched in 1845, was the ill-fated *Birkenhead*. Nor was the path of the shell gun smooth. In 1844 a newly designed 12-inch model was installed in USS *Princeton*. During trials the gun burst killing not only the Secretary of the Navy but the Secretary of State.

It was not until the Bessemer process came into use in the fifties

HMS *Caledonia* at general quarters. She had been laid down in 1860 as a 91-gun second rate, but was completed as an ironclad frigate in 1865

The contest between *Rattler* and *Alecto*

that metal construction became practicable for warships, but USS *Princeton* set another trend that was not reversed, for, unlike most of the British and French warships, she was screw-driven. All commercial experience had favoured the paddle but in 1842 Brunel decided that the liner *Great Britain*, laid down as a paddle steamer, should be converted to screw. This inspired the Admiralty to make practical trials. A screw-steamer *Rattler*, 999 tons and 200 nominal horsepower, was matched against the paddle-boat *Alecto* of equal size and power. Not only did *Rattler* outsteam her in straight competition, she towed her backwards at 2½ knots despite all *Alecto*'s paddles could do.

The triumph of the *Rattler* decided all the principal navies to concentrate on screw-driven major warships. Once again France led the way with the *Napoléon*, launched in 1850 and capable of steaming at 11 knots with her 940 h.p. engines. Two years later the British replied with the 91-gun *Agamemnon* with a comparable performance. Both these battleships were full-rigged ships with their main armament mounted in broadsides. Apart from their smoke-stacks they closely resembled the ships that had fought at Trafalgar. They were able to manoeuvre under steam and, if the wind was not too strong, to sail into it, but their range was limited. As conservative naval officers were not slow to point out, their engines and boilers took up space that could otherwise have been used for ammunition, rations, and water.

These great ships were completed in time for the Crimean War but, from a naval point of view, the most significant event in that war occurred before either France or Britain decided on hostilities. In November 1853 the Russian Black Sea Fleet destroyed a Turkish frigate squadron at Sinope. Unlike overwhelming naval victories in the past, the Russians did not capture their opponents or drive them on the rocks. Every one of the six Turkish frigates was set on fire by

Russian shellfire and burnt to the waterline. The end of wooden warships was clearly signalled and every navy started improvising protection by 'cladding' their wooden ships with iron plates.

The effectiveness of such improvisations was made clear at the beginning of the Crimean War in October 1855 when, with the support of conventional ships, three French floating batteries attacked Kinburn, east of Odessa. These craft were each 60 feet long and mounted eighteen 50-pounders. Built of wood covered with 4-inch iron plates, they were steam driven and barely seaworthy – 'never to be trusted on open water out of sight of more orthodox vessels'. Anchored at 800 yards from the fortifications of Kinburn they proved both effective as batteries and impervious to shot. An observer wrote 'the shot and shell could be heard by the sailors in distant ships slapping and smacking against the sides and then rebounding into the water. One (floating) battery alone received sixty indentations or shot marks, all of which would have been perilous to a wooden vessel.' The Russians were using 18- and 32-pounders against them but could only harm them by getting a lucky shot through a gunport which, necessarily, had to be large (3ft. 4in. x 2ft. 10in.). The only deaths caused on board any of the three were when two French sailors were killed when a cannon ball entered a port in the *Dévastation*. After three hours firing, during which the Russians lost 45 killed and 135 wounded, Kinburn was surrendered by the governor.

The British contribution to the attack on Kinburn was also effective but less well protected. It consisted of some gunboats mounting Armstrong rifled cannon. The advantage of rifled guns was clear. It enabled a lighter gun to fire at almost twice the range. An 8-inch gun weighing 60 cwt. would carry 8,000 yards if it was rifled. A smoothbore of the same calibre would weigh 85 cwt. and have a range of only 4,500 yards. Unfortunately no one could devise a safe breech-loading mechanism and the muzzle-loading of a heavy shell was a difficult and slow procedure.

Although after Sinope there were no fleet actions in the Crimean War, it proved a turning point in naval history. Britain and France each deployed fleets in both the Black Sea and the Baltic but found no enemy to fight. Nor were they much disturbed by a Russian innovation, the floating mine, which was used in considerable quantity but which only succeeded in damaging two small ships. All the fleets were dependent on sail. To the Black Sea the Royal Navy initially sent ten ships of the line, of which only two were steam-assisted. They were supported by seven smaller ships of which six were paddle-steamers. The French fleet there had eight battleships, only one of which had a steam-driven screw, and four paddle-steamers. In the Baltic, which was closer to the engineering resources of Britain, the Royal Navy had thirteen of their nineteen battleships equipped with screws and twenty smaller steamships including a steam-frigate. Only one of the nine French battleships in the Baltic was steam-assisted.

The lessons of Sinope and Kinburn were not lost on either of the

Gloire in Toulon harbour in 1860

Western allies. In 1857 the French declared that no purely sailing vessel would in future be considered as a man-of-war and in the following year the First Lord of the Admiralty announced that, in the British view, 'Sailing vessels, though useful in time of peace, would never be employed again during wars'.

Despite their alliance, naval rivalry between the two countries continued unabated. In 1859 the French commissioned *La Gloire*, a steam-assisted frigate of 5,200 tons capable of 13 knots. She was in fact a wooden two-decker cut down to a single deck and clad from bow to stern with 4¾-inch iron plating. Britain's reply was HMS *Warrior*, 9,200 tons, the first iron-built battleship. To avoid the splinter effect and to increase her strength her hull was constructed of 9/16th-inch iron plating and this was covered with 18 inches of teak. This, in turn, was covered with iron sheeting 4½ inches thick. This armoured construction extended over 218 of the 420 feet of her length and bulkheads of similar strength were built fore and aft of the armoured section. Thus there was an armoured citadel amidships and this contained the engines and most of the main armament. This had been planned as forty broadside-mounted 68-pounders, but was modified to ten 110-pounder breech-loaders, twenty-six 68-pounder muzzle-loaders, and four 70-pounder breech-loaders. Both *Gloire* and *Warrior* were fully rigged sailing ships and on the latter the two funnels were retractable when the engines, which could give her 14 knots, were not in use.

Throughout the nineteenth century it was, despite occasional American intervention, Anglo–French rivalry which dictated the pace of warship development. The French, from Paixhan onwards, had a nagging feeling that they ought to have it in their power to revenge themselves for the humiliating defeat their navy had suffered between 1793 and 1814, a feeling put into words by Adolphe Thiers when he declared in 1840 that the French fleet should be expanded 'not to dominate the seas but to prevent all domination of the seas'. On the other side of the Channel there were recurring fears that a fleet of French steamboats might swarm across and land a large army on England's unprotected shore. As it happened the French lead in pioneering a revolution in naval design resulted in Britain's maritime supremacy being established until the end of the century. The intro-

HMS *Warrior* photographed after her bowsprit had been shortened, but before her armament was revised in 1867

HMS *Warrior* as originally completed. Her fine lines made her fast–she once recorded 13 knots under sail–but difficult to handle and manoeuvre

duction of steam gave Britain a clear advantage since no other nation could match the quality of steam coal that she drew from south Wales. Her scattered colonies ensured convenient coaling stations all over the world and meant that other nations were largely dependent on her to fuel their ships when away from their home waters. The change to iron construction equally favoured Britain. In 1850 world production of iron totalled less than 6,000,000 tons and of this the United Kingdom contributed 2,500,000 tons. By 1870 Britain was producing 6,000,000 tons of iron annually while the combined output of France, Germany, and the United States amounted to only 4,250,000 tons. Britain's main naval weakness during the Napoleonic wars had been that after 1802 all naval building oak had had to be imported while at no time had she avoided dependence on the Baltic trade for the masts for ships of the line. By the middle of the nineteenth century she was entirely self-sufficient for naval building materials. Yet another British advantage was the increased cost of ship-building. *Warrior* cost £377,000 compared to the contemporary price of a wooden frigate, £105,000. As the richest nation in the world Britain was in a very strong position to win any naval construction race.

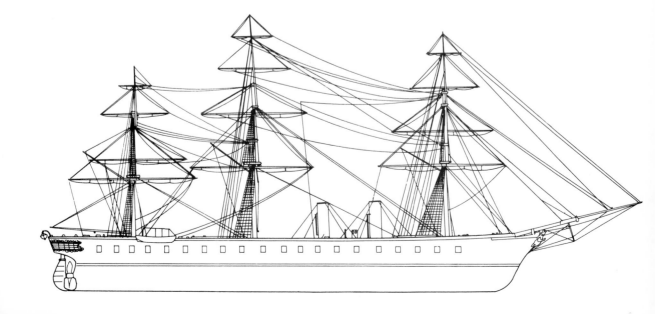

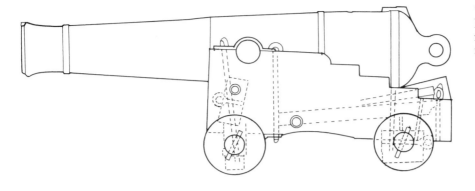

The 110-pound breech-loading cannon which formed HMS *Warrior's* main battery (BELOW) and the 68-pound smooth-bore muzzle-loader which was the secondary armament (LEFT)

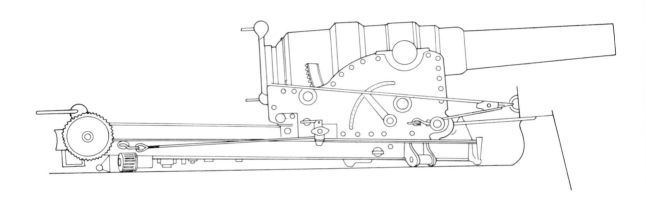

THE FIRST IRONCLAD DUEL

On the outbreak of the American Civil war the US Navy, such as it was, fell entire into the hands of the Federal government. It consisted of seventy-six vessels of which thirty-two were wholly dependent on sail. The Confederacy secured no ships, no building yards, and no cannon foundry until they took Norfolk, Virginia where they acquired not only a shipyard but an arsenal containing 1,198 cannon including 134 8-inch guns. At Norfolk they also took the wreck of a forty-gun frigate, *Merrimac*, which had been burned and sunk to avoid capture. Having refloated her and restored her steam engines to working order they cut her down to just above the waterline. On her deck they built a casemate 170 feet long with walls, inclined inwards at an angle of 35 degrees, constructed of 20 inches of pine covered with 4 inches of oak and, on the outside, two layers of iron plating each 2 inches thick. Within the casemate they mounted on each broadside a 6-inch rifled gun and three 9-inch smoothbores. Fore and aft of the casemate they added a 7-inch rifled gun which could fire on either beam as well as ahead (or astern). The small freeboard

RIGHT: The crew of USS *Monitor* on deck, showing the massive central turret

BELOW: The engagement between *Monitor* and *Merrimac* in Hampton Roads

remaining of the 280-foot hull was left unarmoured, but a cast-iron ram, projecting 4 feet, was attached to the bow.

News of the *Merrimac*'s transformation caused consternation in the north where there was no ship capable of dealing with her. They replied by building a small but revolutionary craft designed specifically to fight her. This was the *Monitor*, built in 118 days to a design by Captain Ericsson. She was only 172 feet at the waterline but had an armoured superstructure which projected 14 feet at the bow and, to protect the screw and rudder, 32 feet at the stern. She

was surmounted by a revolving turret, 9 feet high and 20 feet in diameter, which mounted two 11-inch smoothbores. The turret was protected by eight layers of 1-inch iron plating.

On 8 March 1862 *Merrimac* (unmemorably renamed *Virginia*) set off on her trials from Norfolk. Her engines would barely keep way on her and her steering was so inadequate that it took her thirty-five minutes to turn. Her officers had seceded from the US Navy but her crew were volunteers from the Confederate army. Since a considerable squadron of Federal ships lay in Hampton Roads it was appropriate that Holy Communion was administered to the ship's company before she sailed.

Her debut was a triumph. She rammed and sank the wooden *Cumberland* (30 guns) and then turned on *Congress* (50 guns), drove her ashore with gunfire, set her on fire, and forced her to surrender. On board *Merrimac* there were only ten casualties and a slight leak had developed. That night *Monitor*, under tow from New York, reached Hampton Roads.

Next day the two ironclads duelled and two hours of mutual bombardment produced no result. *Monitor* had brought wrought-iron shot which did not fit her guns and her cast-iron shot shattered on contact with her opponent's cladding. *Merrimac*, expecting only to fight wooden ships, had only shell on board and this could not harm *Monitor*. The latter tried to disable *Merrimac* by driving her bow into her propeller but the two ships only grazed and, even at point-blank range, the 11-inch guns made no effect on the armoured casemate though the iron was driven in at the point of impact. *Merrimac*, as soon as she could be manoeuvred into position, tried to reply and, making her full speed of 5 knots, struck *Monitor* amidships. No damage was done since her ram had been left in *Cumberland*'s side on the previous day and the only result was to increase *Merrimac*'s leak. By that time *Monitor* was running short of ammunition and took to shallow water where *Merrimac* could not close with her. The Confederate ship therefore withdrew and the two never met again. *Merrimac* was eventually scuttled to avoid capture when the Federals recaptured Norfolk and, soon afterwards, *Monitor* was overtaken by a gale at sea and lost.

The action in Hampton Roads proved nothing except that primitive ironclads were proof against unsuitable ammunition. A result might have been obtained if *Monitor* had shipped the right size of shot or if her gunners had been prepared to load their weapons with a charge larger than 15 lb. of powder. Later trials established that her Dahlgren guns could safely be used with a charge of 30 or even 50 lb. but the disaster to USS *Princeton* eighteen years earlier (see p. 61) had made a very deep impression on the US Navy.

The lessons learned by the world's naval designers from the action were both misleading. The first was that ironclads were impenetrable; the second was that the ram was a better weapon than the cannon. The sinking of the *Cumberland* made a deep impression which was not dissipated when in 1864 Admiral Faragut indulged in much ineffective ramming as he forced his way past Fort Morgan at

Mobile and captured the *Tennessee*, the largest ironclad the Confederates attempted to build. Ramming, however, became a fashionable tactic and was to distort naval architecture in America and Europe for more than a decade.

At sea the other significant event in the American Civil War was the first sinking of a warship by a submarine. During the Napoleonic War an American, Robert Fulton, had invented a submersible boat which he offered to Napoleon. When the Emperor was unimpressed, Fulton took his plan to the British Admiralty who gave it a practical trial and in 1805 an unmanned underwater craft sank a French pinnace in Boulogne harbour. Unfortunately news of this success never filtered back to England and further work was stopped.

The basic problem was one of propulsion since it was obvious that neither sail nor steam was suitable while submerged. Once more it was France which eventually took the lead and in 1863 *Le Plongeur*, driven by compressed air, began her trials. In the following year a different type of craft scored a practical success in America. The Confederates were almost in desperation for lack of means to break the ring of Federal blockading ships and, to attack them, developed a series of semi-submersible craft known as 'Davids'. Only one of them, the *Hunley*, managed to achieve anything and that only at considerable cost. Her crew consisted of nine men of whom eight were entirely occupied in winding hand cranks to turn the propeller. Her only weapon was a 'spar torpedo', an explosive charge on the end of a long pole which could be fired either by a trigger or by a timing device. *Hunley* had no conning tower and her low freeboard made her vulnerable to even small waves and on her trials she sank on five occasions, drowning thirty-five out of the forty men who had been trained to sail her. She was, however,

One of the 'Davids' aground in Charleston Harbour, showing the primitive 'schnorkel'

rewarded in the end. Remanned, she attacked and sank the Federal corvette *Housatonic* outside Charleston harbour on 17 February 1864. It is scarcely surprising that the explosion of her own torpedo was too much for her and the *Hunley* sank with all hands.

The British fleet at anchor in Plymouth Sound about 1870. In the centre lies the central battery ironclad HMS *Hercules*, an enlarged version of *Bellerophon*, with HMS *Warrior* immediately beyond her

THE LAST WOODEN SHIPS

By 1865 the revolution in warships was half way through its course. Every man-of-war was steam driven but all sea-going ships still carried the elaborate paraphernalia of a full-rigged sailing ship. All major ships were now ironclads and the thickness of their armour was steadily increasing. HMS *Bellerophon*, completed in 1864, had 1½-inch plating with 10 inches of teak and 6 inches of iron overall, and this extended the whole length of the ship. This was an increase of a third over the thickness of the armour carried by *Warrior* a few years earlier, and reflected the improvement in guns over the same period. All major navies now used rifled guns and their projectiles would carry as much as 10,000 yards although their effective range, largely controlled by difficulties in sighting them, was reckoned as only 2½ miles.

With the increase in the efficiency of guns went an increase in their weight and, added to the huge weight of the iron cladding, it was becoming apparent that a large number of broadside guns could not be mounted, the more so since their gun ports were obvious weak points in the armoured belt. Designers were turning their minds to mounting a smaller number of guns behind armoured screens on deck where they could have a wider arc of fire. The first turret man-of-war, designed before *Monitor* gave a practical demonstration of the potentiality of turrets, was HMS *Royal Sovereign*. She was designed by Captain Cowper Coles and mounted

five guns, each weighing 12½ tons, in four turrets on the centreline of the deck. Each turret had 10 inches of armour round the gunports and 5 inches elsewhere, while the hull had an armoured belt of 4½ inches of iron. *Royal Sovereign* was a makeshift, being a wooden three-decker cut down until she had only ten foot of freeboard, but her sister ship, *Prince Albert*, with the same dimensions and armament, was a purpose-built iron ship. Neither carried sails, and only three light signalling masts, but both were specifically intended as coast defence ships and not designed for the open sea. There was still doubt as to whether it was practicable to use iron ships for long voyages. In 1861 the Admiralty view was that they 'are not acceptable on distant stations where frequent cleansing of bottoms is not feasible'. As the First Lord graphically remarked, an iron vessel on a long commission on an equatorial station would soon have a bottom like a lawyer's wig.

When the Royal Navy's last new built three-decker wooden ship was commissioned as flagship of the Mediterranean Fleet in 1864 there was an outcry from 'progressives' in Parliament and press but, as the Secretary to the Admiralty explained, if you put men 'on board armour-plated ships (in hot climates) they would, from want of ventilation, speedily become useless and have to go to hospital. And therefore, until we can find means of ventilating our armour-plated ships, we must be satisfied to have attached to our squadrons one or more of these large roomy ships'. It was not until 1873 that reasonably satisfactory ventilation could be installed in large warships, and three years before that, the Royal Navy's last wooden battleship, HMS *Rodney*, paid off for the last time at Portsmouth after serving as flagship to the China squadron.

CHAPTER FIVE

Sebastopol and Solferino

A QUARTER OF A CENTURY after Waterloo the flintlock was in process of ending more than a hundred years of supremacy on the battlefield as it was replaced by the percussion cap. Smooth bores would also pass from the hands of the infantry as soon as a satisfactory way could be devised for forcing a ball down a rifled barrel. Once again Captain Delvigne was a pioneer. In 1841 he devised a ball which was the precursor of all subsequent rifle bullets, a shape which he described as cylindroconical. It had a hollow base of which the rim, from the explosion of the propellant charge, was expanded into the rifling. His design was improved upon by Captain Claude Étienne Minié, of the School of Musketry at Vincennes who added to the cylindroconical lead ball an iron plug at the base. The force of the charge drove this forward into the lead, expanding it to fit the grooves. After the rifling itself had been improved by his colleague, Captain Tamasier, the Minié rifle was adopted by both the British and French armies. It had a calibre of 0.702 inch, weighed 10lb., a fraction less than the smoothbore musket, and was sighted to 1,000 yards although it was accurate at scarcely half that range. In the British army it was officially known as a 'rifled musket' since the Duke of Wellington, Colonel Commandant of the Rifle Brigade, insisted that if the infantry of the line were allowed to fancy themselves as Riflemen 'they will be asking next to be dressed in green, or some other jack-a-dandy uniform'.

Although the British adopted the Minié rifle in 1851 and began to issue it to their troops over the next three years they were not satisfied with it and, before any infantryman had one in his hands, a committee was set up to design a successor weapon. The secretary was Captain Pitt-Rivers of the Grenadier Guards who, as part of his duties, made a collection of firearms of all types. From this he took to collecting artefacts of all kinds which illustrated the progress of human invention. Thus, as a by-product of his secretaryship, he became the founder of systematic archaeology.

The committee recommended adoption of the Enfield 'rifled musket' which incorporated improvements to the rifling and the bullet suggested by William Ellis Metford, an Indian railway

The Scots Fusilier Guards advance during the counter-attack on the Great Redoubt during the Battle of the Alma

engineer. This was a smaller weapon than the Minié, weighing less than 9lb. and having a calibre of only 0.577 inch. It was sighted to 1,200 yards but those who used it considered that its effective range was little more than 250. Although adopted in 1853, the Enfield was not available in sufficient quantities to equip the army which sailed for the Crimea. The early battles there were fought with the Minié although the Enfields were shipped out as they became available. They were in India in quantity, and it was the grease necessary to force the bullet down the barrel which was the ostensible cause of the outbreak at Meerut which in turn led to the mutiny of the Bengal Army in 1857.

In fact both the Minié and the Enfield were obsolete before they were designed. In 1843 the Prussian Army had adopted the *Zündnadelgewehr* or needle gun, the first practicable military breech-loader. Designed by Nicholas Dreyse this rifle was the first which enabled the soldier to load and fire lying down since inserting the rounds through the breech made it unnecessary to use the ramrod, an operation which could only be done standing. It also raised the possible rate of fire from the two rounds a minute possible with a rifled muzzle-loader, to eight or even twelve rounds a minute. It was not until the third quarter of the century that the needle gun was recognised as a revolutionary weapon, although the Prussians used it in their almost unnoticed campaign in Denmark in 1864, and meanwhile even more advanced weapons were being evolved in the United States.

In 1848 an American, Christian Sharp, patented a breech-loading lock on what is known as the 'drop-lock' principle, by which a lever

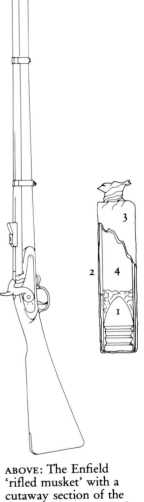

ABOVE: The Enfield 'rifled musket' with a cutaway section of the Minié bullet showing the bullet (1); the cardboard tube (2); the paper envelope (3); and the propellant powder (4)

LEFT: The Whitworth experimental 3-pounder during test firing at Liverpool. The breech and breech-screw can be seen

behind the trigger guard is pulled down thus causing the breech block to swing down from its position. At about the same time, largely in France, fixed ammunition, paper or cardboard cylinders enclosing percussion cap, propellant, and bullet, was being developed. Sharp's rifle, with these 'pinfire' cartridges, was much used by the Federal troops in the American Civil War but the most advanced design was the brainchild of a 20-year-old American, Christopher M. Spencer. He used Sharp's dropping breech block but introduced into the butt a spring-loaded tube which could contain seven cartridges, one of which was forced into the breech each time the breech block dropped, while an ejector working on the rim of the cartridge removed the spent case. It will come as no surprise that in 1861 the military authorities in Washington refused to contemplate the first magazine rifle. Spencer, however, contrived an interview with President Lincoln who examined the weapon and tested it in the garden of the White House. Before the Civil War ended 61,685 Spencer carbines had been issued to the Union cavalry.

During the same twenty-five years artillery at last began to emerge from the stagnation in which it had remained for more than a century. The first stirring came with the introduction of a percussion tube to replace the slow match (or in the navy the flint gun-lock) as a firing device. It was a surgeon who produced the model adopted by the Royal Artillery in 1845. In this a tube containing one of Forsyth's percussion caps was struck with a hammer but, six years later, a more sophisticated tube, in which a roughened bar was drawn through fulminate, was taken into service. At about the same time Captain Boxer R.A., produced a fuse based on a wooden tube filled with powder and bored at timed intervals. This greatly improved the effectiveness of shells and shrapnel.

All artillery pieces were still smooth bores and the artillery taken to the Crimea by both the British and French armies was scarcely distinguishable from the guns used by the two armies at Waterloo. When heavy guns were needed for the siege of Sebastopol the navy came forward with some 68-pounders and some 8-inch guns which had been converted to rifling on the Lancaster principle. Under Charles William Lancaster's scheme, spin was given to the projectile not by rifling grooves but by making the entire bore of the barrel oval and twisting it so that it would make one turn in thirty feet. The projectile was also oval in shape. At Sebastopol Lancaster guns made good practice at ranges of up to 2,600 yards but, since three of the eight guns employed blew up when being fired, there was little enthusiasm for them among the gun crews and Lancaster's ideas were allowed to lapse.

Nevertheless it was inevitable that rifled guns, which gave accuracy at twice the range that could be obtained with smooth-bores, would have to be taken into service and, in all armies, the arguments centred round whether the new models of field gun should be loaded through the muzzle or the breech. Defenders of the old-fashioned system pointed out, not without cause, that no one had yet devised a reliable method of closing the breech and it could not be denied that

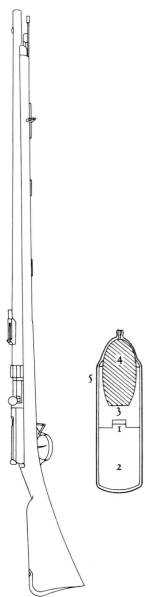

ABOVE: The Prussian needle gun with a cut-away of the cartridge showing the percussion cap (1); the powder charge (2); the papier mâché wadding (3); the bullet (4); and the outer paper tube (5)

as long as guns recoiled several feet each time they were fired the saving of effort resulting from breech loading was not as great as might now be supposed.

In Britain the advocates of progress won a temporary victory. In 1859 a start was made with re-equipping the field and horse artillery with rifled 12- and 9-pounders which were breech-loading on the principles laid down by William Armstrong. By this system the breech was closed by a vent-piece which dropped into place in grooves and was held there by a breech screw which was so bored that the shell could be loaded through it when the vent-piece was raised. This was a simple and, on the whole, efficient design but suffered from the defect that the vent-piece, even on a field gun, was cumbersome and heavy to handle. Hardly had the issue of these Armstrong guns started when the French produced a shell which fitted the bore and was equipped with studs which could move easily down the rifling from the muzzle. The British thereupon appointed a committee to reconsider the merits of breech and muzzle loading and its report, published in 1860, was emphatic 'that the breech-loading guns are far inferior to muzzle loading as regards simplicity of construction and cannot be compared to them in this respect in efficiency for active service'. It was consequently decided that the Royal Artillery should revert to muzzle-loaders just at the time when in Germany Herr Krupp was perfecting an improved breech-loader for the Prussian army.

THE CRIMEAN WAR

There was no particular reason why Britain and France should have become involved in one of the Russo–Turkish wars which were endemic throughout the eighteenth and nineteenth centuries. In Britain there was a continuing concern about Russian expansion to the south and east but, with the exception of Lord Palmerston, the Home Secretary, Lord Aberdeen's government was almost as pacifically minded as it was muddle-headed. It was public opinion, inflamed by *The Times*, that drove a reluctant cabinet to war. As Thomas Carlyle wrote in his diary, 'It is the idle population of editors, etc., that have done this to England. One perceives clearly the ministers go forward into it against their will.' In France even public opinion was opposed to war but Louis Napoleon, newly established as Emperor and anxious to make his reign as memorable for military glory as that of his illustrious uncle, allowed himself to be persuaded into war by his new-found British allies.

War against Russia was declared on 27 March 1854 and, with commendable promptitude, both allies sent expeditionary forces to the Mediterranean. The initial British contribution consisted of 27,000 men. Their commander was Lord Raglan who, as Lord Fitzroy Somerset, had been Wellington's Military Secretary in the Peninsula and at Waterloo – where he had lost an arm. At 65 he had a competent knowledge of tactics, outstanding courage, a mastery of the complex by-ways of military administration, and no experience of commanding so much as a platoon in action. He had, however, the essential quality of earning the devotion and loyalty of everyone who met him. The French sent 30,000 men under Marshal St Arnaud who, despite some creditable service in Algeria, was primarily a political soldier and had organised the *coup d'état* which had brought Louis Napoleon to power. He took up his command knowing that he was a dying man.

According to the orders given to Raglan and St Arnaud: 'The first and immediate object is to protect the Turkish Empire from Invasion.' This was a plausible mission since the Russians had invaded the Ottoman provinces of Moldavia and Wallachia (modern Romania) and were laying siege to Silistria (Silistro) on the south bank of the Danube in what is now Bulgaria. To support the Turkish defence the Anglo-French army began to land at Varna on the Black Sea coast at the end of May.

Since neither of the allies had brought any transport with them, there could be no question of making an immediate move towards Silistria, and before waggons could be obtained – but not before cholera had taken a firm grip on both armies – the Russians raised the siege and retreated from all the Turkish territory they held. Since the allied object had now been obtained the obvious course for the expeditionary forces was to go home, but once again public opinion demanded action. It would not be proper to end the war without a victory and, as *The Times* trumpeted, 'We hold that the taking of Sebastopol and the occupation of the Crimea are objects which would repay all the costs of the present war . . . We cannot but

A photograph by Roger Fenton of stores being unloaded on the quay at Balaklava

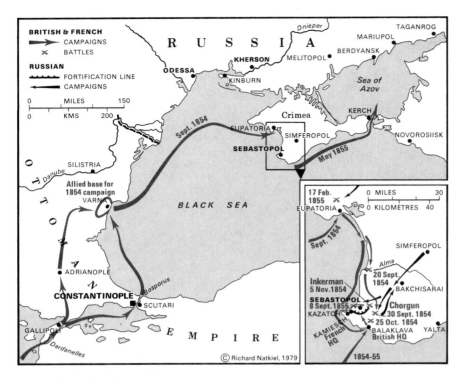

The Crimean theatre of
war showing the major
engagements and the
course of the Allied
naval expedition to the
Sea of Azov in spring
1855

suppose that 40,000 men of the allied armies, supported by their
fleets, would be able to keep in check any number of troops which
Russia can throw into the Crimea.'

The nation rose to this improbable lure and bayed for glory.
When the Prime Minister 'imprudently spoke in the sense of desiring
peace, he was howled down in the House of Lords. Reluctantly
cajoling the French Emperor to co-operate, orders were sent to the
allied commanders for an invasion of the Crimea and the capture of
Sebastopol. Raglan and St Arnaud were less than enthusiastic. They
had no information of the defences that they would have to overcome
and the estimates sent to them of Russian strength in the Crimea
varied between 45,000 and 140,000. Their doubts were shared by few
of their troops. The general view in the armies was summed up at
Varna by the British Inspector General of Hospitals who wrote,
'They might as well be killed there as die of cholera here.'

The Russians had plenty of warning about the coming invasion.
As one of them remarked, 'Why should we need spies when we have
The Times?' The immediate garrison in the peninsula was not very
large, two commands which totalled 50,000 soldiers who could call
on the support of 18,000 sailors and marines. Nevertheless, only 300
miles away in Bessarabia was a large army which, with Moldavia and
Wallachia evacuated, had no employment. Further reinforcements
and supplies would be a greater problem as there was no railway
south of Moscow and it was a four-month march from there to
Sebastopol. The land defences of that port were weak. A defence line
based on eight great bastions linked with earthworks had been traced

out but, thanks to lethargy and lack of funds, little had been done to make the project a reality.

The active strength of the Russian army was 834,000 regulars and 90,000 embodied Cossack irregulars. Behind them stood 100,000 Cossack reserves. There was a regular army reserve of 159,000 men but, since conscripts did twenty-five years with the colours before being posted to the reserve, the minimum age of the reservists was 45 and they were not a very formidable body of men.

The reputation of this enormous army had stood high ever since its successful resistance to Napoleon I and it had a very favourable opinion of its own merits. Its ideas of tactics had changed little since its triumphal entrance into Paris and were a curious blend of formality and improvisation. The soldiers were the most meticulously drilled in the world and would have gladdened the heart of Frederick the Great except that they were deployed in the column which the early French revolutionary generals had devised to compensate for their lack of well-drilled soldiers. Thus the Russians managed to have the worst of both tactical worlds. Their columns were a magnificent sight on the parade ground and a magnificent target in the field. As if to ensure that no enemy could miss them they had, in almost their only tactical innovation, dispensed with skirmishers since their experience in fighting Turkish irregulars had shown skirmishers to be vulnerable to guerrilla fighters. There was thus nothing to obstruct regularly-trained troops from bringing their own fire to bear on the Russian columns which could reply with the smallest possible volume of fire.

Lack of fire power did not worry Russian generals. The great Suvarov had laid down that 'the bullet is a fool, only the bayonet is wise'. All Russian tactics were based on the bayonet. Even in defence troops were not deployed in line, their main strength was held back in vast columns ready to counterattack with the bayonet. Such dispositions would have been of dubious validity in the days of the smooth bore musket; with the coming of the rifle they were a prescription for slaughter.

They were, in fact, still living in the days of the smooth bore. Even the regular battalions were using muskets recently converted to percussion caps and were thus at a grave disadvantage when confronted with the Miniés of the British and French. Reserve battalions were still armed with flintlocks. In each corps of three divisions there was one specialist rifle battalion and each regiment (three or four battalions) had one rifle company. The rifle used was the Littiksky model of 1843, a Belgian-made version of the Brunswick rifle which the British rifle regiments had recently discarded with some pleasure (see p. 50), but such was the stress laid on the supremacy of the bayonet that little thought or training had been devoted to the effective use of the few rifles available.

Staff work had never been a strong point in the Russian army. In the infantry the company officers had, for the most part, been promoted from the ranks and were barely literate. The officers from the nobility who graduated into the higher ranks through the Guard and the cavalry tended to regard administration as a chore for lesser men. Most of the staff officers were Germans, many of them from the Baltic provinces of the Russian Empire who were despised by officers from old Russia.

In their Crimean army the administrative problem was more complicated than usual owing to the character of the commander-in-chief. Prince Alexander Sergeivich Menshikov had served as an officer of artillery and in the Guard before being a staff officer at Borodino and Leipzig. Being a favourite of Czar Alexander I he had been promoted to major-general within seven years of his first commission but Nicholas I had transferred him to the navy, appointing him a rear-admiral and chief of naval staff. He had also done a spell as a diplomat and his overbearing attitude while ambassador to Constantinople had been a contributory cause of the Crimean War. Despite his staff experience and his high reputation as a naval administrator, Menshikov did not care for having his own staff officers and seldom employed the officers allocated to him as more than supernumerary aides-de-camp. Nor did he believe that the allies were capable of landing in the Crimea. When Colonel Todleben, one of the outstanding engineer officers of all time, was sent to assist him with the fortifications of Sebastopol, his first reaction was to send him back to Bessarabia. It was not until the allies were actually marching on the city that Todleben was permitted to begin work on the defences.

The Russians could rely on the traditional bravery and toughness of their soldiers to compensate for some of these disadvantages and their field guns were marginally better than those of their opponents but the British and French had some clear advantages. Their rifles gave them fire superiority and their staff work, though far from perfect, was very much better than that of the Russians. Their communications with their home bases, though far longer in distance were considerably shorter in terms of time. A ship from England would reach the Crimea in a quarter of the time that a waggon would take on the overland journey from Moscow. To set against this the allies lacked much in unity. Despite their recent experience in Algeria, the French in the Crimea went into battle almost exactly as they would have done under Napoleon I. The British manoeuvred in the same way that they had used to defeat him. No steps were taken to establish a common tactical doctrine and none to form a joint command. Operations were arranged by discussions between two equal and independent commanders-in-chief and the agreements reached were frequently far from specific. On occasions no agreement was reached and opportunities went by default.

The allied armies began to go ashore on 14 September 1854. The point chosen was close to the small port of Eupatoria, 50 miles north of Sebastopol and the orders for landing 27,000 British, 30,000 French, and 5,000 Turks with 128 guns were closely modelled on those issued by Sir Ralph Abercromby for his landing against the French near Alexandria in 1801. In the British army the instructions called for all ranks to wear 'full dress without plumes'. The French can scarcely have been encouraged that the date chosen was the anniversary of Napoleon's entry into Moscow.

Since Menshikov believed his army to be too weak to fight on the beaches the landing was unopposed but was observed by a few officers escorted by Cossacks. The Russians meanwhile were establishing themselves in a strong position on the heights above the Alma river, a day's march to the south. The soldiers were astonished at their view of the allied ships:

The whole of the allied fleet was lying off the salt lakes to the south of Eupatoria, and at night their forest of masts was illuminated with lanterns of various colours. Both men and officers were lost in amazement at the sight of so many ships, especially as many of them had seldom seen the sea before. The soldiers said, 'Behold the infidel has built another Holy Moscow on the waves,' comparing the masts of the ships to the church spires of that city.

THE BATTLE OF THE ALMA

It was not until 19 September that the allied army was ready to move out of their beach-head and the following morning found them facing the Russian position. The French and Turks were on the seaward flank, the British taking the inland route since they had the only mounted troops with either army, a single light cavalry brigade. Facing them were the Alma heights, a line of hills stretching 5½ miles from the cliffs above the sea to a point where the ridge fell away and a mass of cavalry marked the right of the Russian line. The main road to Sebastopol crossed the river 3 miles from its mouth and ran

The Battle of the Alma

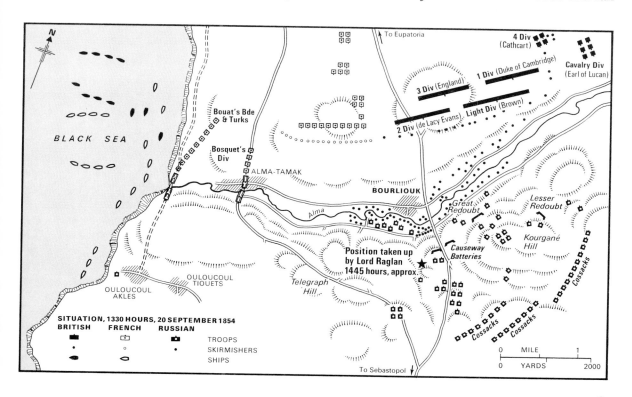

SITUATION, 1330 HOURS, 20 SEPTEMBER 1854

BRITISH	FRENCH	RUSSIAN	
			TROOPS
			SKIRMISHERS
			SHIPS

gently up a causeway through what Raglan described as 'a great amphitheatre'. This was flanked on the west by a height crowned by a signalling tower and known as Telegraph Hill, and on the east by the Kourgané (Kurgan) Hill. The latter was a long feature and its eastern end formed the right of the main Russian position. The Alma river was fordable almost everywhere and there was a strip of cultivated and enclosed ground on each bank. The approach from the north was over open and gently rolling country which gave no cover to the attackers.

The Russians had every advantage of ground but Menshikov had barely enough troops to hold its entire length. Although the four battalions of the Moscow regiment had reached him on the evening of 19 September after a forced march in which they covered 160 miles in five days, he had only 35,000 men. This did not diminish his confidence in his ability to hold his ground and he solved the problem of numbers by ruling that the seaward end of the line was unassailable. The first mile inland was, in fact, a precipitous slope rising 300 feet from the river but Menshikov had made no reconnaissance of it and

ABOVE: The Guards brigade in action during the Battle of Inkerman

RIGHT: Two watercolours by Colonel the Hon. George Cadogan who served throughout the Crimean campaign. Troops on reconnaissance watch a field battery up on the heights open fire, while cavalry skirmish with Russians in the valley below (TOP). Zouaves come to the rescue of British guardsmen during the Battle of Inkerman (BOTTOM)

did not know that it was cut into by a number of negotiable gullies. To cover it he allocated only a single battalion and on the western slopes of Telegraph Hill he stationed only four reserve battalions armed with flintlocks. In their rear was a regular regiment formed in column for immediate counterattack.

The main strength, five regiments, was stationed for the defence of the great amphitheatre and the artillery was similarly massed at this point. Eighteen field guns were deployed beside the causeway on the eastern slope of Telegraph Hill where they commanded the road bridge at a range of 700 yards. On the other side of the road twelve guns occupied an earthwork (known to the British as the

Great Redoubt) and defiladed the road down to the bridge. A smaller earthwork (the Lesser Redoubt) armed with six guns was built higher up the Kourgané protecting the approaches to the Great Redoubt. The reserves, eight battalions of infantry and two regiments of hussars, were posted in rear of the amphitheatre and the right, beyond the Kourgané, was entrusted to a large body of Cossacks. Menshikov divided responsibility for the front between two subordinates but failed to make clear where the boundary between them lay, consequently neither of them accepted responsibility for the eastern slopes of Telegraph Hill and the troops on that side of the amphitheatre were left to their own devices throughout the action. Similarly, although the Prince put the regiments in reserve under the command of the two sector generals he later marched them away under his own orders and without notifying his subordinates.

On the evening of 19 September the allied commanders held a conference. According to an English observer St Arnaud was 'fired with a more than healthy enthusiasm' and proposed that part of the French army should engage the Russians' attention to the front while the remainder attacked their seaward flank. Raglan received this suggestion 'impassively'. Since there was no part in this scheme for the British there was little more that he could do but St Arnaud added as an afterthought that Raglan's men might care to try and work their way round the Russian right. There was every kind of objection to such a move but Raglan remained non-committal and, when the meeting broke up, all that had been resolved was that the French right would advance at 5 am next morning and that the rest would follow two hours later. On leaving Raglan assured his ally that 'he might rely on the vigorous co-operation of the British Army'.

On 20 September the extreme right-hand division, General Bosquet's, with the 5,000 Turks were on the move by 5.30 am and the rest of the French army marched off at 7.00 but, having covered half the distance to the river, the entire force halted, lit fires, and made coffee. Meanwhile the British, who had breakfasted before they marched, were deploying into line and filling the gap on their right which had been unexpectedly left by the French. Meanwhile the two commanders-in-chief rode forward and confirmed what Raglan had always suspected, that the Russian position was far too wide to be held in check by part of the French army. They therefore decided that the British would attack to the east of Telegraph Hill and that the French would deal with the front between that height and the sea. The result was described by a French historian as 'two separate but juxtaposed battles'.

During the coffee break Bosquet had been making his own reconnaissance and had discovered that, while the mouth of the Alma was fordable, the gullies leading up the heights would only permit men to advance up them in single file. He decided to entrust the climb to Bouat's brigade, and the Turks, while he sent his other brigade upstream to the fords of Alma-Tamak which were on the front on the next division on his left.

Both brigades reached the crest without opposition but Bosquet had omitted to order his battery to move by Alma-Tamak and Bouat wasted some time trying unsuccessfully to force the guns up a gully. When he desisted and sent the guns to the ford they became entangled with the flanking division which was trying to cross at that moment. Meanwhile Bosquet's infantry remained below the crest in obedience to a standing order that French infantry should not attempt to advance without artillery support.

His skirmishers, however, engaged the few Russians within range and this roused Menshikov to panic action. He galloped to the extreme left and sent orders for all the reserves to follow him. He took no further part in the direction of affairs on the main front, leaving matters in the hands of his subordinates who now had no reserves to support them. In his own little battle, the Zouave skirmishers caused heavy casualties among the Russian columns as they came up, but the Russian guns kept the Zouaves in check while their ammunition lasted. It was soon found that the Russian ammunition waggons had been left 2 or 3 miles to the rear and their artillery fell silent.

On the allied left the British formed in two lines each of two divisions and each division in two-deep line. The forward lines consisted of the Light and Second Divisions but the Light deployed so far to their right that the Second was squeezed out. In front of the Light was a whole battalion of the Rifle Brigade and, according to Russian participants, it was the fire power of this battalion and their skill at skirmishing that enabled the Light Division to break through. So galled were the defenders of the Great Redoubt that the Light Division surged into it with very little resistance. They could not hold it. As the inevitable counterattack developed an order to retire was passed round the triumphant but disordered attackers. At the time this order was attributed to an English-speaking Russian officer but misunderstanding is a more likely explanation. Whatever the cause, the Light Division fell back about 300 yards when it was halted and reformed.

There was total confusion on the Russian side. Even the counterattack on the Great Redoubt was led by two generals each ignorant of the other's presence. On Telegraph Hill General Kiriakov, moved either by panic or by mistrust of Menshikov's ability to hold Bosquet's impending attack, withdrew the regiment that held the summit and redeployed it to his left. It is scarcely surprising that it took the French some time to realise that this vital height was bare of defenders and before they did so a bizarre event had occurred. When Lord Raglan had set his four attacking divisions in motion, he turned to his staff and said, 'Now we'll cross,' and trotted down to the river beyond the British right. As they forded the Alma two of the staff were wounded by shots from the Causeway battery and Raglan remarked, 'Ha! If they can enfilade us here, we can certainly enfilade them from the rising ground beyond. Order up Turner's battery!'

The Commander-in-Chief then rode on up the hill, passing through the *tirailleurs* of the French left and established himself on a

piece of flat ground on the inland slope of Telegraph Hill. Nothing could have been more demoralising to the Russians than the sight of this group of cocked-hatted officers sitting their horses quietly in the centre of the Russian position, and their consternation was soon increased when, with enormous exertion, two 9-pounders were manhandled up to Raglan's position. While the gunners were struggling to bring the rest of the battery into position, the two guns were manned by officers of the artillery staff and opened fire on the Causeway battery. Their second round blew up an ammunition waggon and the Russian gunners, thinking themselves disastrously outflanked, limbered up and withdrew.

By this time two French divisions were attacking Telegraph Hill from the seaward side and, on the extreme left, the British First Division, Guards and Highlanders, swept across the river and recaptured the Great Redoubt. The Russians fought bravely and made several damaging counterattacks but their generals had lost all control and by mid-afternoon their army was in a confused retreat by regiments and battalions. Their casualties amounted to 5,700 men, of whom 735 were listed as missing. The French lost 1,350 men and the British 2,000.

For a force defending a strong position to lose almost twice as many men as their attackers was a remarkable tribute to the superiority of the rifle over the smooth bore although the Russian columns gave the rifle every possible chance. The Russians were astonished by the British attack in two-deep line. They had never conceived that troops could be used in such a formation and, while criticising the slowness of the British advance, one Russian officer admitted that only rifle fire or canister (grapeshot) could stop it. In saying that he failed to recognise that canister was no longer a practicable defence. It had never been effective at more than 300 yards and, with the Minié, the infantry could shoot down the unprotected gunners before they were in canister range.

ABOVE LEFT: French troops storm the Malakoff bastion, key to the defences of Sebastopol

ABOVE: The scene inside the Malakoff after its capture

RIGHT: A Zouave sentry by one of the French batteries during the winter of 1854

THE SIEGE OF SEBASTOPOL

There had been little enough inter-allied agreement before the Battle of the Alma; there was none in the immediate aftermath. Raglan proposed that the enemy should be pursued by the light cavalry, the horse artillery, by his Fourth Division, which had not fired a shot all day, and by such French troops as were fit to march. St Arnaud refused to agree, saying that no move could be made until the French had recovered their knapsacks from the north side of the Alma. Next day Raglan again proposed an immediate advance, urging that the demoralised Russians should be harried and that the northern defences of Sebastopol should be seized by a *coup-de-main*. Again St Arnaud refused and it was not until 23 September that the armies moved from the ground they had won on the 20th. By the following evening they were within sight of Sebastopol and again Raglan advocated an *attaque brusqué* on the northern defences. St Arnaud collapsed during this meeting. He died four days later but his successor, Canrobert, continued to refuse to risk an assault.

Eventually it was decided that the armies should march round the city and attack the southern side. This would have the advantage that they could base themselves on the little ports of Balaklava, Kamiesch, and Kazatch rather than have to rely on the long overland haul from Eupatoria. What the decision ignored was the fact, suspected by Raglan, witnessed by the fleet, and attested by every Russian account, that the northern side of Sebastopol was utterly defenceless and that the Russian army was dispirited and effectively leaderless. The only Russian officer who was showing any sign of activity was Colonel Todleben and he was only at the start of his task of constructing bastions and earthworks.

The march round Sebastopol was chiefly memorable for the remark of one British general that 'he had received many orders in his day, but that it was the first time he had ever been ordered to march by compass'. The manoeuvre almost brought about a major action when the allied columns almost clashed with the Russian field army. Menshikov believed the defence of the city to be such a forlorn hope that he abandoned it with most of his troops, leaving it to be garrisoned by sailors, marines, and reservists. It says little for the competence of the cavalry on either side that the two armies could come so close without warning being given to the commanders, allied or Russian.

Once arrived at the south side of Sebastopol no attack was made. Instead the complex rituals of siegecraft were invoked, battering guns were landed, and on 17 October, almost four weeks after the victory on the Alma, the allies opened a bombardment. By that time Todleben had had time to build some fortifications at which they could fire.

Henceforward it would be difficult to say who was besieging whom. The allies had penned themselves up in the Chersonese Peninsula, an area 10 miles long and, at its widest, 5 miles deep. Their investment faced only the southern side of Sebastopol and it was as easy for Menshikov to bring supplies and reinforcements into the city from the north as it was for the allies to get their replenishments from the sea. Before the end of October Sebastopol had a garrison of 25,000 men and the Russian field army outnumbered the British and French to such an extent that even Menshikov's extreme misgivings could not prevent him having to obey peremptory orders from St Petersburg to assault the allied lodgement.

His first attempt, known as the Battle of Balaklava, was made on 25 October. The Russian attacks were ill-co-ordinated and gave to the British three epics for their history books. The defence made by the 93rd Highlanders – 'the thin red streak – tipped with a line of steel'; the charge of the Heavy Cavalry Brigade; and the charge of the Light Brigade all demonstrated courage of the highest order but added little to the science of war. The incident that precipitated Lord Cardigan's charge with the light cavalry is, however, a classic example of the difficulties under which a commander laboured when all orders had to be transmitted by messenger. The message sent by Raglan to Lord Lucan, commanding the Cavalry Division, read:

Lord Raglan wishes the cavalry to advance rapidly to the front and try to prevent the enemy carrying away the guns. Troop of horse artillery may accompany. French cavalry is on your left. Immediate.

This might be difficult to understand from the position in which Lucan received it (although earlier messages should have made the intention reasonably clear) but, by tradition, an aide-de-camp carried with him the authority of the originator of the order and was responsible for interpreting the commander's intentions. In this case the messenger sent, Captain Nolan, was an intelligent officer with a high reputation and there could be no reason for Raglan to expect that he would behave to Lucan with such insolence as, in effect, to refuse to explain what was meant. The fact that Lucan and his subordinate (and brother-in-law) Cardigan were barely on speaking terms was an additional hazard which did not fall within normal staff procedures.

On 5 November Menshikov made a second attempt, the Battle of Inkerman. Some 57,000 Russians were set to attack the allied open flank and, although 22,000 of them failed to join the battle, they came within measurable distance of overwhelming the predominately British defenders. Attacking before dawn, they were favoured by a mist so thick that the longer range of the Minié could not be used and, but for brilliant leading by junior officers and NCOs, might have won the day by weight of numbers. As it was the Russians were forced to withdraw having lost 10,700 casualties. The British lost 2,400 and the French 880.

After Inkerman the campaign sank into a stalemate which lasted until the following spring when the bombardment was resumed in earnest. In the intervening months all the armies were chiefly concerned with keeping alive through the cruel winter. The Russians, whose supply system was rotten with corruption, suffered the worst while the French administrative machine showed itself to be marginally better than the others but it was the collapse of the British

supporting services which attracted the most attention.

The seed of this administrative disaster lay in London where a multiplicity of departments were responsible for functions which frequently overlapped. It was serious enough that the infantry and cavalry were the responsibility of one member of the cabinet and the artillery and engineers of another, but the most serious failings were in the Commissariat which was not under military control. Instead it was a branch of the Treasury which hedged it about with minute regulations designed to prevent peculation in peacetime garrisons. As Wellington had said forty years earlier, 'The great business of a Commander-in-Chief is to discover a mode of carrying on the business of this important department as much in conformity with the instructions to the Commissary General as is possible.'

In time of peace the Commissariat establishment was kept to a minimum of sedentary officers and, when war was declared, a field organisation had to be improvised. The junior staff of the department in the Crimea had been recruited by advertisement in the streets of Valetta on the voyage out from Britain. The task of the Commissariat was not only to provide all stores other than clothing but to provide land transport for them. No peacetime transport service was maintained, the Treasury assumed that it would be possible to hire waggons and draught animals at the seat of the war, an assumption that proved ill-founded both at Varna and in the Crimea. There was therefore no possibility that either the supply or the transport system could be efficient in the early months of any war and bad luck ensured that the breakdown became total. The winter of 1854–5 was the most severe in living memory and a hurricane on 14 November

ABOVE: Lord Cardigan leading the charge of the Light Cavalry Brigade against the Russian guns during the Battle of Balaklava

sank sixteen ships in Balaklava harbour with the loss of huge quantities of stores and all the army's winter clothing.

The combination of a supply failure and a hard winter ensured that the British army would suffer heavy casualties and the incompetence of the medical services saw to it that many of the casualties became fatal. The medical department was a ramshackle affair which, despite being responsible to three distinct ministers in London, was not responsible for its own supplies. These were controlled by two separate sections of the Treasury, which were usually at loggerheads with each other, were grossly understaffed, and, like the Commissariat, were pinioned by minute regulations. The army in the Crimea lost, apart from 2,873 men permanently incapacitated, 19,584 officers and men dead. Of these only 3,754 were battle casualties, the remainder died of disease, largely as a result of the chaos into which the medical services fell.

A photograph of British troops recovering cannon balls from the 'Valley of the Shadow of Death'; despite Tennyson's poem this is not the valley in which the charge of the Light Brigade took place

This high rate of casualties was self-perpetuating. The army had no reserves and, to replace losses, all that could be done, apart from raising 'legions' of foreigners, was to recruit young, untrained men who fell sick as soon as they reached the Crimea.

When fighting was resumed in the spring of 1855 the allies were joined by an army from the Kingdom of Sardinia. This army had made a very poor showing when they tried conclusions with the Austrians in 1848 but in the Crimea, where it was kept under close French surveillance, did much to restore the reputation of Italian soldiers. It was not, however, until mid-June that the first assault was made against Sebastopol and it failed miserably. One French column attacked forty minutes too early and the rest of the attacks were made piecemeal and unsuccessfully. The French lost 3,100 men and the British 1,500. Lord Raglan died a few days afterwards, much mourned by his men who believed, probably rightly, that his death was caused by his grief at their losses.

Before another assault could be mounted, the Russians, now led by Prince Gorchakov, made a final attempt to break into the open flank of the allied position. They were frustrated by the French and Sardinians in the Battle of the Chernaya (16 August) and lost 8,000 men. Soon afterwards Gorchakov gave orders for a pontoon bridge to be built across Sebastopol harbour, a tacit admission that the evacuation of the city could only be a question of time.

General Brown, commander of the Light Division, with his staff in the Crimea

The camps around Balaklava harbour during the summer of 1855

The end came on 8 September when the French succeeded in storming the Malakov bastion. French attacks on bastions 5 and 6 failed and the British, mostly inexperienced troops, failed in a humiliating fashion when they tried to storm the Redan (bastion 3). The Russians, however, had had enough and on the following day the garrison filed across the pontoon and Sebastopol surrendered. Fighting in the Crimea dragged on in a desultory fashion until the end of February 1856 and, in this second winter of the war, it was the French administrative system that crumbled so that the British, whose Commissariat was now in working order, were able to help their allies with supplies and medical assistance to repay their debt for the help the French had given them in 1854–5. There were no regrets in either army when the conclusion of peace allowed them to evacuate the Crimea.

The war in the Crimea is usually remembered as a series of administrative disasters punctuated by episodes of great but pointless heroism on both sides. Despite the introduction of the rifle as the weapon of every infantryman, the British and French fought their battles in exactly the style that they would have done forty years earlier and the poor armament of the Russian infantry enabled them to do so with success. With field artillery virtually indistinguishable from that used in the Napoleonic wars, the Crimea contributed nothing to the advance of tactics. There were, however, some innovations which pointed the way to future developments. It was the first war in which a tactical railway was built. In January 1855 the British started constructing a line from Balaklava harbour to their

The siege guns around Sebastopol; part of a 21-gun battery in 1855

siege lines. By April it was capable of handling 240 tons a day, a load which transformed the entire supply system. It was also the first war in which the electric field telegraph was used. Not only were 25 miles of cable laid between headquarters and various points in the siege lines but in April 1855 Royal Engineers put a cable across the Black Sea from Balaklava to Varna in eighteen days. This was only four years after the world's first submarine cable, from Dover to Calais, had come into operation. From Varna the line was extended to Bucharest by French army engineers and there it was linked with the main European telegraph system. It was unfortunate that the chief effect of this link was, on the French side, to permit Napoleon III to interfere with the tactical dispositions of his generals while from London the War Office saw it as a golden opportunity to pose minor administrative queries which further overburdened the staff at the front.

One other novel feature of the Crimean War was to add to the burdens of commanders in the field as much, or more, than direct communication with their governments – the presence of newspaper correspondents. William Howard Russell of *The Times* was not the first war correspondent, his paper had had a reporter at the Battle of Corunna, but he was by far the most influential. His despatches from Balaklava brought down Lord Aberdeen's government and some of

94

his purple patches turned minor episodes into memorable, if imaginary, epics. Many of the abuses to which he drew attention were all too real but he would never hesitate to invent, or draw from tainted sources, evidence to support his contentions. Nor could he or his editor be persuaded to omit information on plans and numbers of troops which could be, and frequently were, invaluable to the enemy. Moreover his attacks on Lord Raglan and his staff were unforgivably personal and, on occasions, demonstrably untrue. Nevertheless the war correspondent was to be a feature of all future wars. Fortunately Russell's successors have learned to avoid his grosser excesses.

FRENCH INVOLVEMENT IN ITALY

The hopes of military glory which Napoleon III had nursed had scarcely come to his regime from the costly war in the Crimea but three years after its end he saw another opportunity of gaining laurels over country where almost every place name was redolent of the triumphs of his uncle. As has been seen the Kingdom of Sardinia (better known as Piedmont) had sent troops to the Crimea and that country's prime minister, Camillo Cavour, was anxious to exploit his French alliance to further his overriding ambition, to secure for Piedmont the hegemony of Italy. To achieve this, he had to defeat the Hapsburg Empire, which held Lombardy and Venetia, and a preliminary foray in 1848, when the Austrians under Marshal Radetzky had won an almost Napoleonic triumph, showed clearly that the Piedmontese army had no chance of achieving this on their own. Cavour, therefore, cemented his alliance with France and set about provoking a war.

By massing the entire Piedmontese army, 74,000 men, on the border with Lombardy he extracted an Austrian ultimatum demanding a reduction in Piedmont's armaments. This was rejected on 26 April 1859 by which date French troops were already crossing into Sardinian Savoy. Three days later a powerful Austrian force, 150,000 men apart from garrisons, crossed the Ticino river into Piedmont and began a tentative advance on Turin, tearing up the railway lines as they went forward. The Sardinians fell back on the river Dora Baltea where a fortified line had been prepared.

The Italian campaign of 1859 was the first in which men went to war by train. In the last ten days of April the railways of France carried either to the frontiers of the Sardinian kingdom or to the Mediterranean ports a daily average of 8,421 men and 512 horses and, as they proudly announced, this was achieved without interrupting their normal services. It was thus possible to bring men to the front in ten days, a journey that would have taken sixty days on the march. In consequence troops reached the front fresh and without either the necessity or the temptation to straggle. So short was the range for the artillery of the time that it was, given convenient lines, possible to detrain regiments within sight of the enemy and march them straight into action.

Particularly on the Austrian side the railways were far from

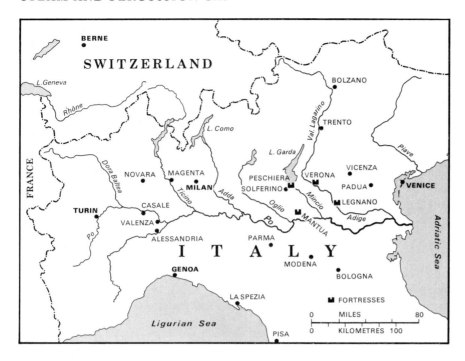

The north Italian
campaign of 1855

perfect. The Hapsburg lands in Italy were connected to the
Austro–Hungarian homeland by two lines. That from the Tyrol was
incomplete and the troops had to march from Innsbruck to Bozen
(Bolzano). The other ran into Venetia from Carniola (Slovenia) and
this had not been built between Udine and Trieste. On the
Franco-Piedmontese side the Alpine tunnel had still to be
constructed and the French had to detrain at St Jean de Maurienne,
march over the snow-covered Mont Cenis pass, and join the train
again at Susa, west of Turin. Consequently four of the six French
corps were embarked at Marseilles and taken by ship to Genoa.
Nevertheless the movement of French troops by either route went
with great efficiency but their administrative services were poorly
organised and operations were constantly delayed when stores of all
kinds failed to arrive. It was little consolation that the Austrian
supply situation was even more chaotic.

The initial French concentration on Genoa and their continuing
dependence on that port for supplies meant that their first operations
were based around Alessandria, near the battlefield of Marengo, and
on 20 May they won a minor action in the vicinity at Montebello, site
of Lannes' victory in 1800. Thereafter they were faced with the
problem of crossing the broad Po in the face of the Austrian artillery.
In 1796 Napoleon I had solved this problem by moving to his right
and violating the neutrality of the Duchy of Parma. Napoleon III
marched to his left, crossed the river at Casale within Piedmont and,
basing himself at Vercelli, threatened the Austrian right. By doing so
he left his vital rail link at the mercy of the Austrian guns at the point
where the railway runs beside the Po at Valenza. Missing this

opportunity, as they were to miss every other during the campaign, the Austrians withdrew and by 3 June the whole Franco–Sardinian striking force, 133,000 men, was near Novara with only the Ticino river and one Austrian corps between them and Milan.

Austrian troops were, however, on the move and on the following day 60,000 of them were deployed to defend the approach to the capital. Their main strength was around the village of Magenta near which the railway to Milan crossed the Ticino. This was a strong position for the river, which is multi-branched, is a formidable obstacle and unfordable. A combined road and rail bridge crossed the river and an Austrian attempt at demolition had done no more than cant the carriageway to one side leaving it passable to infantry and easily reparable for artillery. Under the impression that the demolition had succeeded the Austrians did not defend the bridge and they also failed to block the next bridge upstream, at Turbigo, 7 miles away.

On 4 June Napoleon planned to attack at Turbigo with the Voltigeur division of the Imperial Guard supported by MacMahon's corps and a Piedmontese division. As soon as this attack was heard to be in action a second column, led by the heavy division of the Guard and Canrobert's corps, was to strike up the line of the railway. The only electric telegraph used in this campaign were the permanent cables laid beside the railway so that communication between the two wings of Napoleon's attack depended on aides-de-camp riding from one to the other by way of Turbigo.

Unconcerned about the safety of the railway bridge, the Austrians concentrated the bulk of their strength against the Turbigo attack which they halted but the firing in this engagement was heavy enough to be the signal for the other French column. They crossed the bridge without incident but beyond stretched 1½ miles of featureless plain, flat except where it was broken by watercourses. The plain ends in a steep irregular bank 60 feet high through which road and railway pass in deep cuttings. The Austrians had 136 guns available and these should have had no difficulty in massacring the Zouaves and Grenadiers of the Guard while they crossed the plain. Any survivors should have been easy targets for riflemen as they struggled up the steep bank. Moreover the French artillery could not pass the Ticino and was out of supporting range and Canrobert's corps was three hours late in reaching its start line. In the event only eighteen Austrian guns were brought into action and the Guard reached the top of the bank with little loss.

This, however, was not the end of their problem. Beyond the crest was a tableland across which ran a canal, the *Naviglio Grande*. On the maps available this appeared to be a negligible obstacle but it was found, on the ground, to have very steep sides covered with a thick growth of robiglia, a type of acacia with long hard thorns. On a front of 1½ miles only four bridges gave a possibility of crossing and the Austrians succeeded in blowing two of them, although at one of them they managed to leave, on the French side, sufficient planks to fill the gap caused by the demolition. A dashing attack by Zouaves

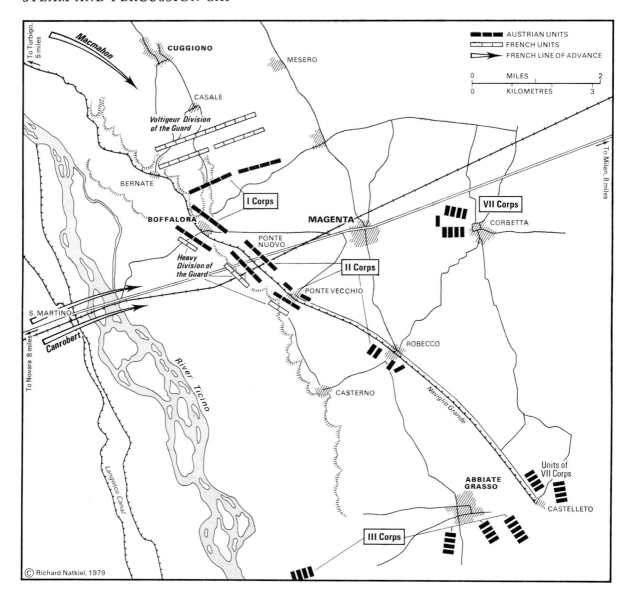

The Battle of Magenta

and Grenadiers succeeded in forcing a crossing and soon afterwards contact was established with the Turbigo column. Heavy fighting continued for some time but French reinforcements arrived in time to secure a victory. The Austrians withdrew, made a half-hearted attempt to renew the battle on the following day, but then abandoned Milan and set out on a long retreat to the east.

The battle cost the French 4,444 casualties. The Austrians lost rather more in battle and a further 4,000 deserters. These were Hungarians, Czechs, Slovenes, and Croats, disaffected to the empire. Their Italian battalions had already been sent away from the front so that the bulk of the fighting fell on German-speaking Austrians. These, however, were traditionally as staunch as any

The attack of the
Imperial Guard at
Magenta

infantry in Europe and even the fact that they had had no rations for
forty-eight hours cannot explain the deplorable defence they put up
near the railway where 5,000 Guardsmen beat 15,000 defenders. The
fault lay in the Austrian command. Field Marshal Count Gyulai,
who was 61, had his headquarters in the village of Abbiate Grasso, 5
miles from the canal bridges, 12 from the Turbigo bridge. Before
9.00 am he was warned that large French forces were coming from
the Turbigo bridgehead but it was some hours before he took any
action to counter them and when he did so he sent too many of his
men to his right. He first visited Magenta village at 2.00 pm. He
stayed there half an hour, during which time he sent a division to
reinforce the canal bridges. Then he rode 3 miles to the rear to ensure
that a corps of reinforcements took the right road, hardly a task for a
commander-in-chief. He did not return to the front. With such an
example of lethargy and indifference it is not surprising that his
subordinates showed neither activity nor initiative.

Accompanied by the King of Sardinia, Napoleon rode in triumph
into Milan on 8 June. The Austrians continued to retreat until, after
80 miles, they took up a very strong position with their right secured
on Lake Garda and their left on the all-but impregnable fortress-city
of Mantua, their front being covered by the Mincio river. The French
and Sardinians followed, their slow advance being conditioned by the
demolitions carried out at every riverline. They were not expecting
the enemy to fight again before they reached the shelter of the
Quadrilateral, the four fortresses – Mantua, Verona, Peschiera, and
Legnano – which had defended northern Italy through the centuries.
On 21 June the allies were beginning to cross the Chiese river, the
last before they reached the Mincio which was 15 miles further
ahead.

The Austrians had fallen back on reinforcements and were now 130,000 strong and divided into eight corps. They had also been joined by the young Emperor Franz Joseph who assumed personal command. On the advice of his chief-of-staff, Major-General Hess, and contrary to the opinion of every other senior officer with the army, the Emperor decided to abandon a defensive strategy and attack while Napoleon's men, about 120,000 of them, were astride the Chiese. It was late on 23 June when he came to this decision and by that time the enemy were already mostly across the river. The fact was that the Austrians had no patrols out and had no idea where the Franco–Sardinian army was. Nevertheless, seven corps were ordered forward and might well have brought on an encounter battle since Napoleon had also been negligent about reconnaissance and was working on the assumption that the Austrians were going to stand on the Mincio. At this stage a new factor came on the scene. With the French army were the brothers Godard, who had invented a new type of captive balloon. This had been sent aloft two days earlier and had seen nothing but, before dusk on 23 June, it was flown from the village of Montechiaro on the Chiese. A sceptical commentator with the army remarked, 'The distance was too great to learn much, for the Austrians were 10 to 12 miles from Montechiaro and it requires a powerful glass, combined with favourable circumstances, to distinguish infantry from cavalry at 5 miles; but the observers might, and probably did, perceive long columns of approaching dust. This would be enough to indicate that some movement of importance was taking place.' Napoleon did indeed realise that the enemy were advancing but concluded that it was a reconnaissance in strength being undertaken by '25 or 30,000 men'.

This warning was sufficient to allow the French army to close up

Napoleon III and his staff during the Battle of Solferino

and in a bloody battle on the following day they won a victory which was enough to break the Austrian will to continue the war. Only on their extreme right, where Benedek's corps beat off a Piedmontese attack, did the Austrians succeed in holding their ground. In the centre Bazaine's corps, with the Imperial Guard in support, broke through to Solferino village while the Austrian left might well have been turned and their whole army cut off from Mantua had not Marshal Canrobert behaved with 'a caution amounting to timidity'. One Austrian general led sixteen squadrons of cavalry at a sharp trot towards Mantua as soon as the firing started, an act for which he was sentenced to ten years in a fortress prison. The victory cost the Franco–Sardinians 18,000 casualties. The Austrians lost 22,000 but of these 8,638 were listed as missing and were, for the most part, deserters.

The chief feature of this short war was the incompetence of the Austrian command which, at all levels, showed itself incapable of reacting to situations as they arose. There were two other significant features. The first was the *élan* and determination of the French infantry in the attack. This was no new phenomenon, the *furia francese* had been the rock on which the great Napoleon had built some of his greatest victories, but since Waterloo and especially in Algeria, French infantry had been trained in self-reliance and speed of manoeuvre, in the belief that the *attaque brusqué* would sweep away even the most formidable opposition. At both Magenta and Solferino they also had the advantage that they had been fed and the Austrians had not. On both occasions the speed and confidence of their attacks were too much for the plodding if resolute minds of their opponents.

The other revelation was the range and accuracy of the new French artillery which was brought into action for the first time at Solferino. These were muzzle-loading rifled 4-pounders cast in bronze which were reputed to be able to hit a man on a horse at 3,400 yards, at least twice the effective range of the Austrian field guns. Technical advance in the French army was also demonstrated by the presence in the baggage train of steam-driven gunboats which had been built in Paris and brought forward in sections to be assembled if it became necessary to use them on the Italian lakes.

In the peace which followed the campaign Sardinia acquired Lombardy but, to Cavour's fury, Austria retained Venetia. A year later Napoleon III extracted his pound of flesh from Sardinia in the form of Savoy and Nice. He also acquired a spurious reputation as a field commander.

VOLUNTEERS WANTED!

1776! 1861!

AN ATTACK UPON WASHINGTON ANTICIPATED ! !

THE COUNTRY TO THE RESCUE !

A REGIMENT FOR SERVICE

UNDER THE FLAG OF THE UNITED STATES

IS BEING FORMED IN JEFFERSON COUNTY.

☞ NOW IS THE TIME TO BE ENROLLED !

Patriotism and love of Country alike demand a ready response from every man capable of bearing arms in this trying hour, to sustain not merely the existence of the Government, but to vindicate the honor of that Flag so ruthlessly torn by traitor hands from the walls of Sumter.

RECRUITING RENDEZVOUS

Are open in the village of WATERTOWN, and at all the principal villages in the County, for the formatiom of Companies, or parts of Companies. ☞Officers to be immediately elected by those enrolled.

WATERTOWN, APRIL 20, 1861.   WM. C. BROWNE, Col. Comd'g 35th Regiment.

Ingalls, Brockway & Beebee, Printers, Reformer Office, Watertown

CHAPTER SIX

The War between the States

THE AMERICAN CIVIL WAR (more properly but less conveniently known as the War of Secession) is frequently referred to as the first modern war. In terms of *matériel,* this is scarcely true. Most of the tactical innovations – railways, telegraphs, balloons, and the rifled cannon – had already been used with effect in the Franco-Austrian War of 1859. What was new was the scale of the war. From first to last the North enlisted 3,000,000 men and had as many as 1,500,000 under arms at a time. The South enlisted almost 1,000,000. To clothe and feed armies on this scale would have set Napoleon an insoluble problem but, unlike President Lincoln, he did not have behind him the Howe-Singer sewing-machine which made it possible to make uniforms for the Union soldiers whose boots had the sole stitched to the uppers by another machine. Nor did the French emperor have large quantities of mechanical mowers, threshers, and reapers which, in the Union, made it possible to feed the armies.

Essentially it was a war of amateurs. When it broke out the army of the United States was only 16,000 strong and, even including reservists, there were only 2,000 trained officers. Only one of them Major-General Winfield Scott, had ever commanded as many as 14,000 men and that was when, fourteen years earlier, he had marched from Vera Cruz to Mexico City against no very serious opposition. The only other active service that the army had seen was the occasional punitive expedition against Indians in which, as one brigadier expressed it, 'In twenty years of service I learned all about commanding fifty United States dragoons and forgot everything else.' In 1861 Scott, who had made his reputation fighting against the British in the war of 1812, was 75 but he still was in active command of the army.

There were a handful of other senior officers who had been through the Mexican War. The most notable was Major-General Robert E. Lee, who had been Scott's chief engineer on the march from Santa Cruz. Both sides looked to him for his help. In April 1861 President Lincoln offered him command of the Union armies but, on the 16th of that month, his home state seceded and he felt

One of the earliest Union recruiting posters

obliged to resign his United States commission and offer his services to Virginia.

The first shots were fired on 12 April 1861 when Beauregard's Confederate guns opened on Fort Sumter, an island in Charleston harbour. There followed a pause of three months while the two sides strove to turn a mass of recruits into armies. On paper the resources of the North were overwhelming. The twenty-three states which remained within the Union had a population of 22,000,000. The eleven states of the Confederacy had only 9,000,000 of whom a third were slaves who could not be used as soldiers although, for the most part willingly, they kept the southern economy going and performed all manner of non-combatant functions. The difference in the horse population was even more striking, especially as the horse was still the key to all tactical mobility. The North had an inexhaustible supply while the South was always hard put to it to find remounts for cavalry and artillery.

In the North were 20,000 miles of railway. The South had less than half of this and what it did have was frequently discontinuous and varying in gauge. All the Confederate locomotives and rolling stock came from factories in the Union, their repair facilities were very limited and, as the war continued, their railway system sank steadily into chaos. To make matters worse several of the Confederacy's strategic lines touched the coast where they were vulnerable to seaborne raids from the Union which had managed to secure the whole of the US Navy and, as the war progressed, expanded it from 76 to 670 ships.

There was little to choose between the two sides in the arms they used. Both started with the Springfield muzzle-loading rifle, accurate up to 250 yards, and, as a field gun, the 12-pounder 'Napoleon', a smooth bore, accurate to 880 yards and effective at a mile. In the years that followed there was a steady improvement in arms with breech-loading guns and rifles becoming common. Here again the advantage lay firmly with the industrial strength of the Union where there were 110,000 factories employing 1,131,000 workers against 20,000 factories employing 110,000 in the Confederacy. It was only because large quantities of arms were seized from Federal arsenals, that the South could conduct a war. Replacements were a constant problem and at best improvised workshops could only produce 500 rifles a day. Once the Union effort got under way they could manufacture 5,000 a day.

In the early days of the war both sides relied largely on imported munitions. The North bought 428,000 Enfields from Britain and 298,000 other muzzle-loading rifles from the continent of Europe. In the South import was more difficult since the Union navy immediately clamped a blockade on the Southern ports. At first especially the blockade was far from complete, and many Southern ships broke through, but the type of ship, light and fast, which made a successful blockade-runner was, by definition, unsuitable for carrying heavy armaments. Nor had the Confederacy any reserves of foreign currency for buying arms. The wealth of the south lay in the

The war between the states was the first in which railways played a decisive role; a Union military railway depot at City Point, Virginia, in 1864

export of cotton and this, except in very small quantities, the blockade interdicted. It was not only foreign currency that the South lacked. When the Confederate government was established there was, apart from the coin in the pockets of the citizens, only 1,000,000 dollars which were seized in Federal mints. Every internal transaction had, therefore, to be conducted in hastily printed paper money secured against nothing but hope. It depreciated at a brisk rate.

Nevertheless the Confederacy was not without advantages. Its declared aim was to be left to manage its own affairs so that it had no need to invade Union territory and could stand everywhere on the defensive with interior lines of communication. Conversely the North had the task of subduing a vast area, 800,000 square miles, stretching 800 miles from north to south and 1,700 from east to west. If the Confederacy found its railways unsatisfactory it could console itself that the lines would be in a far worse condition if the Union tried to make use of them for an invasion. For the most part the invaders would be faced with vast tracts of scantily-populated lands served only by abominable roads.

Another Confederate advantage was that their territory reached to the gates of the Federal capital, separated from it only by the Potomac river. Until 1864 there was always the possibility that they could seize Washington, a possibly fatal blow to the prestige of the Union. In the meanwhile the Union President and his generals were

Armies of the American Civil War

The American Civil War was the first to be dominated by the rifle and one of the results of this dominance was a simplification of uniforms. The private of 116th Pennsylvania Infantry Regiment (BELOW RIGHT) wears a uniform which, while by no means wholly inconspicuous, is designed more for utility and less to impress the enemy than, for example, that of the Waterloo period infantryman on page 27. At least his képi is less of an encumbrance than the headgear of fifty years earlier and he has no cross belts to give the enemy an aiming point. Nevertheless the lethal potentiality of the rifle had not been fully appreciated and Pickett's charge at Gettysburg (BOTTOM LEFT) was carried out in close formation across open country. Although railways played a significant part in the war, tactical mobility still depended on legs. The Union guns at Gettysburg (BELOW LEFT) were brought into action much as batteries had moved in the Napoleonic war and the guns were, for the most part, little changed from those of 1815. In the end, industrial capacity triumphed over military skill and the Union troops forced their way into the Confederate capital at Richmond, Virginia (BOTTOM RIGHT)

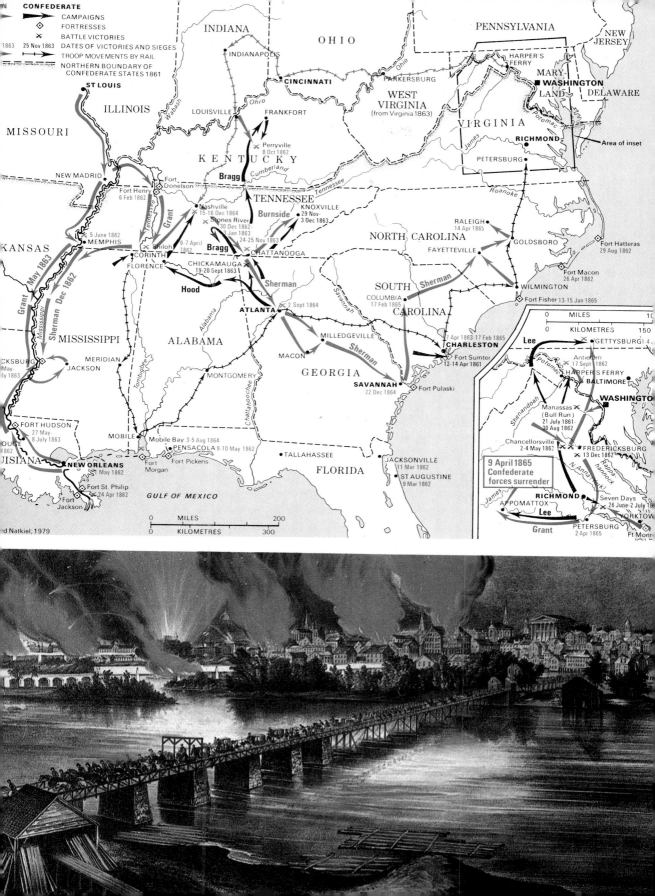

certain to be largely preoccupied with the safety of their capital. It was unfortunate that this advantage was largely wasted when the Confederacy established their own capital at Richmond, Virginia, only 130 miles from Washington, so that its security had to be one of their own overriding concerns.

THE OPENING SKIRMISHES

The South was quicker to get its improvised army into some sort of order. The credit for this must go, at least in part, to Jefferson Davis, the Confederate President, who had been trained at West Point and had served both as a regular officer and as Secretary for War. They were also fortunate that, in building their military machine, they were not tied to the peacetime organisation of the US Army which, like the British, had in its higher echelons a number of independent departments, each jealous of its prerogatives and more likely to compete than to co-operate. To make matters worse the Union, when it started a vast expansion of its army, frequently allowed the soldiers to elect their officers, a recipe for disaster where every man was as ignorant of war as his fellow. In the Confederacy officers were appointed for efficiency rather than popularity and as a result the Southern battalions were better officered and better disciplined.

Robert E. Lee, photographed by Matthew Brady in 1865

The presidents on both sides exercised their constitutional powers as commanders-in-chief but Davis contented himself with laying down an overall defensive strategy and seldom intervened directly. Lincoln, by contrast, having no military experience except for a short period of militia training, constantly interfered with his generals, frequently for reasons that were more concerned with political ends than with military considerations. Davis, by luck or skill, showed himself good at choosing generals. Except where they died in battle, the Southern generals who commanded at the beginning of the war were still at their posts when it ended, while the Union generals of 1861 and 1862 followed each other into retirement with brisk regularity. Nor was Davis narrow in his choice. Prominent among Southern commanders until he was killed in 1864 was Lieutenant-General Leonidas Polk who, in civil life, was Bishop of Louisiana. Chief among the Confederacy's assets was Robert E. Lee, the greatest general of the war.

Three months after the bombardment of Fort Sumter, the first battle was brought on by pressure from Lincoln and the politicians who overrode the views of Winfield Scott and the other Union generals. Twenty-two thousand Confederate troops under General Beauregard were in position to cover Manassas Junction behind the Bull Run stream, within 30 miles of Washington. The attack was entrusted to Major-General Irwin McDowell who planned to assault with 35,000 men on 19 July 1861 and had arranged, unsuccessfully, that another column should pin down the Southern forces in the Shenandoah valley, 50 miles to the north-west. The inability of the Union troops even to make a short march meant that the attack had to be postponed for two days but McDowell managed to achieve a fair

Thomas 'Stonewall' Jackson, photographed by George Minnes in 1863

measure of surprise and almost broke Beauregard's left which was supported only by the brigade of Thomas Jackson, standing 'like a stone wall' on Henry Hill. However, two brigades from the Shenandoah had joined Beauregard and when, during the battle, more men from there arrived by rail, the balance tilted in favour of the South. As General Sherman remarked, 'Both armies were fairly defeated, and whichever had stood fast the other would have run.' It was the Northern troops that ran and, as another observer wrote, 'The men seemed to be seized simultaneously by the conviction that it was too late to do anything more, and they might as well start home. Cohesion was lost, the organisation being disintegrated, and the men walked quickly off.' Soon the walk turned into a run, retreat became rout, and most of the Union soldiers threw away their arms and fled for Washington.

Things were little better on the other side. According to Beauregard, 'Every segment of the line we succeeded in forming dissolved while another was being formed; more than 2,000 men were shouting each some suggestion to his neighbour, their voices mingling with the noise of the shells hurtling overhead, and all words of command drowned in the confusion and uproar.' Riding up to see the battle, President Davis met so many panic-stricken deserters that his companions were convinced that the Confederacy had been defeated. In fact both sides had lost about 2,000 killed and wounded while the North lost a further 1,000 'missing' and 28 guns.

The immediate result of this First Battle of Bull Run was that McDowell was superseded by George B. McClellan who was appointed General-in-Chief of all the Union Forces in succession to Scott on whose staff he had, like Lee, served in Mexico. He had many military qualities but he was most reluctant to undertake operations until he had an army with the rudiments of training and discipline. To buy time he sent the President a series of reports stressing the strength of his opponents. Since there was no military intelligence organisation, he obtained his information from Pinkerton's detective agency. Meanwhile the Southern commanders were equally pursuing a strict defensive strategy and when Lee, still no more than one of the generals in the Virginian forces, pressed for some offensive action he was relegated to coast defence in South Carolina.

President Lincoln continued to urge attacking the enemy and in April 1862 McClellan was persuaded to make a seaborne attack aimed at Richmond. He decided to strike up the peninsula between the York and James rivers where the Union-held Fort Monroe offered a convenient landing place. McClellan was most reluctant to take the offensive and he was no happier to discover from the newspapers that he had been relieved of his post of General-in-Chief while retaining command of the attacking army. Scarcely had he digested this tactless demonstration of apparent lack of confidence on the part of the government when he heard that Lincoln had withheld 40,000 men from his army on the pretext that Washington was in danger. From a combination of pique and native caution the general proceeded on the campaign with extreme circumspection. He spent a month besieging

Yorktown and even when, by mid-May, he was within a few miles of Richmond, he made no serious attempt to break through. The campaign lapsed into deadlock until on 1 June the Confederates, anxious for their capital, appointed Lee to command the Army of North Virginia. Before the end of the month he had defeated McClellan at Gaine's Mill and cut his communications with the shore base at West Point on the York river. This roused McClellan to show his true value as a general. He switched his base to Harrison's Landing on the James river, and stood at bay with his back to the water and the guns of the navy to support him. There, in the Seven Days' Battle around Malvern Hill, he fought off every attack Lee made upon him. Nevertheless his campaign was in ruins and he withdrew the army from the peninsula having lost 36,000 rifles and 60 guns. He was immediately superseded by John Pope while the chief command of the Union forces went to Henry W. Halleck.

Pope did not enjoy his command for long. At the Second Battle of Bull Run (30–31 August) Lee, although leading only 50,000 men against 75,000, utterly defeated him and inflicted 20,000 casualties – taking 30 guns and 20,000 rifles. Halleck assured the President that Washington was lost and McClellan was reinstated to save the capital. Lee, however, struck at Maryland and, on 15 September, took Harper's Ferry with 12,500 prisoners, 13,000 rifles, and 73 guns. McClellan marched against him and on 17 September the two armies fought each other to a standstill beside the Antietam Creek. Each side lost one man in four of those engaged and, although Lee was not defeated, his offensive could not be continued. McClellan was again superseded, this time by Ambrose E. Burnside who, having been disastrously repulsed from Fredericksburg on 13 December, was replaced in his turn by 'Fighting Joe' Hooker.

In the early months of 1863 the majority in the North would have been content to concede independence to the Confederacy. In two years of war nothing had been achieved at an enormous cost in lives and money. The need to find 2,500,000 dollars a day, the cost of keeping the war going, was crippling the Union. The state elections

ABOVE: Ulysses S. Grant, photographed by Matthew Brady

BELOW: President Lincoln with General McClellan and his staff during a visit to the battlefield at Antietam

William Tecumseh
Sherman

of 1862 had shown a total lack of confidence in President Lincoln, desertion from the army was on a massive scale, voluntary recruitment was minimal, and in New York City riots against the drafting of conscrips cost hundreds of lives. It was only the resolution of the President, supported by the ingenuity of the Secretary of the Treasury, Salmon P. Chase, that kept alive the North's determination to continue the fight.

The Union's move that was to cripple the South was already under way. While the eyes of the government and the world were fixed on the Potomac, troops were moving in the west. An unknown general, Ulysses S. Grant, had obtained the consent, rather than the approval, of General Halleck for the capture of Forts Henry and Donelson in Tennessee. This he achieved in February 1862, thus giving the Union access to the great artery of the Mississippi. Two months later he narrowly beat the western Confederate army at Shiloh (6–7 April). Soon afterwards Admiral Farragut, a southerner who commanded the Union navy, seized New Orleans and started working his way up the great river. By midsummer the Mississippi was under Union control except for the stretch between Fort Hudson and strongly fortified Vicksburg with a garrison of 30,000 Confederates. The only Southern force within reach consisted of 24,000 while Grant had 70,000 in his command.

General Grant had been to West Point and, in time, had risen to the rank of captain before abandoning the army to try his hand at farming and the leather trade. He was not notably successful at either but, on the outbreak of the war, he was recalled to the army and made a colonel. He soon showed himself the best of the Northern generals. He lacked Lee's tactical brilliance but, almost alone, he grasped the strategic clue that the Confederacy could only be defeated by being ground down until the will to fight was destroyed.

His colleagues in Virginia started 1863 badly. Hooker tried to blast his way through to Richmond with 130,000 men, twice as many as Lee could deploy. He crossed the Rappahannock successfully and passed his cavalry round Lee's flank believing that this would force his opponent to retire. Instead he found himself blocked in the close 'Wilderness' country. However, still believing Lee to be trapped, he retired to a strong position at Chancellorsville which he had previously fortified and where he believed himself impregnable. Thereupon Lee and Jackson made their most daring combination. Dividing their greatly outnumbered army and marching on exterior lines they not only defeated Hooker but came within measurable distance of cutting off his retreat. Between 2 and 4 May they inflicted 17,000 casualties and drove Hooker's force back across the Rappahannock in disorder with its general unconscious. Nevertheless, it was a dearly-bought victory for the South because one of their dead was Stonewall Jackson.

After Chancellorsville, the initiative was firmly in Lee's hands and he was determined to move the seat of war away from north Virginia since the country between Washington and Richmond, having been fought over for two years, and never fertile, was quite incapable of supporting the armies through another campaign. There were two options. One, favoured by President Davis, was to march west into Kentucky and Tennessee with the intention of diverting Grant in his Mississippi campaign. Lee refused to undertake this move which would have to be made without the support of a railway and which would leave Virginia open to the Union army near Washington. The alternative, which Lee favoured, was for a march to the north crossing Maryland and striking into Pennsylvania. The threat to Philadelphia and even New York would further discourage the bankers, already reluctant to lend Chase the money needed to pay for the war, and the Confederate army would be able to feed itself at the expense of the North. While such a move would also leave Richmond unprotected, Lee correctly judged that Lincoln would insist on his army keeping between Washington and the enemy.

The Confederate army began to move to the west of Washington. Lee had 57,000 infantry, 9,000 cavalry, and 250 guns and he moved in three widely-spaced corps hoping to convince Hooker for as long as possible that the Rappahannock was still strongly held. Hooker was not deceived and, finding a single southern corps at Fredericksburg with no support within 40 miles, sought permission to smash it and drive on Richmond. As Lee had foreseen, Lincoln refused to agree. Instead he replaced Hooker and gave his successor, George Meade, orders to 'manoeuvre and fight in such a manner as to cover the capital and also Baltimore'. Meade was no genius but he could be counted upon to avoid the gross errors of Burnside and Hooker. He would be no match for Lee in the open field but he could be counted upon to behave cautiously and to hold his ground on a strong position.

By the end of June the Confederate army was in the area Carlisle – Chambersburg – Cashtown and within striking distance of the Susquehanna river and the heartland of Pennsylvania. On their march they had captured several Union garrisons and much material but, unfortunately, they had mislaid their cavalry. Lee's cavalry commander, the dashing J. E. B. Stuart, had obtained permission to make a raid towards Washington in the hope of misleading the Federal commanders and of disrupting their communications. Stuart excelled at this kind of sortie and on two previous occasions he had succeeded in riding round the enemy's army spreading disorder. On this occasion he miscalculated and let himself be forced to follow Meade's army as it marched north after Lee. Thus between 24 June and 2 July Lee was without his horsemen and had no means of discovering what Meade was doing. When Stuart finally rejoined, his troopers and horses were too fatigued to be of immediate service.

Meade knew little more about Lee's doings than Lee knew about his. He knew that the Confederates were marching towards the Susquehanna but expected them to turn south and strike at Baltimore. He therefore set about entrenching a position behind the Pipe Creek which would cover both Baltimore and Washington. Neither he nor Lee expected an encounter battle and neither wished for one.

THE BATTLE OF GETTYSBURG

Meade's advance guard consisted of an incomplete cavalry division, about 2,000 men, with two batteries and was commanded by Napoleon B. Buford. On 30 June, while searching for Lee's army, they entered the little town of Gettysburg. Hardly had they arrived when a Confederate infantry brigade approached hoping to find boots in the town. Buford, one of the few generals before the twentieth century to induce cavalrymen to fight on their feet, stood his ground and sent for reinforcements. His enemy, finding the town defended, made no attempt to attack it but returned the way they had come while Buford, recognising that Gettysburg was the meeting place of eleven main roads, dug in and waited while two corps marched to support him. On the Confederate side the reactions were sluggish and when a serious force approached the town on 1 July they found the Union troops firmly in possession.

Gettysburg stands between two streams running north and south, the Willoughby Run to the west of the town and the Rock Creek to the east. Between the town and the Willoughby Run is a low ridge on which stands a seminary. This was not strong ground and on 1 July, when about 22,000 men were engaged on each side, the Confederates took both ridge and town without difficulty. In doing so they drove their opponents back on to much more formidable ground which rose immediately south of Gettysburg. It was a ridge shaped like a question mark. The curved end, above the town, was formed by Cemetery Hill, in line with the main ridge, and Culp's Hill, a thousand yards to the east. The stalk of the question mark stretched 2½ miles southwards ending in two features, Little Round Top and Round Top.

Deprived of Jackson's loyal support, Lee had difficulty in imposing a plan of attack on his three corps commanders. They would have preferred to make a stand where they were or to fall back to some position where an enemy attack could be received with confidence. Lee replied that they could not afford to stand and wait anywhere since, especially since Stuart's cavalry was still missing, it would be impossible to feed the troops. When it was agreed that the army must attack, one of the commanders, James Longstreet, was vehement that they should march against Meade's southern flank thus interposing themselves between the enemy and Washington. To this Lee replied that, without the cavalry, there was no way of telling where Meade's flank lay. It could be far to the south of Round Top. When the conference broke up late on the evening of 1 July the only decision that had been reached was that an attack would be made on the following day 'as early as practicable'.

Lee finally issued his orders at 11.00 am on 2 July. They called for two assaults to be launched simultaneously. Ewell's corps was to march on Cemetery and Culp's Hills while Longstreet, from the west, would move through Peach Orchard to reach the crest of the ridge somewhat to the north of Little Round Top. He would then

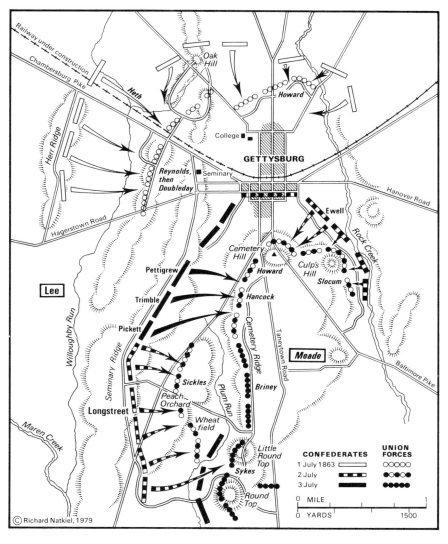

The Battle of Gettysburg

wheel to the north and roll up Meade's army along the ridge. At noon there had been 40,000 men of the Union army in position but before Longstreet started his advance at 4 pm Meade had 65,000 men on the ridge. It may be that Longstreet did launch his divisions as soon as was practicable but, though he made no secret of disapproving of his orders, he stuck rigidly to the letter of them. Thanks to the errors of General Sickles, his immediate opponent, Longstreet was able to drive up the Peach Orchard slope but, as he was about to wheel to the north, it was reported to him that there were no Federals on Round Top. This was a moment for inspired disobedience for, with Round Top firmly in Confederate hands, the position of Meade's army would be unenviable. Longstreet, however, decided that he must obey his orders and turned north without sparing even a brigade for Round Top. He changed his mind when his drive along the crest was halted but by that time there was a

Union garrison on Round Top. Meanwhile Ewell's men had failed at Cemetery Hill and though they gained a foothold on Culp's Hill they were driven off it by a dawn attack on the following day.

On the morning of 3 July Lee's position was desperate. Stuart's cavalry had arrived but were too jaded to be used. Meade now had superior numbers and a strong position. His men were concentrated on a line of 2½ miles while the Confederates, holding a line curving round them, were spread out over 6 miles. There was no way of breaking off the action since to retreat with a smaller army in the presence of a large and active cavalry could only bring disaster. The only solution was to win the battle that day by a single smashing blow.

Lee decided to deliver this attack from Seminary Ridge and to direct it at Ziegler's Grove, about 1,000 yards south of Cemetery Hill. 15,000 infantry were to spearhead the movement with the divisions of Pickett and Pettigrew in first line and a third in immediate support. Three more divisions were to follow the attack but the orders to them appear to have miscarried as did orders to Ewell to renew his assault on Cemetery Hill.

Pickett's division belonged to Longstreet's corps so that it was up to that general to start the movement. This he was most reluctant to do, exclaiming, 'I do not want to make this charge. I do not see how it can succeed. I would not make it but that General Lee has ordered it and is expecting it.' When Pickett asked permission to advance, Longstreet could not bring himself to speak but merely nodded.

Pickett's charge was a magnificent failure – the Light Brigade's charge at Balaklava repeated on foot and on a grander scale. The divisions had to cover 1,200 yards of open ground broken only by some standing corn, a small stream, and several fences. On the crest their enemy was entrenched or shielded by stone walls and had the support of ninety guns. These guns were very short of shot and shell but they had a plentiful supply of canister which was devastating at up to 300 yards. From the top of the ridge the defenders could see:

Regiment after regiment, brigade after brigade, move from the woods and rapidly take their place in the lines forming the assault . . . More than half a mile their front extends; more than a thousand yards the dull grey masses deploy, man touching man, rank pressing rank, and line supporting line. The red flags wave, their horsemen gallop up and down; the arms of fifteen thousand men, barrel and bayonet, gleam in the sun, a sloping forest of flashing steel. Right on they move, as with one soul, in perfect order, without impediment of ditch or wall, over ridge and slope, through orchard, meadow and cornfield, magnificent, grim and irresistible.

It could not last. The Federal guns opened with terrible effect as soon as the grey lines came within canister range. Soon afterwards the rifles of two divisions started firing volleys. The long lines continued to struggle up the ridge, always closing to their left to close the gaps in the ranks. Meade rushed reserves to the threatened sector and the gunfire rose to a crescendo only to die away as the ammunition failed. The rifle fire continued and Pettigrew's division crumpled and fell back. A Federal regiment swung up its outside flank to enfilade the remainder. Pickett's Virginians were not to be stopped. They broke into a double, stormed the stone walls ahead and planted their colours on the summit. Some Philadelphians opposed to them broke and fled; 100 Virginians established themselves in the centre of the Federal position. They looked back for their support and there was nothing to be seen. Longstreet had two divisions standing idly by but he would not move a man to help. A brigade of Vermonters counterattacked and the business was settled. Pickett and some 700 of his magnificent men straggled sullenly back through the corpses of their comrades. The Battle of Gettysburg was over. The Confederates had lost 20,000 men but they had inflicted 23,000 casualties.

Lee could do nothing but retire and, had Meade been a general of any enterprise, the Army of North Virginia, encumbered by a vast train of waggons and wounded, must have been destroyed. As it was, the retreat was unimpeded by the enemy. Even when Lee was delayed for a week by the flooded Potomac, Meade was content to wait until the Confederates went away. In the whole campaign Lee lost only seven guns.

THE END OF THE CONFEDERACY

After Gettysburg there was no chance that the Confederacy could win the war. On the day the retreat started General Grant ensured that they could not even look to forcing a draw. On 4 July he took Vicksburg and its garrison of 32,000 men and when, four days later, Fort Hudson fell, the Mississippi was wholly in Union hands and the South was cut in half. Texas, Louisiana, and Arkansas were isolated

Pickett's charge reaches the Union line at Gettysburg

Dead on the field of
Gettysburg;
photographed by
Alexander Gardner

and 55,000 soldiers there could do nothing more to intervene in the war. In a week Grant and Meade had deprived the South of 114,000 irreplaceable soldiers. There was worse to come. On 19–20 September, General Bragge won for the South a partial and expensive victory at Chickamauga and, following-up, marched into Tennessee to besiege Chattanooga. He was still there at the end of November when Grant routed him in a three-day battle, driving him back into Georgia.

On 9 March 1864 Ulysses S. Grant was given command of all the Union armies. He devoted his own energies to the front around Washington where the Army of the Potomac was still nominally under Meade. To the command of the western army he appointed his friend and subordinate from the Mississippi campaign, William T. Sherman. Grant saw with brutal simplicity how the war must be continued. If the Confederacy was determined to fight to the last they must be crushed by the superior reserves of manpower and industrial strength in the North. 'I am determined to hammer continually against the armed forces of the enemy and his resources by mere attrition, if in no other way, until there should be nothing left for him but submission.' This was the thinking that led to Verdun and Passchendaele, yet what other way was there to overcome a resolute and skilful enemy armed with weapons that gave every advantage to the defence? Grant was, in fact, the apostle of the war of attrition which was to dominate the battlefields for the next half century and more. It was unfortunate that he was to apply the small measure of skill that such a war permits a commander with a callousness that makes von Falkenhayn and Haig appear as tactical masters.

On 4 May 1864 he led the Army of the Potomac southwards and followed Hooker's plan of trying to force his way through the Wilderness south of Chancellorsville. Two days fighting (5–6 May) cost him 17,500 men without a gain of any kind. He then tried to turn Lee's right and get between him and Richmond. He failed in the confused series of actions near Spotsylvania Court House (8–19 May) which cost him 18,000 men. Remarking that 'I propose to fight it out on this line if it takes all summer', he again made for Lee's left. On 3 June he attacked a fortified position at Cold Harbour with a lack of subtlety which would have made General Burnside shudder. In one hour he lost 7,000 men and would have renewed the attack had his men not refused to advance again. He left his wounded lying in the broiling sun for three days before Lee suggested that he might ask for a truce to collect them. What were a few hundred wounded to a general who had, in five weeks fighting, inflicted on his own army 55,000 casualties against an army which had never exceeded 60,000 men?

His next plan was to revert to McClellan's tactics and to establish his army across the peninsula between the York and James rivers. He made one brutal and unsuccessful attack in an attempt to take Petersburg, hoping to sweep round the south of Richmond. Then he relapsed into blockading the Confederate capital from the north and

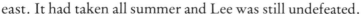

LEFT: General Grant looking at a map over the shoulder of General Meade at Massaponax, Virginia

east. It had taken all summer and Lee was still undefeated.

Sherman won the war. Like Grant he had a two-to-one superiority over his opponent, Joseph E. Johnston, who retreated skilfully before him and even struck back sharply at him at Kenesaw mountain. In an evil moment President Davis superseded him with John B. Hood who rashly took the offensive and was twice defeated losing 15,000 men. Sherman took Atlanta on 2 September and spent the autumn marching through Georgia ravaging the land, the railways, and the buildings. He did not molest the inhabitants but there was little for them to live for. On 22 December he reached Savannah and the Confederacy was now cut into three sections. Trying to divert him Hood attacked his communications and invaded Tennessee, only to be defeated at Nashville by yet another Union army.

In his siege lines opposite Richmond, Grant started the year with some more unsuccessful assaults on the Confederate trenches. All he now had to do was to wait for the opposition to disintegrate. In March 1865 Davis, at last, gave Lee the command of all the Southern armies but it was too late. He reinstated Joseph E. Johnston but Sherman was now irresistible and he marched into Charleston pushing Johnston before him into North Carolina. At Richmond food was short and ammunition still shorter. The railway system had collapsed, the army was melting away. At last Grant judged that the time had come. With 140,000 men he struck again at Petersburg and, on 2 April, he broke through. His cavalry alone now outnumbered Lee's army who were living on half rations of green corn. The Army of North Virginia set out on its last march and on 9 April Lee and 26,765 magnificent but starving soldiers surrendered at Appomattox

ABOVE: A Union observation balloon being inflated

BELOW: Men of the US Signal Corps erecting telegraph poles. Photographed by Timothy O'Sullivan in 1864

Court House. Johnston surrendered to Sherman a few days later.

The Civil War cost the lives of more than 500,000 soldiers, the Confederates alone losing 258,000 men. On both sides the armies fought with a determination and ferocity unknown in previous wars. This, added to the ham-handedness of most of the Federal generals, meant that battle casualties were extraordinarily severe. This was only part of the story. During the war the Union lost 360,000 soldiers dead but only 110,000 of them were killed in action or died of wounds, the remaining 250,000 died of disease. Weapons had improved but medical and sanitary science had not kept pace with them. It was not to be until well into the twentieth century that weapons were able to claim more deaths than the various pestilences that have beset the soldier throughout the centuries.

Nevertheless this was the first war in which the rifle clearly showed its potentiality. Even the muzzle-loading Springfields and Enfields firing two rounds a minute, which formed the main armament of the infantry on both sides, were sufficient to demonstrate that frontal attacks were a useless waste of lives, as was shown with brutal clarity at Fredericksburg, Gettysburg, and Cold Harbour. The lesson of the war was that with two equally-matched armies campaigns must deteriorate into bloody stalemates unless there was room for manoeuvre. Where there were open flanks a talented commander could still defeat a pedestrian opponent. Lee's shining talent was thus able for years to redress the balance in men and *materiél* which was so heavily weighted in favour of the North. Lee's tragedy at Gettysburg was that, without his cavalry, he dare not search for Meade's flanks. Cavalry was still a vital part of any army. Although the importance of Stuart's dashing raids has been exaggerated, the cavalry of both sides played a useful role throughout the war. Partly this was due to the fact that there was room enough for them to stay away from the rifles of the infantry, partly they were

successful because, unlike their European colleagues, they were prepared to dismount to fight.

The dominance of the rifle was ably seconded by the field gun. Here the Federals had the advantage both in numbers and in types of guns, particularly as time wore on and they acquired large numbers of rifled breech-loaders. This advantage was usually nullified by the extremely enterprising tactical handling of the Confederate artillery. Nevertheless, both sides suffered from the flat trajectory of the pieces they used. All their field guns had to be fired from positions where their crews were exposed to enemy riflemen. If the Northern artillery deserves the greatest share of credit for repulsing Pickett's charge, it did so at dreadful cost. Had the reserve divisions followed Pickett's men up the ridge they would have advanced without the scourge of canister. Even had there been ammunition remaining, there were too few gunners left to load it.

In one feature the Federal army was an example to the world. Their commissariat was excellent and set a standard which has ever since made the US army the envy of other nations. It was, wrote Colonel Henderson, 'often plentiful even to luxury. All the resources of civilisation followed the troops into the field. Before some of the greatest battles, when men were lying down waiting for the signal to advance, the newsboys went down the ranks crying the latest edition of the daily news; and certainly in one of the camps were posted notices stating that agents were present to arrange for the embalming of those who fell in action, and for forwarding to their friends in the very neatest coffins at the very lowest prices.'

Gatling guns, repeating rifles, and observation balloons were all used but had a minor effect on the course of the fighting. Railways, however, had become an essential part of the tactical, strategic, and administrative scene and, at a tactical level, the electric telegraph greatly eased the commander's burden, giving him a safe and immediate means of controlling his subordinates. The telegraph, however, also had a baleful influence. For the first time it enabled politicians to exercise direct control over generals in the field. President Lincoln, in particular, used it to interfere with tactical decisions and his interventions were almost uniformly unfortunate until, when Grant accepted the supreme command, he was induced to desist.

The telegraph should have brought the news of the war to Europe. The first transatlantic cable had been laid from Ireland to Newfoundland in 1858. Unfortunately it broke after three months in use and could not be permanently repaired until 1866. The war did, however, see the first signal organisation in any army. The Union established a corps to supervise 'all telegraph duty in the army' and which also employed flags, rockets, and balloons for communication purposes. Apart from the permanent telegraph lines which, as was usual in all countries, followed the railways, field lines up to 5 miles long were laid and signal officers were posted to all headquarters down to divisional level. Before the war ended the US Signal Corps was a sizeable organisation with 168 officers and 1,350 enlisted men.

PART THREE

Breech Loaders

CHAPTER SEVEN

The Rise of Prussia

A T THE END OF THE EIGHTEENTH CENTURY Prussia's military reputation was at a low ebb. Under Frederick the Great her army had been the finest in Europe and his methods had been copied, to a greater or lesser extent, in all other armies. In the wars of the French Revolution Prussia's part had been despicable and, when she finally decided to take a part against Napoleon, her disastrous defeats at Jena and Auerstadt showed how hollow her reputation for military prowess had become. There followed a period of radical reform after which her troops behaved creditably both when fighting for Napoleon in 1812 and against him in 1813–14, although a British general who saw them at the Battle of Lützen (2 May 1813), commented, 'I am quite unhappy to see the Prussians slaughtered from mismanagement. They are fine material, but they require exactly what has been done with the Portuguese – the loan of British leaders to train their own.' The leadership of Blücher, unsubtle but indomitable, exactly suited the Prussian army as it then was and the Waterloo campaign confirmed their reputation for hard fighting even if bad, possibly perverse, staff work almost resulted in their arriving too late to take part in the final battle.

Many of the reforms of 1806–12 were discarded when peace returned but conscription remained. At the age of 20 every able-bodied man became personally liable to three years service with the colours followed by two in the reserve. Thereafter he served, until the age of 40, in the *landwehr*. This was a thoroughly unsatisfactory body, resembling the British militia in so far as it was under civilian, rather than military, control and in being almost incapable of moving out of its own district. Apart from the conscripts it included every man who, for one reason and another, had not been called up so that it included a substantial minority with no training of any kind. On two occasions, 1831 and 1848, the *landwehr* was called out and both times it was found to be militarily useless and rotten with disaffection.

Both at home and abroad the entire Prussian army was widely regarded as being an ineffective body but much forward-looking military thinking was going on behind the scenes. One product of this was seen in 1843 when it was decided to introduce the needle gun designed by Nicholas Dreyse. In fact, as is usually the case with the introduction of new weapons, there was a long pause between this decision and its implementation. It was 1848 before two complete regiments were issued with the needle gun and 1867 before it became the weapon of all Prussian infantry. The *Zündnadelgewehr* was the world's first military breech-loader in general use and the first to have a bolt action. When the bolt was withdrawn a paper cartridge was inserted into the breech. This comprised, from front to rear, a bullet, a primer, and a bag of powder. Inside the bolt was a long needle, spring-loaded, which when the trigger was pressed, passed through the powder and struck the primer. By the standard of later bolt-action mechanisms it was a primitive device since, after each round, the needle had to be retracted and the action cocked, but the breech sealing was reasonably secure and the rate of firing was four times that of any muzzle-loading rifle. As previously mentioned, it could also be fired while lying down.

The next significant advance came in 1857 when Helmut von Moltke was appointed chief-of-staff. Later he was to show himself as an excellent tactician and a better strategist but his immediate impact on the army was on its staff. Of the forty officers who graduated annually from the *Kriegsakademie* Moltke selected twelve whom he trained personally, ruthlessly rejecting any who failed to reach his exacting standard. He contrived in this way to ensure that a staff officer, trained to an agreed tactical doctrine, stood at the side of every formation commander and, as time went by, these staff officers became brigade and divisional commanders and the whole hierarchy became permeated by men who thought and reacted alike when faced with any usual tactical problem. Moltke was also a man with a keen appreciation of the military importance of railways. As a youngish man he had invested his savings in the Berlin-Hamburg railway when it was being built and he became, in time, one of the company's directors. He extended the General Staff to include a Lines of Communication Department and formed a civilian-military joint commission to operate the railways in time of war.

As chief-of-staff there was a limit to what Moltke could achieve. Prussia's population was 19,000,000 but her regular army, including the trained reserves, amounted to only 200,000 men and this was insufficient to make her a considerable military power, the more so since she was exposed to potential enemies on three fronts – France to the west, Russia to the east, and Austria to the south. Austria, Prussia's century-old rival for the leadership of Germany, was the power Berlin most wished to overawe and the Prussian army was in no state to be an effective weapon of policy. It could only be made one by bringing the *landwehr* under military control and reformed so that it was capable of acting with the regulars. Such a step would require the assent of the Assembly where it would be faced with the opposition of the liberally-minded Prussian bourgeoisie who would be able to block any increase in military expenditure.

In 1858 Prince Wilhelm became Regent. He was the first

PREVIOUS PAGE: Prussian troops bringing out French wounded from the ruins of Le Bourget during fighting in December 1870

professional soldier to rule the country for eighty years and he was much impressed by a memorandum submitted to him by Albrecht von Roon proposing a thorough-going reform of the army and the *landwehr*. Its implementation, however, seemed impracticable but the need for it was stressed in the following year when international tension caused the army to be mobilised. The resulting chaos determined the Regent to act. He appointed von Roon Minister of War and the army reform plan was put before the Assembly. As was to be expected the fusion of army and *landwehr* was rejected and the wrangle prolonged itself until in 1862 the Assembly refused to vote any funds for the army. Wilhelm, who had by this time succeeded as King Wilhelm I, on von Roon's advice appointed Otto von Bismarck as Minister-President and dissolved the Assembly.

In the parliamentary interregnum which followed, taxes continued to be collected and the army was reformed. The *landwehr* was incorporated and, with regular units, was grouped into districts. There were originally seven of these and, on mobilisation, each would produce one complete army corps. A further corps was to be provided by the Guards. Henceforward every Prussian male would serve three years with the colours and four with the reserve. He would then be transferred to the *landwehr* for a reduced term of years but during the first of them he was subject to immediate recall. Thus on mobilisation the army could count on eight annual contingents instead of five as had been the case earlier.

Still without parliamentary consent, Bismarck involved Prussia in a war with Denmark (1864). Although this short campaign was fought with Austrian support, the result was that the duchies of

Prussian troops after the storming of the fortress of Düppel during the war against Denmark

Developments during the Franco-Prussian War

One result of the development of longer range weapons, of rifling in both infantry and artillery weapons, was the increased importance of cover. The breech-loading rifle meant that a soldier could use his weapon when lying down so that he could conceal himself as he fired. Apart from the sieges of fortresses, eighteenth-century armies usually fought in open country. By the Franco-Prussian War, when both sides were using breech-loaders, fighting in towns and villages became more common since the buildings gave some cover from fire. The Germans storming Dijon (RIGHT) show almost open country fighting in one of the city's squares but the Bavarians at Sedan (BELOW RIGHT) and the Württemberg *Köningen Olga* regiment repulsing a French sortie from Paris (FAR RIGHT) show house to house fighting becoming more common

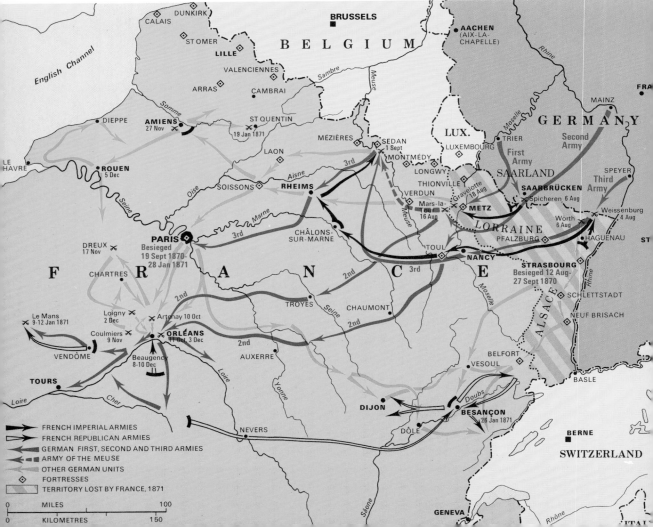

FRENCH IMPERIAL ARMIES
FRENCH REPUBLICAN ARMIES
GERMAN FIRST, SECOND AND THIRD ARMIES
ARMY OF THE MEUSE
OTHER GERMAN UNITS
◇ FORTRESSES
TERRITORY LOST BY FRANCE, 1871

0   MILES   100
0   KILOMETRES   150

Schleswig and Holstein were taken from the Danish crown and their population subjected to Prussian conscription, adding a further army corps to her mobilisation strength.

By 1866 Prussia could put into the field, apart from depot troops, 335,000 men with 130,000 more, the first levy of the *landwehr*, trained and ready for use almost immediately. Also available were 106,500 horses of which 76,000 were required for the cavalry and artillery. The remainder were needed to draw the first line transport consisting of 5,450 waggons. In the artillery, a start had been made in issuing breech-loading steel guns. At this time steel was a suspect material for guns since it was liable to be flawed in casting. Austria and France were still using bronze for their cannon while Britain was using reinforced wrought iron. In Prussia, however, Krupp had succeeded in casting flawfree steel guns and fitting them with a safe breech-closing mechanism.

THE AUSTRO–PRUSSIAN WAR

Now that the army was ready, Bismarck forced a quarrel on Austria. As von Moltke wrote, 'The war of 1866 did not break out because Prussia was threatened or because public opinion demanded war. It was a war for which the cabinet made long and careful preparation not because they aimed for territorial aggrandisement but to establish Prussia as the pre-eminent power in Europe.'

On 15 June Prussia declared war on three of Austria's main allies, Hanover, Hesse-Cassel, and Saxony and immediately sent troops into their territories. The Hanoverians, caught wholly unprepared, managed to win a creditable victory at Langensalza (27 June) before being forced to capitulate but in the other two states the Prussian occupation was almost bloodless although the Saxon army, 25,000 strong, escaped and joined the Austrians who mobilised to defend their allies.

The Austrians had to detach three corps to Italy where, on the promise of receiving Venetia, the Sardinians had declared war in support of Prussia but their main army, 270,000 men including the Saxons, was concentrated around Josephstadt (Mlada-Boleslav) in Bohemia. Their commander was Field Marshal Ludwig von Benedek, the only Austrian commander to have given a good account of himself at Solferino. In supreme command he was to show himself an unskilful general. Bohemia thrusts forward into Germany and is surrounded by mountains and hills. Two courses were open to Benedek. He could hold the passes, all of which gave strong defensive positions, or he could fall back from the salient and fight on the hills north of Brno which form the south-eastern border of Bohemia. Knowing that his army was less well equipped than his enemy, either of these courses would have given Benedek a chance of success but he chose to reject both and base himself on the central Bohemian plain. There he was served only by a single railway while his opponent, who could strike at him from the east through Silesia and from the north through Saxony, could use five railway lines.

Von Moltke decided to strike from both directions, relying on the

Westphalian hussars entraining at Düsseldorf in 1866

traditional sluggishness of Austrian military movements to offset the risk of having his two striking forces defeated singly. Prince Friedrich Karl, commanding the First Army and the Army of the Elbe, was to march south from Görlitz and Zittau while the Second Army, under the Crown Prince, was to march over the Riesengebirge from the east. The two armies were to join in the heart of Bohemia.

In the early fighting the superiority of the needle gun was clearly demonstrated but its effect was to some extent counteracted by the admirable handling of the Austrian artillery, notwithstanding the fact that the Austrians were pitting muzzle-loaders against breech-loaders. Prussian communications were also excellent. Every divisional headquarters had attached to it a field telegraph waggon which reeled out cable behind it so that each headquarters could be kept in touch with the permanent telegraph system running alongside the railways. Thus, within half an hour of a headquarters being established, it could communicate not only with its corps command but with Berlin. Von Moltke, who directed the opening of the campaign in minute detail, did not leave the capital until shortly before the end of June and it was not until he did so that he began to have trouble in directing the scattered forces under his command.

Benedek made no attempt to crush either of the Prussian armies advancing towards him but decided rather to take up the strongest position he could find and allow the enemy to exhaust himself by attacking him. On 1 July he started putting his men into position on a short range of heights north-west of Königgrätz (Hradec Kralove). Four corps were placed in the centre where the ground was highest, the heights of Chülm, and his left, the least threatened side, was entrusted to the Saxons. Two Austrian corps, at right angles to the main front, protected his right. Another corps and a cavalry division formed his reserve. In front of the heights of Chülm his outposts held the village of Sadowa (Sadova).

Von Moltke divided his army into three for his attack. Prince Friedrich Karl with First Army was to hold the Austrian attention to the front while both their flanks were assailed. On the Austrian left the small Army of the Elbe was to work round the Saxons but the main blow was to come from their right where the Crown Prince was to roll up the Austrian centre with Second Army. The attack started at 8.00 am on 3 July and First Army had no difficulty in taking Sadowa but they met stiff opposition in front of the Chülm hills. Moreover, as is usually the case with attacks on exterior lines, the flank columns were late in arriving. It was not until 11.00 am that the Army of the Elbe started exchanging shots with the Saxons and the Second Army was still out of striking distance. Matters were made worse by Friedrich Karl who took the bit between his teeth and made a series of determined frontal attacks on the heights. The Austrian infantry fought, as always, most stubbornly but most of the high casualty rate in First Army was caused by the Austrian guns which were cunningly sited and brilliantly served. By midday Benedek, who did not suspect the approach of the Crown Prince's army, was planning a counterattack that must have routed the First Army.

Prussian troops passing King Wilhelm I and his staff on their way to attack at the Battle of Königgrätz

It was at this time that he learned what was happening on his right wing. The two corps commanders had taken the offensive against First Army on their own initiative and had done so using heavy columns of infantry which might have served their purpose at the Battle of Leipzig but which could only prove suicidal against the needle gun. Nor would these generals desist from their attacks until Benedek sent a third set of orders for them to fall back to their assigned positions. Their weary troops were trudging back when the Crown Prince's advance guard burst into their flank and broke through to the Austrian centre.

Even this disaster did not cause the Austrian army to disintegrate. The bulk of the infantry retreated in good order, covered by their artillery. A Prussian attempt to pursue with cavalry was almost destroyed by a brigade of Austrian cuirassiers who themselves were massacred by the ubiquitous needle guns. The gunners fought their pieces so long that most of them fell into Prussian hands and at the end of the day they had lost 174 guns. They also suffered 31,000 killed and wounded and lost 13,000 prisoners. The Prussian loss was 9,000 men, mostly from First Army.

The Emperor of Austria asked for an armistice immediately after Königgrätz but the Prussians would not agree until their army had reached the Danube. When the preliminaries of peace were signed they were seen to be very mild considering the completeness of the Austrian defeat. The empire only had to give Venetia to the Sardinians who, ironically, she had trounced both on land at at sea. The crux of the settlement was that Austria should give up all claims to the hegemony of Germany. Prussia was to be the leader of the North German Confederation, which included all Germany north of a line drawn east and west at the level of the northern frontier of Bohemia. Austria was not to interfere within the Confederation.

Harsh terms were imposed on Austria's allies. Hanover, Hesse-Cassel, Nassau, and Frankfurt were annexed to Prussia, giving her a further 4,000,000 inhabitants and two more army corps. Saxony retained some vestiges of independence but she was to join the Confederation, surrender control of her telegraph services to Prussia, and contribute a corps to the Confederation's army. Hesse had also to join the Confederation and contribute a division. The southern states had only to buy peace: 30,000,000 guilders were demanded from Bavaria and 8,000,000 from Württemberg.

Prussia's crushing victory, achieved in six weeks, stirred every War Office in Europe. Every army now had to adopt the breech-loading rifle. Designs had been accumulating dust in pending trays for many years but now they were taken out and sent to be manufactured. The earlier opposition to them melted away in the light of the demonstration that had been given. This opposition had come from two sources. First, as might be expected, were the ministries of finance who protested that breech-loaders were too expensive. The other consisted of conservatively-minded soldiers who prophesied that the possible rate of fire was so high that the soldier would immediately fire away all his ammunition and leave himself defence-

less. A smaller minority averred that once a man was lying down
under cover to fire it would not be possible to get him on his feet
again when it was time to advance. Königgrätz showed that neither
of these misfortunes was likely to occur.

In 1866 the French started to re-arm their infantry with the
Chassepot, a more sophisticated bolt-action needle gun with a rubber
plug to seal the breech. It was sighted to 1,600 yards, 600 more than
the Snider which the British adopted in the following year. The
British were still not convinced of the safety of bolt-actions and the
Snider had a hammer action and a hinged breech-block which swung
out sideways. Although originally designed to use a paper cartridge,
it was actually issued with a cartridge made from drawn brass, the
invention of Colonel Boxer, which was the prototype of all subsequent cartridge cases since the brass of the case, expanding on
firing, effectively sealed the breech.

There was less unanimity about artillery. The advantages of
Krupps steel breech-loaders were obscured by the mediocrity of their
handling when compared with the brilliant performance of the
Austrian gunners with their muzzle-loaders. Steel was still suspect.
A British writer in 1867 dismissed it on the grounds that 'it has a
tendency to brittleness under the shock of a sudden blow. Of two
steel guns apparently made under similar conditions, one may last for
many rounds and the other fly to pieces at the first round.' Nor did
the same writer, who was far from being a reactionary thinker, see
much advantage from guns having a long range. Even for heavy
pieces he asked 'What more can possibly be demanded than good
shooting up to 6,000 or even 4,000 yards? Who would throw away

their costly shot at greater distances, unless to bombard a town where accuracy matters little?' This view was echoed in the current instructions issued for the Prussian artillery. These, while laying down that field guns should not engage infantry at less than 6–800 yards (i.e. within the effective range of the needle gun), deprecated firing at a range greater than 1,800–2,000 paces since accurate observation would be impossible. The underlying view of gunners in all countries, at sea as well as on land, was that guns should be used at 'decisive ranges', a survival from the days of smooth-bores which was to persist up to, and in some cases beyond, the end of the century.

FRENCH REORGANISATION AND NEW EQUIPMENT

Naturally it was the French who felt most threatened by the growing strength of Prussia which faced her across the middle Rhine. The French army had regained, if it had ever lost, the good opinion of its own capabilities which it had consolidated under the first Napoleon. Since then it had had battle experience on a scale unparalleled by any other continental power and in the Crimea, whatever the administrative failings, the French soldiers had fought excellently. The Italian campaign of 1859 had given it victory and a tactical doctrine – the offensive at all costs. The *élan* of the French infantry in the attack was rightly believed to be the envy of the Prussian War Office.

To set against its advantages, the French army had serious failings. One of the most serious was that the army was growing steadily apart from the nation. This was largely the deliberate choice of Napoleon III who wished to retain it as a reliable instrument to preserve his rule and the result was that, while being mistrusted by the bourgeoisie, it

A contemporary French print of Krupp's breech-loading field gun. Despite breech defects, this was the mainstay of the Prussian army in 1870–1

was not, as in Britain and Prussia, closely connected with the aristocracy. Both in France and in Algeria the officers formed a distinct and isolated social class. Nor was the recruiting for the ranks in a satisfactory state. Conscription had been retained but in a partial and unjust form. Men were called up by ballot and those who were unfortunate enough to draw a *mauvais numéro* were, unless they were rich enough to be able to buy a substitute, required to serve for seven years with the colours after which they were unlikely to be able to find a satisfactory niche in civilian life and frequently volunteered for long service. Meanwhile more fortunate contemporaries had only to register on a reserve which did no training.

The army resulting from this conscription was not strong enough to protect France from Prussia. When Prussia thrashed Austria it was realised in Paris that France's field strength was only 288,000 men, of whom a large number must be kept in Algeria. Prussia had started the Austrian war with nine army corps, 335,000 men, and, by the treaties signed after her victory, had added to her strength a further four corps.

Napoleon called for an army with a mobilisation strength of 1,000,000 men and suggested achieving this target by introducing military service for all on the Prussian model. No one supported this plan. The view of the soldiers was that only an army composed of long-service professionals could be effective. The liberals, on whose support the empire was becoming increasingly dependent, talked of a 'Nation in Arms' with universal service without substitutes or exemptions but added that only the *Corps Legislatif* had the right to fix the size of the army and that it must not be as large as that which would result from universal service. The republican opposition also talked of the Nation in Arms but aimed to achieve it by disbanding the regulars and relying on a civilian militia on the Swiss model.

In January 1868 a compromise was reached. The scheme was devised by the practical and capable Marshal Niel and arranged that every man would be liable to military service but that, for the majority, this would consist only of five months training. A minority would be chosen by ballot and would be liable for five years with the colours and four on the reserve. Substitutes would still be permitted for those balloted but those who provided them would still be liable for their five months training. It was calculated that by 1875 this scheme would give France an army which, when mobilised, would total 800,000 men. Behind this would stand 500,000 men of the *Gardes Mobiles*. These, a resurrection of the old and unsatisfactory National Guard, would include all those who, for any reason, had escaped the conscription. Niel wanted them to do three weeks training each year but the liberals, forgetting their call for a Nation in Arms, claimed that three weeks training would turn France into a barracks. All that they would agree was that the *Gardes Mobiles* should train on fourteen separate days during the year and, in the event, very few of them had done any training before war broke out.

The greatest access of strength to the French army was the

adoption of the Chassepot rifle, a more sophisticated if less robust version of the needle gun. Its adoption was only achieved by the personal intervention of the Emperor in the teeth of a bitter resistance from the Ministry of War and the cost of equipping the infantry with it was 113,000,000 francs, a sum which effectively put out of court any possibility of re-equipping the artillery with breech-loaders. Thus the French had to go to their next war with the rifled muzzle-loaders that had done well in Italy and the belief, based on the Austrian gunners' success at Königgrätz, that muzzle-loaders were quite as effective as the Krupp breech-loaders. France also had a new weapon, the *mitrailleuse*, an early machine-gun consisting of twenty-five barrels which were revolved by a handle. It could fire 150 rounds a minute to a range of 2,000 yards but it had the disadvantage that it was as conspicuous as an upright piano. Properly handled it could have been a most useful weapon but, so anxious were the French to keep its existence a secret that they undertook no tactical exercises to show how it could best be used and the gun crews had no opportunity to fire the *mitrailleuse* under field conditions.

In 1867 Marshal Niel was appointed Minister of War but he was already a sick man and died within two years. He had done as much as any man could to make the army fit for war but, despite the unwavering support of the Emperor, the opposition was too great, the time was too short, and the task was too gigantic. His successor abandoned many of his reforms and allowed to lapse the civilian-military commission on railways which Niel had set up on the Prussian model. In 1870 the liberal ministry decided that disarmament was the most promising form of defence and reduced the army estimates by 13,000,000 francs. They relied on the supposed superiority of the Chassepot over the needle gun and on the prestige of the French army which had a peace strength of 150,000 men and a potential mobilised strength of less than 500,000. They counted blandly on the support of Austria in any war against Prussia but, as has so often been the case in France, politicians and soldiers alike put their faith in *le Système D*, the belief that *on se débrouillera toujours* – 'we shall always muddle through'.

FRANCE AGAINST PRUSSIA

On 30 June 1870 France's liberal Prime Minister, Émile Ollivier, proudly announced that 'the peace of Europe seems better assured than at any previous period'. Two weeks later, 13 July, his cabinet ordered general mobilisation on the grounds that Prussian manoeuvres to place a Hohenzollern princeling on the throne of Spain were an insult to French honour.

French mobilisation was chaotic. It had been agreed that, with her smaller army, France's best chance would be a quick spoiling attack to disorganise the Prussian army while its complicated mobilisation was incomplete. To speed up this attack it had been decided that regiments should move directly to their war stations while their reservists would report to the depots and be forwarded thence in batches of 100. The calculation was that the entire army would be in position and at its full strength on the fourteenth day of mobilisation. Since Niel's mixed railway commission had not been allowed to do its work the system failed. When the fighting started tens of thousands of reservists were trailing round the railways in increasingly discontented groups under the incomplete control of unknown officers. Of the 385,000 men whom it was hoped to have massed on the western frontier by 28 July only 202,448 were actually present and one in ten of those were in the wrong place.

To make matters worse the French army was not in peacetime divided into brigades, divisions, and corps. These formations had to be formed on mobilisation and their staffs improvised from inexperienced officers who knew nothing of the troops they were to serve. All that had been agreed was that the troops would be grouped into three armies, each commanded by a marshal. Two of these armies, each of three corps, would be close to the frontier, based respectively on Metz and Strasbourg. The third, of only two corps, would be formed in the rear at Châlons-sur-Marne. While mobilisation was in progress Napoleon changed his mind. No armies were to be formed and he would personally direct the operations of the eight separate corps. Even in good health it was a task that he was ill-equipped to undertake. Since at the time he was crippled with the stone, he had barely the physical strength even to try to do so. He was not even able to decide between two schools of strategic thought that quickly emerged. One of these demanded a rigid defensive to protect the national territory while the other called for a vigorous offensive into south Germany, hoping that the French would be greeted as liberators in Bavaria and Württemberg and thus give Austria an excuse to intervene.

Although not without its problems, the German mobilisation brought the forces required to the points where they were needed. Some 309,000 men divided into three armies were concentrated in a great arc from Trier through Mainz to Speyer. There they were ready to converge on the short stretch of common frontier between Germany and France which was not covered by the Rhine. There were thirteen army corps from the North German Confederation with two from Bavaria while Baden and Württemberg each contributed a division. The enemies of four years earlier were now united under arms. Germany had 1,183,000 men ready for war within eighteen days of mobilisation. The high command had its plans laid and the means to carry them out. The German maps of France were better than those available to the French. The French had maps of Germany but none of France.

It was in Germany that the first fighting took place. On 2 August six French divisions marched 2 miles across the frontier and drove three Prussian companies out of Saarbrücken. The town was not occupied but the French took up a position on the heights to the south-west. Napoleon's headquarters spent some exciting days planning sweeping offensives and, with this in view, the front-line armies, so recently united under the Emperor's command, were again divided with Marshal MacMahon commanding on the left and

Marshal Canrobert on the right. This delegation did not stop imperial headquarters sending orders direct to formations. Since the French fear was now of invasion, corps were dispersed to cover every possible German approach road.

Anxious as Napoleon was to exploit his easy success at Saarbrücken, advance was impossible. The army could not be supplied. Stocks had been built up but the railways were still so involved in moving reservists about that there was no rolling stock available for bringing forward ammunition and rations. The French troops, trained for the offensive, were disheartened but their disappointment did not match that of von Moltke who had planned to draw them forward into the Saarland and encircle them there. Seeing that their advance had halted, he had to recast his plans and surround them where they stood. He ordered the First and Second Armies to hold them in front while the Third Army under the Crown Prince swung round their right and took them in the rear.

This scheme was also frustrated. The First Army was commanded by General von Steinmetz who had served under Blücher and inherited his headlong tactical style. On 6 August he hurled his men piecemeal against a French corps on the heights of Spicheren, south of Saarbrücken. He deserved to be soundly beaten but he was saved because every German commander within earshot marched to the sound of the guns while the French generals stayed where they were. The French held the Spicheren position until late afternoon when they retreated on orders since it was believed that their flanks were being turned. They had fought tenaciously all day but, when the retreat started, their morale cracked and great disorder set in. There had been 4,500 Prussian casualties while the French lost only 2,000 killed and wounded. 2,000 more, however, were missing. The Germans could claim a victory but it was one which von Moltke would have preferred not to fight for – the French retreat meant that the Crown Prince could not turn their flank.

The Crown Prince fought his own battle on that day. Like von Moltke he had not meant to fight but was committed to action by an over-enthusiastic subordinate. At Wörth (or Fröschwiller) the French were once more driven back after heavy day-long fighting. Both sides lost about 11,000 killed and wounded but the French had as many as 9,000 missing. Many of the French losses fell on the cavalry for on several occasions brigades of cuirassiers tried to counterattack German infantry only to be massacred by rifle fire. The Germans had their own problems. They were greatly impressed by the range and accuracy of the Chassepot. In fact the French had much trouble with their new rifle. Its bore was less than the needle gun and, since black powder was still being used by both sides, the barrels fouled very quickly. Nevertheless, this was the first time that the Germans had encountered an enemy able to fire as fast as they could themselves and they quickly found their massed formations of infantry very vulnerable. They tried to use looser formations only to find that once an infantryman had gone to ground behind cover it was difficult to get him on the move again if he did not have his comrades beside him. The Germans found the answer – enterprising use of their artillery. This arm had been radically re-trained since the Austrian war and issued with a far more efficient percussion fuse. Forcefully handled and firing with a standard of accuracy hitherto unknown, the Krupp guns were able to crush the feeble response of the French muzzle-loaders, to say nothing of the conspicuous and poorly handled *mitrailleuses*, and to keep the heads of the French infantry down until their own infantry was within storming distance.

THE LONG RETREAT TO METZ

The defeats at Spicheren and Wörth produced a sharp drop in French morale and the long retreat that followed did nothing to improve it. The Emperor handed over the supreme command to Marshal Bazaine but could not resist the temptation to issue orders on his own account. Further orders reached the armies from Paris, some originating from the Ministry of War, some from the Empress. As a result the army became divided. On the right MacMahon with the corps that had fought at Wörth retreated on the reserve army at Châlons-sur-Marne, while Bazaine with 178,000 men made for Metz.

This left wing fought off a Prussian attack at Borny on 14 August but, having reached Metz, Bazaine decided that the fortress was too far to the east and that his force would be better placed at Verdun. He might have saved his army if he had issued his orders as soon as he made up his mind but, on the evening of 14 August, he was exhausted and had been slightly wounded. By the following morning when he made known his new objective there was German cavalry across the road from Metz to Verdun and on the 16 there was infantry to support them.

Bazaine's advance guard came up against this opposition near Mars-la-Tour on 16 August. The French could bring overwhelming numbers to the battlefield and a determined commander could have broken through, but Bazaine was not a determined man. He became obsessed with an illusory threat to his left flank and concentrated all his reserves to meet it. By nightfall he had inflicted 13,000 casualties for the loss of only 11,000 but he had failed to clear the road to Verdun and he ordered the army to fall back towards Metz.

Mars-la-Tour was a disastrous day for cavalry. It was bad enough that French lancers and the Cuirassiers of the Guard met with a bloody repulse when they charged Prussian infantry. What was worse was a local success won by von Bredow at the head of a brigade of Prussian dragoons. In a charge of which Murat would have been proud they broke into the French gun lines doing fearful damage. That they were driven back immediately and lost 380 out of 800 present was soon forgotten. What was remembered was their initial success. Von Bredow's charge reactivated a legend, the legend that cavalry could profitably intervene on a battlefield dominated by the rifle and the field gun. Heavy cavalry was reprieved and in 1914 all the major armies took the field with large forces of dragoons and cuirassiers fit only for a ceremonial parade.

Bazaine did not immediately withdraw into the fortifications of

Metz and on 17 August he had his army deployed on a long position to the west of the fortress. Its southern end was immensely strong. The flank was secured on the Moselle from where ran a line of heights facing the Mance stream. As late as 1944 a few improvised German units stood on these heights and repulsed General Patton's army. In 1870 the French had loopholed a number of stoutly-built farmhouses on the crest and one on the forward slope, turning them into miniature fortresses. The northern stretch of the front, from Amanvillers to St Privat and beyond, was less secure. The continuation of the ridge was a gentler slope and, while it offered magnificent fields of fire to the defenders, there was nothing on which the flank could be secured. It was standard practice in such a situation to 'refuse the flank' by posting troops echeloned back from the main line. The corps commander responsible, Marshal Canrobert, neglected this precaution and instead posted a brigade at St Marie-aux-Chênes, a mile in front of his right wing at St Privat. It can only be supposed that he made this most unwise disposition in order to shield the roads from Metz to Montmédy, which ran through St Privat and still offered an escape route for Bazaine. He did not do so on Bazaine's orders for when the commander-in-chief found what he had done he ordered him to swing back his whole right to a safer position nearer Metz. By that time it was the morning of 18 August and too late to make the change.

On that morning the French army with 113,000 men and 520 guns was deployed on a front of 7 miles. The length of this line meant that there could be few reserves. The only infantry not in the line was the Guard Corps which was stationed near Bazaine's headquarters, Fort Plappeville, one of the outlying forts of Metz. To the Guards' commander, Marshal Bourbaki, Bazaine said no more than that he should act as he saw fit. The commander-in-chief then relapsed into total lethargy.

Von Moltke was deliberately courting a battle. He had with him the First and Second Armies, 118,000 men and 732 guns. The German cavalry had made a poor job of reconnaissance and the whereabouts of the French was largely unknown. Opinion at headquarters was that Bazaine was marching for Montmédy and that only a rearguard was left to attack. The plan was, therefore, that Steinmetz and First Army would make a holding attack from Gravelotte against the southern end of the ridge while Prince Friedrich Karl with Second Army would turn the French right and strike towards Metz. The problem was that no one knew where the French right was so that the Second Army must march across the French front until they found it. While they were doing this they would be very vulnerable to a spoiling attack from the ridge. Fortunately Bazaine was too apathetic to attempt such a move.

The irrepressible Steinmetz had no use for a holding attack. Throughout the day First Army hurled itself at the unassailable ridge in a series of all-out frontal attacks. The limit of their success was the capture of St Hubert Farm on the forward slope. They never came within measurable distance of reaching the crest. Towards evening

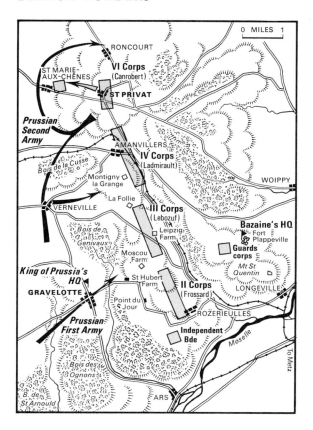

the forward troops after one more bloody repulse broke and fled in panic. A reserve division fired into them believing them to be a French attack. At this point a French counterattack, even with cavalry, must have destroyed Steinmetz's army but Bazaine would give no orders. He only left his headquarters once during the day – to visit a fort somewhat to the rear.

For most of the day Second Army fared little better. Friedrich Karl first decided that the French right was south of Amanvillers and ordered two corps to advance to the north of the village. Just in time to cancel the attack, he realised that a line of French tents, white on the skyline, stretched northward towards St Privat. Ordering his guns to engage the line north of Amanvillers, he sent his reserve corps, the Saxons, to sweep wide round St Privat. His guns soon mastered the French muzzle-loaders but the Saxon advance was slow. They had first to clear St Marie-aux-Chênes. This they did competently enough but it was becoming obvious that it must be some considerable time before they could skirt St Privat and outflank Canrobert. The delay was too much for Prince Augustus of Württemberg who commanded the Prussian Guard Corps. At 6.00 pm, on his own initiative, he launched his men at St Privat neglecting even to call for artillery support. The result was a massacre. The attack collapsed 600 yards from the village with 8,000 guardsmen having fallen in twenty minutes.

ABOVE LEFT: The Battle of Gravelotte-St Privat

ABOVE: A Prussian
brigadier and his staff in
St Privat

An hour later the Saxons with fourteen batteries were in position north of St Privat. Fourteen more batteries fired into the place from the west and Canrobert's men were crushed beneath the weight of shells. They began to retreat and soon they were running for their lives. In their rout they crashed into the Imperial Guard which Bourbaki was bringing up to their support and soon both corps were dashing in disorder for the shelter of Metz. Bazaine stirred himself sufficiently to order the rest of the army back to the fortress. He admitted to casualties of more than 12,000, almost certainly an underestimate, and talked of making a further attempt to break out. He never made any serious move to do so and henceforward the larger part of the French field army was penned up in the fortress.

As they counted their casualties – 20,163 of them – the Germans saw little reason to be pleased. It was midnight before the King of Prussia and von Moltke heard that St Privat had been taken. Earlier, as they watched from Gravelotte, the battle had seemed to be an unmitigated disaster and even after they knew that they had won they realised that First Army was no longer in a state to fight another battle. The wrecking of his Guard Corps was a particularly savage blow to the King of Prussia.

Despite the German misgivings, the Battle of Gravelotte–St Privat decided the campaign. Including the garrison 154,481 regular French troops were shut up in Metz and a shattering blow struck at the

confidence of the remainder. Von Moltke detailed the remains of First Army and half the Second to invest the fortress and formed the remainder, Third Army and three corps of the Second, into the Army of the Meuse, commanded by the Crown Prince of Saxony, for operations against the remainder of the French field forces. These comprised four corps at Châlons-sur-Marne amounting to 130,000 men and 423 guns. Three of these corps had fought on the frontier and were demoralised by their long retreat. The fourth, XII Corps, was a makeshift affair made up of one regular division, withdrawn from the Pyrenees, one division of marines, and one division of recruits. There were also eighteen battalions of *Gardes Mobiles* from the Paris region. They were quite without training and were simmering with sedition.

Napoleon III surrenders

Marshal MacMahon was in nominal command but the Emperor was with the army and, on 17 August listlessly presided over a council of war. It was decided that the army should fall back and manoeuvre against the German onslaught with their flank secured on fortified Paris. Scarcely had this decision been reached when news arrived on Bazaine's repulse at Mars-la-Tour. The retreat was countermanded and only the *Mobiles* were sent back to the capital.

From Paris, from the Empress and the Minister of War, came urgent promptings to advance to join Bazaine. No move was made while supplies were collected but, on 21 August, German cavalry was within 20 miles of Châlons and MacMahon led the army to Rheims. He was reluctant to do so being convinced that the only sensible course was to fall back on Paris. Rations were running short and the sight of his exhausted men on the march depressed him beyond measure. 'Bazaine', he said, 'cannot be rescued. He has neither supplies nor ammunition. He will have surrendered long before we reach him.'

At Rheims he received a message from Metz telling him that Bazaine intended to break out to the north-west. This gave him a faint hope that the two armies might be able to join near Montmédy and on 23 August the Army of Châlons marched off to the east with the pain-racked Emperor trailing along among the baggage. The sight of the way in which his discouraged army shambled along the road finally destroyed any spark of optimism that MacMahon may have retained but he was kept at his task by a peremptory message from the Minister of War: 'I require you, in the name of the Council of Ministers and the Privy Council, to go to Bazaine's assistance'. On 30 August they found the Bavarians across their road near Beaumont-sur-Marne and in a brisk encounter battle lost 7,500 men, twice the loss they inflicted. It was now clear to MacMahon that there was no chance of marching to Montmédy and he gave orders for a retreat of 15 miles to the north-east where the army might get some security from the dismantled fortress of Sedan. It may have been an unavoidable move but it was certainly a fatal one. At Sedan the Germans pinned them against the Belgian frontier. MacMahon's orders for 1 September were: 'The army will rest today.' One of his corps commanders took a more realistic view of the situation: '*Nous sommes dans un pot de chambre et nous y serons emmerdés.*'

There was no rest for the Army of Châlons on 1 September. The German attack opened at 4.00 am and although some of the French, especially the Zouaves, fought with dash and tenacity the result was a foregone conclusion. By 6.30 in the evening a French general was riding into the German lines with a letter from his Emperor to the King of Prussia:

Monsieur mon Frère,
N'ayant pas pu mourir au milieu de mes troupes, il ne me reste qu'a remettre mon épée entre les mains de Votre Majesté. Je suis de Votre Majesté le bon frère,

Napoléon

The Germans had already taken 21,000 prisoners. Eighty-three thousand more became prisoners on the following day when the capitulation was signed. Bazaine's army continued to hold out in Metz until 27 October but Sedan saw the end of the French regular army.

In the whole of unoccupied France there were now only 95,000 trained soldiers available, most of them scattered in depots and drafts. Only two complete regular regiments were at liberty. In six weeks the most highly-regarded army in Europe had been not only defeated but destroyed. This triumph was not primarily the result of tactical skill. Except at the highest level German generalship was little better than French and some German commanders, notably von Steinmetz, made serious and costly mistakes. When in good heart the French soldier fought as well as his German counterpart and, as was shown opposite Gravelotte, the Chassepot in a good defensive position could dominate the battlefield despite the German superiority in artillery. The lesson of the six weeks fighting had been that future wars would be won as much by administration as by weapons. Staff work was the key to victory. The German mobilisation plan and the organisation of their railways gave von Moltke an initial advantage he never looked like losing. French commanders started the fighting with their formations at best partly formed and, while many of the corps commanders were highly-competent soldiers, they never received clear orders, partly because the high command was incapable of taking decisions and partly because the staff system was unable to transmit such decisions as were reached. The high command was further hampered by supply shortages. This was not the result of a dearth of stores but of the inability of the railways to deliver what was required and of the disorganisation of the *Intendance* which could not distribute such supplies as were available.

By contrast the Germans had a commissariat which worked admirably and a railway system which, despite local difficulties, always delivered what was required. Able to rely on being supplied, German corps commanders could concentrate on executing the clear decisions which came down from royal headquarters and which were interpreted for them by staff officers trained by von Moltke to a common doctrine and able to react to the unexpected in a way that would be comprehensible to their colleagues on the staff at all levels. Almost all the German problems were caused by generals who neglected both their staff officers and their orders.

The weakest point of the German high command was its collection of intelligence. Some of these failings were due to the indecision of their enemy and the sheer improbability of their moves but principally they were due to the failure of the German light cavalry to perform their most important function, that of keeping in touch with the enemy and reporting his moves. Communications posed another problem. Despite their efficient field telegraph units, the high command relied chiefly on the railway telegraph cables which could transmit only in morse. In a battlefield situation von Moltke and his subordinates had to rely, both for giving and receiving orders, on aides-de-camp riding about the field on horseback. Thus they were no better equipped in this respect than Marlborough had been, while the action they were seeking to control was on a much wider front and even more obscured by the clouds of white smoke which billowed out from the black powder used in every weapon.

The Germans had expected that the defeat of all the imperial

Napoleon III driving to surrender to the King of Prussia

armies would mean the end of the war but they were soon disillusioned. The empire collapsed ignominiously but an improvised republican government resolved to fight on. It took up its stand in Paris and was invested there on 20 September. The defences of Paris had been reconstructed over the past thirty years and, if not intrinsically formidable, were very extensive. The perimeter marked by the outlying forts stretched for 38 miles so that the German siege lines were more than 50 miles in circumference. To man them von Moltke could only allocate 236,000 men and within the city were 90,000 regulars; 11,000 sailors and marines; 100,000 *Gardes Mobiles;* and 200,000 *Gardes Sédentaires*, the last a kind of untrained Home Guard. Few of the garrison would be formidable on the offensive but, fighting in the streets in defence of their homes, they could soon destroy a larger army than the Germans could ever bring against them. The only hope of General Trochu, Governor of Paris and President of the Council, was that the Germans would attack him. He had no confidence in his troops' ability to break out, an estimate briskly confirmed every time political pressure forced him to attempt a sortie. His hope was to make Paris 'a second Saragossa'.

Von Moltke would not oblige him. He knew he had not the numbers for such an undertaking, particularly since he had to keep, and occasionally reinforce, a covering army to counter the attacks of peripheral French armies, composed of sketchily-trained recruits armed from America, Belgium, and Britain. To make the German situation more difficult they had to rely on a single railway between the German frontier and the armies. It was not until 2 January, when the fortress of Mézières capitulated, that a second

LEFT: The Prussian 150-mm Krupp gun used during the siege of Paris

BELOW: Prussian siege artillery outside Strasbourg

became available and the third remained blocked until the end of the war by the steady resistance offered by the garrison of Belfort.

To the German staff the only course available to them was the reduction of Paris by blockade, to force its surrender by starvation. They doubted the efficacy of shelling the city and dreaded the effect on their tenuous and overstrained supply line of adding to their needs large numbers of shells for their 150-mm guns and 210-mm mortars. Eventually civilian pressure, led by Bismarck, forced the soldiers to open a bombardment. On 27 December seventy-six guns opened on the improvised fort on Mont Avron and compelled the garrison to evacuate it within thirty-six hours. On 5 January 1871 a more general fire was opened on the forts to the south and east of Paris and a few guns were directed on the city itself. This could only be reached by using oversized charges in the guns which gave a range of above 7,500 yards but quickly wore out the barrels. Although three or four hundred shells fell in Paris each day they caused astonishingly few casualties and, if anything, stiffened the population's determination to resist. This, ironically, proved to be to the German advantage. Popular and political pressure insisted that a grand sortie by 90,000 men be made on 19 January. Aiming at St Cloud and Malmaison, the attack failed utterly and with its failure even the government lost heart. An armistice was signed on 28 January and a few days later Marshal Bourbaki, with the last of the peripheral armies, allowed himself and 80,000 men to be interned in Switzerland rather than surrender. In the peace that followed France lost Alsace and Lorraine and was forced to pay an indemnity of 5,000,000,000 gold francs.

The Franco–Prussian War showed that Germany, reorganised on 18 January 1871 as the German Empire, was indisputably the supreme military power in Europe. At the same time it was brought home to her that her power stopped at the coast. Although France's armies had been destroyed and her capital blockaded, her ports (except Dieppe) remained open and the great industrial region of the north-east remained free. She was thus able to continue her international trade since the German fleet was impotent in face of French strength at sea. French credit on the international markets remained good, better in fact than Germany's, and she was able, throughout the war, to import arms and other supplies to any extent she required. This was a lesson which the Germans took deeply to heart. Before she next went to war with France, Germany took care to equip herself with a powerful fleet, one that could overmatch that of France. It was unfortunate for Germany that the possession of such a fleet brought her another enemy.

CHAPTER EIGHT

The Supremacy of the Rifle

THE RAPID DEFEAT of the imperial French armies dazzled all the military thinkers of the world and every army set about modelling itself on the triumphant Prussian armies. Every nation overhauled its mobilisation procedures and redrafted its training manuals. Some armies, including the British, even went so far as to adopt the ugly and absurd spiked Prussian helmet, the *pickelhaube,* despite Queen Victoria's plea that 'She wishes particularly to do away with the *spike* at the top of the helmet'. Much less attention was paid to the impotence of the victorious army when confronted with the defences of Paris. Nations, and particularly Germany, set about acquiring cannon which, in any future war, would be able to demolish any construction of masonry or concrete but nowhere was serious consideration given to the possibility of a massive and well-equipped army being brought to a halt by improvised earthworks held by determined men using the overwhelming defensive power of new weapons. This possibility was to be demonstrated vividly six years after the Franco-Prussian war ended.

In 1877 Russia indulged in yet another of her forays against the Turks with the ostensible purpose of ameliorating the lot of the Christian subjects of the Sublime Porte. She had chosen a time when the other European powers were in no condition to intervene and when Britain, the main prop of the Ottoman Empire, was in a violently anti-Turkish mood thanks to the Bulgarian massacres and Mr Gladstone's inflammatory oratory, culminating in his demand that Turkey should be removed 'bag and baggage' from Europe.

The Russian army had been much improved since the Crimean War. The system of conscription had been overhauled so that those called up, 150,000 men out of the annual class of 600,000, served only six years with the colours, followed by nine in the reserve and five in the militia. The mobilisation procedure had been recast on approximately Prussian lines. The tactical training, however, remained based on the bayonet and consequently on the use of infantry in mass. The rifle had been taken into service and the Berdan, an American model sighted to 1,000 yards, had been issued to the *élite* corps – Guards, Grenadiers, and Riflemen – and to nine

Men of the Black Watch storm an Egyptian gun emplacement during the Battle of Tel-el-Kebir

of the thirty-six line divisions. The rest of the army was still using the Krenk rifle, a converted muzzle-loader equivalent to the British Snider and accurate to less than 600 yards. It was unfortunate that of the troops available on the south-western frontier all, apart from a handful of rifle regiments, were armed with the Krenk.

In arms the Turks had a distinct advantage since all their field infantry had the Martini-Peabody, with a range of more than 1,800 yards and as good a rifle as that in service in any army in the world. In artillery the Turks had breech-loading steel Krupp guns while Russians were still using bronze muzzle-loaders. In every other way the Turks were markedly inferior. Their cavalry was poor and ill-mounted and the draught horses for the artillery were of very poor quality. Their staff and medical services were rudimentary and, although ammunition supply was adequately managed, their commissariat was corrupt and inefficient and the troops had mostly to rely on foraging for their rations. Appointments to senior command went by court favour and most generals viewed their positions principally as sources of profit. There was no peacetime organisation above battalion level.

Having assembled an army of 200,000 men in Bessarabia, the Russians cajoled the Rumanians into granting them transit rights for their troops. The command was given to the Grand Duke Nicholas but the direction of the army was effectively in the hands of his chief-of-staff, General Nepokoitschitsky, who aimed to emulate the 1829 campaign of General Diebitsch who had marched over the Balkan range and dictated peace at the gates of Constantinople. Conditions had, however, greatly changed since Diebitsch's day particularly since, the Russian Black Sea fleet having been destroyed at Sebastopol in 1855 and not replaced, the Turks now had absolute command of the sea. Diebitsch had marched through the Dobruja and Varna, supplying his men from ships. Nepokoitschitsky, on the other hand, had constantly to bear in mind the possibility that his enemy might make a landing in his rear. He planned to make his incursion some 200 miles from the coast, crossing the Danube between Giurgevo and Nikopol and then marching through Turnovo and Adrianople (Edirne).

The Turks had 170,000 men in the threatened area but they were widely scattered. Their commander, Abdul Kerim Pasha, was a septuagenarian who had acquired a military reputation by studying war at Vienna. There he had learned that rivers, however wide, seldom make successful defensive lines and, secure in that knowledge, decided to abandon the line of the Danube although that great river was dominated by a powerful Turkish naval squadron. Far from making use of his naval strength on the Black Sea, Kerim, also remembering Diebitsch's campaign, insisted in keeping his main strength near the coast in the Dobruja. This suited the Russians to perfection and, leaving a single division to watch Kerim, they passed their striking force across the Danube near Sistova (Scishtov) in the first week of July 1877 against light and ill-co-ordinated opposition.

The Russian advance had been planned with great care and skill

A Russian gunboat and torpedo-boats on the Danube in 1877

and the opening moves of their invasion of what is now Bulgaria went with great smoothness. On 7 July a cavalry force, boldly handled by General Gourko, seized Turnovo and went on to capture the main Balkan pass at Shipka with very few casualties. To the west the fortress of Nikopol was captured on 16 July with only 1,300 men lost. Probing south from there a Cossack patrol visited Plevna (Pleven) and drove out its garrison, a company of invalids. The Cossacks then withdrew and Plevna was re-occupied by four battalions which had been detached from Nikopol before its surrender. Abdul Kerim took little notice of these Russian moves. He stayed in the Dobruja hoarding troops and havering on the grandest scale.

THE SIEGE OF PLEVNA
It was fortunate for the Turks that their extreme left wing consisted of a corps of three divisions under the enterprising Osman Pasha. Despite a series of orders from Kerim urging him to detach troops on pointless missions, Osman realised the importance of Plevna, the meeting place of six roads, and collected a field force of 11,000 men. He led them to the town, 110 miles over difficult country from his headquarters at Vidin, in a remarkable forced

march lasting six and a half days and arrived at dawn on 19 July. That afternoon his batteries were in action with the Russian advance guard 3 miles north of the town.

Plevna was an inconsiderable place, little more than a village, which lay in a hollow surrounded by low hills. The approaches from the west were fairly secure, being covered by the Vid river, while a well-marked ridge, the Janik Bair, protected the northern side but the eastern flank was all but open. Until Osman arrived nothing had been done to make Plevna defensible except the digging of a few small trenches on the Janik Bair. Nevertheless when six Russian battalions attacked from the north on 20 July they were driven back with the loss of 2,900 men.

At this stage Abdul Kerim was relieved of the supreme command and his successor ordered Osman to defend Plevna to the last and to collect reinforcements where he could. He was thus able to raise the garrison's strength to 22,000 men and 58 guns. He was also able, by disarming useless cavalry regiments, to issue to the defence a large number of Winchester repeating rifles, the first successful magazine rifle. Meanwhile the Turks were digging industriously. The Janik Bair was entrenched from end to end and the weak eastern flank was strengthened by a number of earth-built redoubts linked, as time went on, by trenches. The soil was clay which could be dug without too much difficulty and could be compacted to form an effective parapet.

On 30 July the Russians launched a second attack using 35,000 infantry supported by 170 guns. It was a disastrous failure. A British officer in the Turkish army who was stationed in a redoubt at the eastern end of the Janik Bair described how, after an intense bombardment, the Russians came on:

They seemed to have no advance-line of skirmishers. Serried ranks of infantry – three battalions I believe – climbed in a solid body the bank of the last ditch and advanced in a line parallel to the redoubt. The attack was purely frontal. Hardly had they appeared when a dozen bugles sounded Fire *and a terrific fire, coming from three sides (the redoubt and the side trenches) brought the enemy to a dead stop. The survivors surged back and were swallowed up by a second, which had meanwhile, commenced to advance. A third followed at a short distance . . . The Russians surged forward and recoiled from the slope like the waves of a tempestuous ocean.*

Some 7,300 Russians were killed and wounded that day. Nothing was achieved.

It was six weeks before they attacked again. Before that the investing army had been built up to 80,000 men with 364 field guns and 24 siege pieces but their third assault captured only one outlying redoubt at a cost of 17,500 casualties. Fortunately for the Russians General Todleben, the veteran hero of Sebastopol, arrived to take charge of the siege at the end of September and he at once forbade further assaults. Instead he concentrated on getting his troops dug into well-constructed trenches and in completing the encirclement of

Plevna. This last was not achieved until the end of October by which time the garrison had been increased to 50,000 men and some supplies had been brought in. Osman, however, saw clearly that the town must soon become untenable and asked permission to withdraw while there was still time. This was refused for by this time the defence of Plevna had become a matter of prestige rather than strategy in Constantinople. He was ordered to fight to the last and promised that Turkish armies would relieve him.

All the Turkish moves to relieve Plevna failed, largely through the incompetence of the generals employed. Twice attempts were made to recapture the exposed and vulnerable Shipta pass. Both attacks failed as the Turkish infantry, despite their bravery, withered under Russian rifle fire. The Russians meanwhile continued to build up their strength and by mid-November they had 100,000 men with 510 field and 40 siege guns round Plevna. In preparation for a winter campaign they had built a line linking the Russian railway system with the Rumanian and started work on another reaching as far south as Turnovo.

It was supplies which settled the matter. By the beginning of December the garrison was on half-rations and it was clear that, however small the allowance of food made, there would be no supplies left by the middle of the month. On 10 December Osman made a despairing effort to break out westward across the Vid. He had some early success but the enemy were too strong and the Turkish troops found themselves penned on the flat ground astride the river while the Russians moved in to the abandoned redoubts. Osman had been wounded and saw that nothing more could be done. He surrendered before nightfall.

Osman Pasha presented to the Czar after his surrender at Plevna

At last the Russians could continue their advance and, since no other Turkish general could stand against them, they captured Adrianople on 22 January. The prospect of a Russian army in occupation of Constantinople, an event likely to bring about the dissolution of the Ottoman Empire, so alarmed the British that the Mediterranean Fleet was sent through the Dardanelles. The sight of ironclads on the Golden Horn stopped the Russian army in its tracks. An armistice was arranged which became permanent in the Treaty of San Stephano by which Turkey was forced to concede the independence of Rumania and to grant a measure of autonomy to Bulgaria. These terms were regarded by the other European powers as being so harsh that the Congress of Berlin was called to modify them. Disraeli claimed that he returned from Berlin with 'Peace with Honour' but one of the arrangements made at the Congress was that Bosnia should be ceded by Turkey to the Hapsburg Empire. It was thus as a direct result of this meeting that the Archduke Franz Ferdinand was in Sarajevo on 28 June 1914.

Starvation brought about the fall of Plevna. Had it been possible to supply them, Osman's men, many of them middle-aged reservists, could have defended the town indefinitely. Yet Plevna was not a fortress; it had been completely unprotected until less than a week before the Russians appeared before it. All the redoubts and all but a few of the trenches were dug in the presence of the enemy and continually improved during the 142 days during which the town held out. Its defence was in stark contrast to that of Kars in Turkish Armenia at the same time. Kars was a permanent fortification with twelve detached forts built of masonry and each equipped with bastions, ditches, and parapets. The Russians bombarded it for six days and then took it in an assault in which they lost only 2,273 casualties. Apart from the character of Osman Pasha, the Turks had more advantages at Kars than they had at Plevna. The fact was that the strength of the Bulgarian town lay in its improvised defences. Forts of masonry, however well designed, gave the siege guns something to destroy. Once they were damaged there was little the garrison could do to repair them while the siege lasted. Earthworks in suitable soil could, by contrast, be continuously patched and improved. All that was needed were picks, shovels, and willing hands. At Plevna the earthworks were not even revetted as there was little or no timber to use for the purpose.

The long defence of Plevna was, above all, the triumph of the breech-loading rifle. The Turkish artillery, though superior in quality, was greatly out-matched in quantity and, due to the investment, could not make use of their greater range. It was rifle fire which beat off the Russian assaults and the casualties inflicted were shattering. In their first attack the Russians lost a third of the troops involved, in the second a quarter. The third attack cost them 31 per cent of the men who advanced, 23 per cent of the entire investing army. In the three attacks 27,500 men were lost and the total gain was one outlying redoubt of very little significance to the defences as a whole. This was against an army which had a very low standard of

A British mountain battery during the Abyssinian campaign of 1868

marksmanship. Turkish soldiers were notorious for doing no more than point their weapons in the general direction of the enemy and fire as fast as they could. It was clear that, against skilled soldiers, defensive fire was going to dominate any battlefield of which the flanks could not be turned.

BRITISH COLONIAL CAMPAIGNS

The British were, nevertheless, to discover in Africa that defensive rifle-fire was not infallible. Their army, although it did not fight against a major power between 1855 and 1914, amassed more varied military experience than any other and found much of it misleading. The Crimea had, however, taught them to organise their supply services. With the Commissariat removed from Treasury control, a rapid improvement took place. In 1860, when an Anglo-French expedition occupied Peking, the British supply service worked excellently. Eight years later Sir Robert Napier, who had commanded a division in China, led a punitive expedition from the Red Sea coast to the Ethiopian capital of Magdala. The military opposition was scarcely formidable but the administrative problems were immense. The force consisted of 15,000 fighting men and included 9-pounder breech-loading guns and two 8-inch mortars. All were landed at a port constructed for the occasion and advanced over 400 miles of mountainous country on a road they built as they marched. Although Napier's men included Indians, so that different rations had to be provided for Hindus, Muslims, and Europeans, the commissariat could not be faulted and the supply of food and ammunition never failed.

Eleven years after Napier reached Magdala and thirteen months after Osman Pasha surrendered at Plevna, a British battalion was destroyed in Zululand. Left to guard the camp of Lord Chelmsford's column which was probing towards Ulundi, the Zulu capital, 1st battalion Twenty Fourth Foot with two companies of their 2nd battalion, some colonial horsemen, and two battalions of somewhat suspect native levies were attacked by a very large force of Zulus at the foot of Isandhlwana mountain on 22 January 1879. The Twenty

Fourth were armed with the Martini Henry rifle, a weapon all but identical with that used by the Turks at Plevna. It was sighted to 1,450 yards and, being a single loader, could fire twelve rounds a minute. Each man had 100 rounds in his pouches and there was plenty of reserve ammunition in the camp. Their opponents had a few elderly firearms but relied entirely on their heavy stabbing assegais.

By nightfall the only survivors of 508 officers and men of the Twenty Fourth were two bandsmen and a groom who had been able to seize horses and ride away. As long as the battalion had been able to fire from behind cover they had imposed crippling losses on the attackers but an ill-advised attempt to support a column of reinforcements which had been foolish enough to make an independent advance led to the Twenty Fourth being deployed in the open with one flank in the air. The Zulus, with an astonishing tactical flexibility and an utter disregard for casualties, engulfed the battalion and slaughtered the defenders. Nevertheless the defensive power of the Martini Henry was conclusively demonstrated that night only 6 miles away. In an improvised fort at Rorke's Drift 100 men from the second battalion of the Twenty Fourth successfully defended themselves against more than 4,000 Zulus and inflicted so many casualties upon them that they abandoned the attack.

The disaster at Isandhlwana was the beginning of a bad period for the British. Eighteen months later they suffered a severe check at Maiwand in Afghanistan where a force of all arms lost 43 per cent of its fighting strength although it inflicted three casualties for every one it suffered. The three infantry battalions engaged (one British and two Indian) each lost more than 60 per cent of their strength. Worse was to come in South Africa. In 1880 the Boers of the Transvaal laid siege to the small British garrisons which were dotted about their country and a small force, initially only 1,100 men crossed the border from Natal to relieve them. Their commander was Major-General Sir George Pomeroy Colley who had been described by General Wolseley as 'the ablest man I know'. It was a description that Sir Garnet may have lived to regret.

Colley's first attempt to enter the Transvaal at Laing's Nek was disastrous. After a brisk artillery bombardment he sent a battalion in close order to attack trenches held by the Boer riflemen. This was, incidentally, the last occasion on which the British took their Colours into action, although other nations were carrying them many years later. Even without the Colours there would have been little chance for the battalion to succeed and they were, in fact, checked with very heavy loss. A month later, on 27 February 1881, he tried to seize the Nek (or pass) at night. He led a small body of men drawn from two regiments and the Royal Navy to the summit of Majuba Hill, which dominates the road. The summit of Majuba is 1,100 feet above the highest point of the pass but it is itself commanded by higher hills to the west. Dawn found him on the summit with 414 men and without having fired a shot but, although the men had carried picks and shovels with them, he refused to let them dig in, believing that the rocks which circled the summit, supplemented by a few small sangars, would give them adequate protection.

Transvaal military organisation was rudimentary but each one of the 3,000 Boers present was a marksman and their Westley Richards rifles were as good as the Martini Henrys of the British. Normally averse to taking the offensive, their council of war decided on this occasion that Colley's situation gave them an opportunity too good to miss. They proceeded to give the British a classic demonstration of fire and movement, the tactic whereby one portion of a force advances (or retires) under the cover of the fire of the remainder, a manoeuvre scarcely appreciated in any European army where fire-discipline was always strict and volley-firing was the normal, almost the only, type of musketry practised. Picking themselves well-covered positions, the older Boers fired to keep down the heads of the defenders while the younger men, divided into three assault parties, scaled the hill from different directions. There was little answering fire. To shoot at their assailants Colley's men had to stand up and lean over the rocks. Every man who did so was shot by the covering party. When the stormers were very near the summit there was a moment when a bayonet charge might have driven them off as the two sides were too close for covering fire to be practicable. Colley refused to agree to the attempt and, once the Boers gained the crest, their fire decided the battle, the more so since they outnumbered the defenders. Most of the British scrambled over the

Evacuating the hospital during the action at Rorke's Drift

rocks and ran for their camp as fast as they could go. They lost 287 men, Colley being among the dead. The Boer casualties were 2 killed and 5 wounded.

Henceforward the training instructions for the British army inculcated the rule that no body of infantry should advance towards the enemy without covering fire. It was unfortunate that in many of the situations in which British troops found themselves this admirable rule of tactics was inapplicable. In their world-wide campaigns they were frequently confronted with enemies, such as the Zulus, who attacked with such vast masses that all that could be done to beat them off was to hold one's ground and fire volleys as fast as possible. It was a dilemma that was to remain until the introduction on to the battlefield of a practical machine-gun.

The next British campaign was one in which fire and movement played no part. In Egypt there was a military coup led by Colonel Ahmed Arabi, known in England as Arabi Pasha. Egypt's finances were in chaos with 37 per cent of the revenue mortgaged to foreign bondholders and the entire revenue of the Suez canal going abroad. Anti-foreign sentiment was already strong and a reduction of one-third in the army, forced by the foreign creditors, was enough to spark a revolution. Determined to assure the security of the Suez canal, Britain decided to intervene, acting in the name of the Sultan of Turkey who had a nominal suzerainty over Egypt. As it happened the Sultan had just conferred the Order of the Medjidie (First Class) on Arabi Pasha, the supposed rebel. On 11 July 1882 the Mediterranean Fleet, taking advantage of some rioting in Alexandria, bombarded the batteries of the port and landed troops to occupy the city. Previous to the bombardment the ships had used electric search-lights to observe work being done on the defences under cover of darkness. The Egyptian authorities regarded this unprecedented use of artificial light for military purposes as 'discourteous'.

The landing at Alexandria focused Egyptian attention in that direction but Sir Garnet Wolseley, who was commanding an expeditionary force, had no intention of landing there. Determined to reach Cairo as soon as possible, he took his men up the Suez canal and landed at Ismailia between 19 and 23 of August. The landing was unopposed. Apart from line of communication troops, he had a striking force of 17,000 men including three regiments of cavalry and three native battalions from India. His artillery comprised sixty field guns, a 40-pounder naval gun, and six gatlings and, for the first time in history, a British expeditionary force landed with its complete establishment of first line transport. It also brought locomotives and rolling stock sufficient for four complete goods trains.

Advancing up the Sweetwater canal, which leads directly to Cairo, the army reached Kassassin by 12 September having experienced no more than a few skirmishes. A few miles ahead they discovered that Arabi had entrenched 20,000 men and 75 guns on the north bank of the canal opposite the town and barracks of Tel-el-Kebir. Their position was an extremely strong one, consisting of a low ridge, at right angles to the canal and facing a perfectly smooth plain which extended for several miles. Along the crest of the ridge had been dug a well-sited trench which had a powerful parapet and a ditch. At intervals there were redoubts armed with field guns and there was a single advanced redoubt where the gentle slope up from the canal met the plain which covered the main front. The rifles of the Egyptian army were as good as those of the British and their Krupp guns better than the Royal Artillery's field guns. Their right flank was secured on the canal and their left on desert so rough that it was impracticable to march infantry through it. The only solution was a frontal attack which was likely to be extremely costly.

Wolseley decided that his only course was to make a night approach, aiming to storm the entrenchments at dawn on 13 September. This caused some misgivings in his army since it was many centuries since any European commander had made a successful night attack except in the limited sense of storming a fortress that had already been breached. The view of all senior commanders was that 'in every night march there is a danger of confusion from the darkness and a possibility of panic'.

As it happened Sir Garnet had a number of unusual advantages on his side. As any British soldier who endured Kassassin camp during and after the Second World War will remember, the approach to Tel-el-Kebir is composed of hard, gravelly sand which is perfectly flat and resembles nothing so much as a gigantic parade ground. In addition, since a naval brigade formed part of his force, he had available a number of naval officers who were accustomed to navigate by the stars. He therefore aligned his attacking force, two divisions, on a front of 3,200 yards parallel to the entrenchment and 6,600 yards from it. To avoid any possibility of the inner flanks of the divisions coming into collision, the bulk of the field artillery, 42 guns, was stationed between them. On the left flank and slightly held back a brigade of infantry advanced on either side of the canal, while on the desert flank, also held back, rode the cavalry and horse artillery.

The advance, scheduled to be at a speed of one mile an hour, went well although it proved difficult to keep the leading brigades in line and the formation became an echelon back from left to right. The left-hand brigade, the Highlanders, were within 100 yards of the ridge an hour too early while the right of the line was still half a mile from the enemy and, at that stage, the unexpected appearance of a comet was mistaken for the first flush of dawn. The Highland Brigade immediately attacked and was able to reach the trench before the Egyptians could make their fire tell. There was some very brisk hand-to-hand fighting before the remainder of the attackers managed to double forward to the enemy but, as the light broke, the cavalry was seen to double the desert flank and ride for Tel-el-Kebir bridge. Seeing their retreat cut off, the Egyptians, who had fought with great stubbornness, gave way and fled. Their army never reassembled. The British and Indians, who had lost 439 killed and wounded, were left in possession and the cavalry rode on and occupied the citadel of Cairo on the following day.

As soon as the success at Tel-el-Kebir was certain, Royal Engineers ran out 3 miles of cable from Wolseley's headquarters to the railway station, the task taking thirty minutes. News of the victory reached London within an hour of its completion.

Technological advances and obstacles

Field telephones were used for the first time in the Egyptian campaign of 1882, only six years after Alexander Graham Bell had invented the telephone and three years after the first London telephone exchange had opened (with seven subscribers). The instruments used at Tel-el-Kebir had only a very limited range but they marked the beginning of a revolution in military communications. For the first time a commander could send orders on the battlefield faster than a horse could gallop. As with other military details, the British had some special problems with communications. In the Ashanti campaign of 1874 the mobile telegraph unit of the Royal Engineers had laid a most efficient cable 85 miles long only to find that in order to keep the operators out of hospital they had to be given such massive doses of quinine that they became totally deaf.

Tel-el-Kebir marks the effective end of the single-loading rifle. Four years later the French adopted the 0.315-inch bore Lebel, the first infantry magazine rifle to be taken into service. Two years later the Germans followed suit with a magazine Mauser (0.311-inch) and the British at last went over to bolt-action with the 0.303-inch magazine Lee Metford which was sighted to 2,800 yards. The French, however, had a distinct advantage since, with the Lebel, they introduced *Poudre B*, a propellant based on Nobel's 1861 discovery of nitro-glycerine. Not only did this give them a greatly increased range – the Lebel was said to be lethal at 4,000 yards – but it literally changed the face of the battlefield for *Poudre B* was all but smokeless. Since firearms had first been introduced in the Middle Ages all battles had been shrouded in the thick white smoke produced by black powder. In future battles, commanders were not only going to be able to pass their orders by telephone, they were going to be able to see what their troops were doing and where they were.

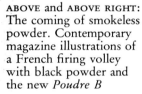

ABOVE and ABOVE RIGHT: The coming of smokeless powder. Contemporary magazine illustrations of a French firing volley with black powder and the new *Poudre B*

The new visibility on the battlefield was not an unmixed blessing. It enabled the general to see his battle but it also allowed the enemy to understand what was going on. In the days of black powder the most important attribute of a uniform had been that it should be recognisable at a distance. In the days when the musket had been the principal weapon there had been little point in giving a soldier a uniform which would enable him to merge into the landscape. When the musket gave way to the rifle it was still arguable that fewer men would be hit by enemy fire at 300 yards than would be by friendly artillery firing at them in error. Consequently all the armies of Europe were dressed distinctively in various shades of blue, in scarlet, in green or, in the Austrian army, in white. The coming of smokeless powder and effective ranges for rifles of over 1,000 yards made distinctiveness far too dangerous.

It was the British who led the way. When Harry Lumsden raised the Queen's Own Corps of Guides in 1846 for service on the Indo-Afghan frontier he wanted to dress them so that they would be inconspicuous yet distinct from the inhabitants of the region. This he achieved by giving them uniforms of home-spun cotton dyed with mulberry juice to give a yellow-drab or mud-coloured effect and, since the Urdu for mud is *khak*, the colour came to be called khaki. It was widely used by British and Indian units during the Sepoy Mutiny but it was later forbidden except in the Punjab Frontier Force. It was not until 1881 that it was officially recognised as the colour for units on active service in India and, a few years later a different shade was authorised for service use in Africa. At Tel-el-Kebir the troops wore scarlet, green, or blue and on the abortive expedition to rescue General Gordon in 1885 British fought in scarlet for the last time. There were problems in finding a sufficiently stable dye for khaki and it was not until 1902, after experiments had been made with uniforms of grey tweed, that it was finally adopted for service dress in all parts of the world under the official nomenclature of 'drab mixture'. Other nations were slow to follow the British lead and most German units started the 1914 war in a light shade of 'field grey' and wearing the elaborate and distinctive *pickelhaube*, which had no value as armour. The French infantry at that time were conspicuous in blue tunics and

The first machine-gun in
the British army—a
Nordenfeldt gun
privately purchased by
the Central London
Rangers

scarlet trousers while their cuirassiers went into action wearing breastplates and with long horsehair plumes on their elegant Grecian helmets. The Household Cavalry of Belgium, *1er Régiment des Guides*, rode off to meet the German invader in green tunics and amaranth breeches, and the Austrian cavalry had breeches of madder.

The move towards inconspicuousness was not before its time as the machine-gun was rapidly becoming a practicable weapon. Both the gatling-gun, which had been used in the American Civil War, and the *mitrailleuse*, which had proved such a disappointment in the Franco-Prussian War, relied on a multiplicity of barrels. So did the first British machine-gun, the Nordenfeldt which a colonel of Volunteers, W. J. Alt of the Central London Rangers, bought for his battalion with his own money. All such multi-barrel guns were cumbersome and more suitable for light naval vessels than on a battlefield. Nevertheless gatlings manned by sailors did useful work on land both in the Zulu War of 1879 and the Egyptian campaign of 1882. The breakthrough occurred in 1883 when Hiram Maxim, an American coachbuilder who acquired British nationality, invented the single-barrelled machine-gun. The principle employed was that the recoil of one shot ejected the spent cartridge and put a live round in its place while the ammunition, which in earlier models had been fed in through a hopper, was held in a web belt containing 250 rounds. Since the rate of fire was 600 rounds a minute, the barrel was cooled with a waterjacket. The British army adopted the Maxim-gun in 1888, reducing the original 0.75-inch calibre to 0.303-inch to match that of the newly-adopted ammunition for the Lee Metford rifle. Soon every army in the world was using Maxims or weapons closely modelled on the design, while navies were adopting Maxim's 1-pounder pom-pom which worked on the same principle.

Artillery also benefited from the new nitro-glycerine based

propellant charges and had need to do so. In the Franco-Prussian War the Germans had relied on their field guns to counteract the superiority in range of the chassepot over the needle gun. Had the French been armed with the Lebel using *Poudre B* they would have outranged the German gunners. Nevertheless it was hard to convince artillery officers that long ranges were useful, particularly since they made accurate observation increasingly difficult. In all artilleries, as in all navies, the delusion persisted that guns must be brought to 'decisive ranges'.

The more powerful propellants, however, did finally mean that the muzzle-loader was at last displaced. This occurred not because everyone was convinced that the breech-loader was more efficient but because the powerful new charges meant that barrels became longer and it was increasingly difficult to load and ram them from the muzzle. It might have been thought that the excellent performance of the German gunners in 1870 would have convinced the world that breech-loaders were superior but this was not the case. There was widespread admiration for German artillerymen but when it was heard that after the Battle of Sedan two hundred German guns were out of action because of breech defects there was a widespread reaction against them. The British, who were already re-equipping with breech-loaders, reverted to muzzle-loaders and did not finally adopt breech-loaders until 1885. Nevertheless, it was they who pioneered the next considerable advance when in 1892 they introduced lyddite as a bursting charge for shells, a great improvement on the black powder used hitherto for this purpose.

The great obstacle in the way of any great advance in the use of field guns was the failure to devise some method of absorbing the shock of their recoil. In heavy guns for coastal defence, which were installed in fixed emplacements, it was possible to equip them with heavy springs or hydraulic machinery. Such apparatus was too cumbersome for mobile pieces and although experiments were made with spades for the axle and the trail or with shoes on the wheels none was satisfactory. Consequently every time a gun was fired it recoiled several yards and had to be dragged laboriously forward into position and on its target.

There was another way in which armies had not been able to keep abreast of the technological advances in other fields. It was still dependent on the horse. Once away from the railways, waggons and guns could only be moved by teams of horses, and horses provided the only means of moving tactically above the pace of the foot soldier. Above all every commander was dependent on his light horsemen for reconnaissance, for his knowledge of enemy movements. It was unfortunate that in every army, cavalry, despite the lessons of 1866 and 1870, continued to fancy itself as a potent fighting arm and continued to believe that in future wars they would influence battles by making massed charges, an archaic manoeuvre on which they wasted most of the time allotted to them for training, time which could more profitably be spent on learning how to fulfil their still-vital functions as mounted infantry and in reconnaissance.

CHAPTER NINE

The Ram and Armour Plate

ITALY WAS PRUSSIA'S ALLY against Austria in the war of 1866. Her aim was to acquire Venetia and she marched her army into the Quadrilateral only to be handsomely beaten at Custozza (24 June) on a field where she had already been humiliated in 1848. With the Austrian army defeated in its turn at Königgrätz, Vienna promised to cede Venetia but Italian *amour-propre* demanded that her armed forces should win at least one victory. For this she had to rely on the navy which, at great expense, she had built up since the war of 1859. Her battle squadron consisted of twelve ironclads including two battleships recently bought from the United States; a fast and powerful 'turret ram' from Britain; and two smaller rams from France. These most modern ships were armed with Armstrong rifled guns. In support there were a large number of obsolete steam-driven wooden ships.

The Austrian fleet, based at Pola, was only half as powerful. There were seven ironclads and one steam-driven wooden battleship with a number of gunboats and small wooden vessels. Large rifled guns had been ordered (and paid for) from Krupps but, not unnaturally, had not been delivered and the fleet relied on smooth bores. Another potential source of trouble was the presence on board all the ships of a substantial number of Venetian sailors. To offset these weaknesses the Austrians had an excellent admiral in Wilhelm von Tegetthof, a man who was not afraid of his enemy, inspired his sailors, and had trained his captains, in the Nelson manner, to think as he did in the presence of an enemy.

The Italian admiral, Carlo di Persano, was a very different man. Although he had shown, particularly during the Crimean War, that he was a competent sea officer he was incapable of making up his mind. In late June, Tegetthof, with only part of his fleet, had trailed his coat within sight of the Italian base at Ancona, Persano had felt unable to take his ships to sea. Ordered out by his government, he made a short cruise towards Pola but returned without sighting Tegetthof's ships or even the enemy coastline. Peremptory orders drove him to sea again on 16 July with the aim of capturing the Austrian island of Lissa (Vis). After four ineffective days off the coast

ABOVE: The Battle of
Lissa–*Ferdinand Max* has
just rammed *Re d'Italia*,
Palestro is on fire to the
left

of the island, news arrived that the Austrian fleet was approaching.

Persano formed a ragged line of battle with nine of his ironclads while three more tried vainly to catch up and the wooden ships were aligned astern. For some reason his first formation was facing in the wrong direction but this was rectified before Austrians came within range. Tegetthof, knowing that he was heavily outgunned, decided to rely on the ram and to break through his opponent's line. He had his ironclads formed into an arrowhead formation with the wooden ships inside its arms. He led the fleet himself in his flagship *Ferdinand Maximilian* which flew the signal *Armoured ships to charge the enemy and sink him.*

Persano directed his fleet from the centre but, as soon as his line was formed he decided to abandon his flagship, *Re d'Italia*, and board the turret ram *Affondatore* believing that it would be convenient 'to take up my position outside the line in an ironclad of great speed, to be able to dash into the heat of the battle, or carefully to convey the necessary orders to the different parts of the fleet'. This may have been a wise decision but his implementation of it caused chaos. He omitted to inform any of his captains what he intended so that they continued to look to *Re d'Italia* for orders that never came. The signalling equipment on *Affondatore* was far from adequate so that none of his many subsequent signals was received by his subordinates. To make his transfer he failed to call up the fast turret ram until it was alongside the flagship but merely stopped the *Re d'Italia* until the *Affondatore* caught up. As a result the van of the fleet steamed blithely ahead while the rear bunched behind the flagship.

Tegetthof was unlucky that his first charge led his fleet straight into the gap thus created but, undismayed, he reversed course and

PREVIOUS PAGE: HMS
Devastation; completed
in 1873, she was the
world's first true
battleship

attacked the Italians from the rear. There was a heavy but ineffective exchange of fire during which all the Italian shots went over the masts of the Austrians whose own missiles did no more than dent the Italian plating. As the fleets closed there was a confused mêlée during which red-hot shot set fire to the Italian ironclad *Palestro* and the rudder of the *Re d'Italia* was carried away. The flagship was now help- less and Tegetthof rammed her squarely with the *Ferdinand Maximilian* driving forward at her maximum speed of 11½ knots and, immediately on impact, reversing her engines to back away. *Re d'Italia* heeled once to starboard then swung back to port, her masthead all but fouling the Austrian's bow. Then she sank.

The rest of the battle was confused and indecisive. The Austrian wooden battleship, *Kaiser*, with 90 guns in broadside, rammed the other modern Italian ironclad, *Re di Portugallo*, but succeeded only in breaking off her own bowsprit while bringing down the foremast. Temporarily crippled and stopped, Persano came at her with the *Affondatore* but, at the last moment, he swerved aside. He later claimed that he did so because it would be inhumane to sink a ship already disabled. A more probable explanation is that he realised that if *Affondatore*'s 26-foot ram buried itself in *Kaiser*'s wooden side both ships would sink locked together. Whatever the reason, he next led his fleet back to Ancona, the *Palestro* blowing up on the way. Soon after their arrival *Affondatore* sank in harbour from damage received in the battle. Persano was relieved of his command and later dismissed from the service.

The impression made by the success of the ram in the Battle of Lissa was reinforced by the almost total failure of gunnery during the action. Its only success was the lucky hit which set *Palestro* on fire. 381 Italian sailors died when she blew up; these, the 600 men lost when *Re d'Italia* sank, and 8 other men killed, represented all the Italian casualties that day. The losses inflicted by Italian gunnery were even less impressive. Only 38 Austrians were killed of whom 24 were in the wooden, unarmoured *Kaiser*. In the Austrian ironclads there were only three men killed. The apparent lesson to be learnt from Lissa was that guns were powerless against iron plating.

BELOW: *Kaiser* showing the damage sustained at Lissa when she rammed *Re di Portugallo*

THE REVOLUTION IN DESIGN

The potency of the ram continued to be demonstrated in a series of spectacular accidents. In 1875 HMS *Iron Duke*, cruising at seven knots off the Irish coast, carved her way into HMS *Vanguard* (5,899 tons) and tore a hole 25 feet square below her armoured belt. *Vanguard* sank within the hour, her crew being rescued. Three years later the Prussian battleship *König Wilhelm* accidentally rammed her consort *Grosse Kurfürst* off Folkestone, sinking her with the loss of 250 seamen. In 1893 a misjudged manoeuvre caused HMS *Camperdown* to ram the flagship of the Mediterranean fleet, the three-year-old *Victoria*. A hole 125 feet square was torn in her side and she sank with the loss of 321 lives including the admiral.

Every large navy in the world altered its tactics to give primacy to the ram and this trend had its effect on the disposition of the guns. For centuries the main armament of warships had been mounted in broadsides and, on larger ships, this disposition was continued after the coming of steam power. However, guns were growing steadily in weight and, added to the huge weight of the iron cladding, ships were in danger of becoming top heavy and turning turtle in a heavy sea. Matters were made no better because every sea-going ship continued to carry the masts and sails of a full-rigged ship. This was not through mere conservatism or over-insurance against engine failure. Early steam engines were extremely inefficient and coal bunkering space was very limited. Thus HMS *Warrior* (see p. 64) had a steam-driven range of only 1,400 miles, far less than was acceptable to any navy with widespread commitments.

Masts needed rigging and, if the guns were mounted anywhere except in broadsides below deck level, it was likely that they would shoot away the rigging of their own ship. Thus broadsides were retained although, as in the case of *Warrior*, the main armament was concentrated in a central citadel which fired, in effect, an attenuated broadside. This, of course, did little to solve the weight problem for guns in broadside could only fire to one side of the ship and it was obvious that the weight of guns could be halved if each one could be brought to bear on either side.

The revolving turret had been demonstrated in the *Monitor* and, in Britain, in *Royal Sovereign* and *Prince Albert* (see p. 70–1), but all these were coast defence ships and relied entirely on their engines and had only vestigial masts. They were wholly unsuitable to ocean-going duties. Many ingenious devices were conceived in an attempt to install turret-mountings in ocean-going ships but none could succeed as long as full-rigging was a necessity. The vogue for the ram suggested a way out of this *impasse*. If the ram was to be the decisive weapon it was obvious that ships would have to have their bows towards the enemy and thus their main armament would have to point forwards. This meant that, provided the forestay could be avoided, there would be no problem with the rigging and guns could be mounted either in turrets or, as the French in particular preferred, in barbettes – open-topped armoured redoubts.

RIGHT: Two views of
HMS *Captain* showing
one of her two turrets
(TOP) and the fatally
low freeboard (BOTTOM)

As time passed and engines grew more efficient rigging became
less essential but it was a disaster which prompted its final
withdrawal. In 1871 HMS *Captain* was Britain's most modern battleship being 320 feet long and displacing 7,767 tons. She had an
armoured belt of up to 7 inches thick and her armament included
four 12-inch and two 7-inch guns. These were mounted in four
turrets, two on each side and built below the main deck so that,
although only half her main armament could fire on either beam, she
had no problem about shooting away her own rigging. She was
designed by Captain Cowper Coles, the inventor of the turret, and
he had intended her to have a freeboard of 8 feet 6 inches. When she was

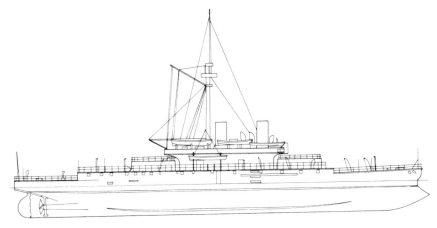

HMS *Devastation*:
despite her low freeboard
she was an excellent
seaboat and her main
armament remained
operational in heavy
weather

built it was found that her freeboard was only 6 feet 8 inches but Coles asserted that she was nevertheless seaworthy. He was aboard her on 6 September 1871 when she foundered in the Bay of Biscay with the loss of all but 13 of her crew of 500. Subsequent enquiries established that the cause of her loss was less the lowness of her freeboard but the fact that, despite her very adequate engines, she carried the masts and sails of a battleship of Nelson's day. Henceforward the trend was to cut down masts to whatever was considered necessary for observation and signalling. The transformation in design was not accomplished overnight and, five years after the loss of *Captain*, the Royal Navy laid down HMS *Temeraire* which had four 10-inch guns but carried the masts and sails of a brig.

The advocates of the ram were the archpriests of the 'decisive range' school of thought but they overlooked the steady improvements in guns and the increase in the weight of their projectiles. The answer was to increase the thickness of the iron cladding. In 1873 HMS *Devastation* had a 10-inch armoured belt, a thickness which, it was believed, would protect her against projectiles comparable to those she herself fired – 700-lb. shells with a range of 4,800 yards. Eight years later HMS *Inflexible* had to be built with 24 inches of wrought iron cladding and it was doubtful whether any ship with thicker armour would be able to stay afloat. As it happened *Inflexible* showed how the weight problem was to be evaded. Her main guns, four 16-inch rifled muzzle-loaders each weighing 81 tons, were mounted in turrets with only 17 inches of iron over them. They had, however, a facing of steel which made them as strong as the 24 inches of the remaining armour and saved 600 tons of weight into the bargain. By 1893 the *Majestic* class could have nickel steel armour of only 9 inches and three years later *Canopus* and her sister ships were regarded as adequately protected with only 6 inches of Krupp-processed steel. The reduction in thickness of armour reduced the draught of the *Canopus* class so much that they became the first battleships able to use the Suez canal.

Devastation was, nevertheless, a great turning point in battleship design. She was launched in 1871, before *Captain* sank, underwent a number of modifications before her sea trials and emerged as the prototype of all subsequent battleships. Her light mast was situated amidships with her funnels and her main armament, four 12-inch guns, each weighing 35 tons, were mounted in pairs in turrets fore and aft. Her engines developed 6,650 horsepower and drove twin screws (first used in a battleship in 1867), which gave her a maximum speed of more than 13 knots and a range at 10 knots of 4,700 miles. In only one way did *Devastation* and her sister ship *Thunderer* hark back to an earlier era. Their guns though rifled were muzzle-loaders but in 1879 one of *Thunderer*'s guns burst killing eleven men. Investigation showed that the disaster had been caused by double loading, an error that could only occur with muzzle-loaders, and it was this that finally induced the Royal Navy, almost last among the world's fleets, to change to breech-loading.

Devastation and several of her successors were built with rams but this was little more than the addition of a weapon which did not detract from the ship's performance and might, in certain circumstances, be useful. The increase in the power of guns even five years after the ram's triumph at Lissa meant that it would be suicidal to attempt to close a hostile battleship to ramming distance. Even so the idea of ramming died slowly and in 1881 the Royal Navy built the *Polyphemus*, a pure-bred ram which carried only light guns and torpedos. The intention was that she should accompany the battle-fleet and, so that her final approach to the enemy might be as inconspicuous as possible, she was built very low in the water and given engines capable of almost 18 knots. Unfortunately her low freeboard made her unsafe in any kind of breeze and the idea was abandoned.

The most significant development in naval warfare during the second half of the nineteenth century was the perfection of the torpedo. This was the triumph of Robert Whitehead, a British engineer working in Fiume (Rijeka). Basing his experiments on an Austrian idea, he produced in 1866 a cigar-shaped steel cylinder packed with gunpowder at the front and with a compressed-air engine at the stern. The secret of his success was to harness the pressure of the water, which increases with depth, to activate fins which kept the weapon at a constant depth. His first model was capable of only 8 knots making it useless against a moving target and it was scarcely better against a stationary one until an American naval officer contrived a gyroscopic device which would keep it on course.

HMS *Inflexible*: she was originally brig-rigged with full sails, but these proved so ineffective that her masts were converted as seen here in 1885

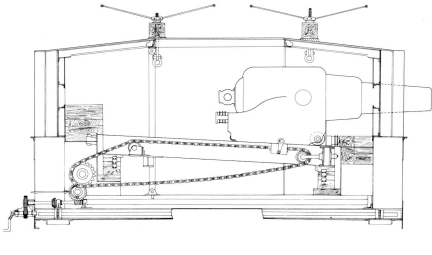

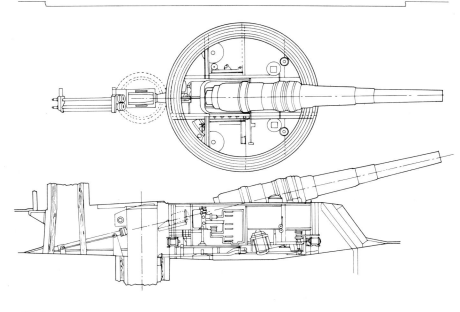

The development of naval gunnery was affected by two technological changes – from shot to explosive shells and from breech to muzzle loading – and the need to make guns more trainable and better protected. Early ironclads (page 64) were armed with simple broadside weapons, but on HMS *Captain*, Edward Coles developed the armoured turret (CENTRE LEFT) which could be rotated and trained, and into which the twin 12-inch rifled muzzle loaders could be pulled for reloading. Throughout the 1870s and 1880s naval designers wavered between the turret – as on *Devastation* (page 172) – and the open barbette. The Royal Navy used the 13.5-inch breech-loader as its standard armament, mounting some in barbettes as on HMS *Rodney* of the Admiral class of 1882 (TOP LEFT). Difficulties with producing the 13.5-inch led to 16.25-inch guns (BOTTOM LEFT) – the largest ever used on a British battleship – being mounted singly in barbettes on the Victoria class of 1885. In 1895 a new 12-inch gun proved superior to the 13.5-inch, and was adopted as the Royal Navy's standard armament until 1909. The twin-gun turrets on the Canopus class of 1896 (RIGHT) were the first to allow all-round loading at any elevation from a protected magazine deep in the ship, and were used in future classes, among them the King Edward VII class of 1901/2 (TOP RIGHT) which also carried an intermediate armament of four 9.2-inch guns plus ten 6-inch quickfirers

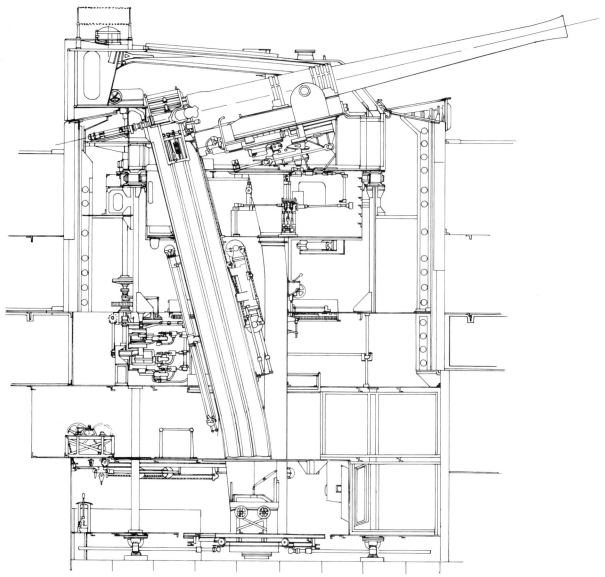

HMS *Polyphemus* in dry dock showing her massive ram

The first hostile use of a Whitehead torpedo occurred in 1876 when the British iron frigate *Shah* fired one at the rogue Peruvian turret ship *Huascar*. It missed but the inventor was constantly at work improving his design. An improved engine gave a speed of 18 knots (it was to be 30 knots before the end of the century) and the substitution of gun-cotton for gunpowder tripled the explosive effect. The first warship to be sunk by one of these weapons was the

HMS *Lightning* in 1877, showing the amazingly exposed steering position

Chilean cruiser *Blanco* which was attacked by light craft in 1891.

Torpedo tubes became standard fittings on all large warships during the 1870s but at the same time a new kind of craft was being evolved to deliver torpedoes. This was the torpedo boat and the first was HMS *Lightning*, commissioned in 1876, with a designed speed of 19 knots. She was 90 feet long but so narrow in the beam that her motion at high speed exhausted her crew. It was clear that she could only have a defensive role while her intended function had been to attack enemy battleships at sea. Her successors were built even longer but none were found to be seaworthy until in 1889 Britain, in desperation, built HMS *Vulcan* which was designed to carry six small torpedo boats which she would launch when they were required. Simultaneously all the naval powers were concerned about the threat posed by torpedo boats to their capital ships and developed larger craft known as 'torpedo boat destroyers' for use against them. It was realised in time that these TBDs were a more practical way of delivering torpedoes and, with their names shortened to destroyers, they took over the functions of the craft they had been designed to destroy.

The torpedo posed a greater threat to the battleship than the gun had ever done and, despite the unsatisfactory means of delivering them, the torpedo caused changes in the design of big ships. They were divided up into watertight compartments and every capital ship protected itself with fences of steel mesh held at a suitable distance from the hull by a series of booms. It was only a question of time before torpedoes were designed with mesh cutters incorporated in their nose-cones.

Britain's wealth enabled her to keep her navy, as was her tradition, stronger than that of any possible rival. Throughout the century it was assumed that, as had so often been the case in the past, her most probable enemy in a maritime war would be France. In the mid-1880s she had sixteen first class battleships against France's twelve and a two to one superiority in cruisers but the complex diplomatic events at that time, notably the Penjdeh incident of 1885 and the Bulgarian crisis of 1885–6, resulted in an alliance being formed between France and Russia. The latter had been an object of British suspicion ever since the fall of the first Napoleon and she was the third naval power in Europe. Britain therefore found herself faced with the threat of war against the French and Russian navies whose combined strength was greater than her own fleet. A wave of alarm swept the country and Lord Salisbury's government was stampeded into proclaiming the adoption of a 'Two Power Standard' whereby the Royal Navy was always to be kept at a strength equal to that of the next two naval powers. Ten battleships, eight of them first class, were to be built in the three following years and the number of modern cruisers was to be increased to ninety-two, compared to the nineteen which the French were expected to have. Ironically, in seven of the eight first-class battleships to be built under this programme, the Royal Sovereign class, the four 13.5-inch guns in each were to be mounted in the French style, in barbettes. Only in *Hood* were turrets used.

The Naval Defence Act of 1889 which called this expansion programme into being signalled the start of the naval building race which was to last until 1914, but the war which then began was to be waged with Britain, France, and Russia as allies. Their main enemy, Germany, had only a small coast defence navy in 1889. It was not until 1892 that she launched her first sea-going battleships. These were strongly urged by Kaiser Wilhelm II who, in that year, gave to his chief of naval staff, Admiral von Tirpitz, the right of direct access to the imperial presence, a right previously held only by the chief military adviser.

Not the least of the factors which induced Germany to become a naval power was the work of an American writer. It was in 1890 that Captain A. T. Mahan, USN, published *The Influence of Sea Power*. Mahan was a fine historian but he was even better as a propagandist. His theme was that 'Control of the sea is the chief among the merely material elements in the power and prosperity of nations', and his aim was to persuade the American government to build something better than the collection of obsolete warships which formed the US navy and to secure some colonial bases which he considered essential to a first-class naval power. His success was remarkable. Not only did the United States begin a building programme and, in due course, acquire some colonies but every nation with a seaboard set about acquiring or augmenting its navy. The Kaiser was among the most avid of Mahan's disciples.

PART FOUR

Smokeless Powder and the Dreadnought

CHAPTER TEN

Battleships and Submarines

A FEW YEARS after Commodore Perry, USN, at the head of a powerful squadron forced the Emperor of Japan to open his ports to foreign trade (1854), a British squadron shelled the coastal towns of Shimonoseki and Kagoshima to exact reparations for the ill-treatment of British and other European nationals. These two demonstrations of naval power decided the Japanese that they required a fleet of their own. They modelled it largely on the British navy and, among other trainees, they sent to England a young officer, Heihachiro Togo, who beside serving for two years on the training ship HMS *Worcester*, attended courses in gunnery, mathematics, and naval engineering.

Japan had no shortage of sailors but her shipbuilding industry could not produce large warships which had to be bought from the west, largely from Britain. She could, however, build destroyers and torpedo boats in large numbers and her repair facilities were capable of supporting a large fleet. Her navy had a trial run under active service conditions when, in 1894, she picked a quarrel with China and set about annexing Korea. The Chinese navy was, on paper, the more formidable of the two but it was creakingly inefficient and, thanks to the elderly design of her ships, could only use the tactics of the era of the ram. Their engines were ill-maintained, ammunition was in short supply, and the ships were so damp that the crews were in the habit of storing rice and other comestibles in the gun barrels to keep them dry. It is said that the captain of one of their larger ships had pawned a 12-inch gun from his main armament. Wisely their admiral, Ting, kept his main fleet concentrated in the harbour of Wei-hai-wei until he was unequivocally ordered to escort a troop convoy to Korea.

On 17 September 1894 Admiral Ting was off the mouth of the Yalu river with five ironclads, five cruisers, two revenue cutters, and two torpedo boats. His two most powerful units were the battleships *Chen Yuen* and *Ting Yuen*, both 14 years old and built at Stettin (Szczecin). They had armoured citadels covered with 14-inch iron plates and the main armament, four 12-inch Krupps on each, was mounted in pairs in echeloned barbettes at the forward end of the

citadel. Thus each could only use her full gun power forward and even then great care had to be exercised to avoid blasting overboard the 6-inch chase gun mounted in the bows.

On that day the Japanese fleet came in sight consisting of eight cruisers, two ageing ironclads, and two lesser vessels. Ting, seeing no chance of escape ordered his ships into their battle formation, a long straggling line steaming towards the enemy, and opened fire at 6,000 yards. The noise of the 12-inch guns was so great that many on the bridges of the two battleships suffered concussion and Admiral Ting had to be taken below. His opponent, Admiral Ito, who had divided his fleet into two squadrons, steamed in line ahead across the front of the Chinese on a converging course. With the dense black smoke from the funnels of the Japanese ships rolling down on them, the Chinese gunners scored no hits and did only occasional ricochet damage. It was not until the range was down to 3,000 yards that the Japanese opened fire using not only their main guns but their 6-inch and 4.7-inch quick firers and putting down a volume of accurate fire which wholly overmatched the Chinese return. At almost the same moment their van squadron, four British heavy cruisers, turned the Chinese right flank and set about the weaker ships on that wing, none of which could bring substantial armament to bear on their beam.

Two paintings which show clearly the changes in naval design over thirty years. Sail- and steam-powered battleships during the bombardment of Alexandria in 1882 (RIGHT); and dreadnoughts at the Royal naval review in 1911 (ABOVE)

PREVIOUS PAGE: The Japanese battleships opening fire during the Battle of Tsushima. From left to right are *Asahi*, *Fuji*, *Shikishima*, and *Mikasa*

Meanwhile the two Chinese battleships were ploughing forward at their maximum speed of 6 knots and came within striking distance of the slower and less well-protected vessels in the rear of Ito's line. The *Hiyai*, an elderly wooden-built ironclad, was in such danger of being rammed that she turned towards the enemy and steamed between the enemy battleships and the *Akagi*, a gunboat with a single 6-inch gun, narrowly escaped destruction. Seeing this the van squadron turned back to assist and the main squadron also wheeled and tried to take the *Chen Yuen* and *Ting Yuen* in broadside. The Chinese, trying to keep their main guns pointing at the enemy, kept wheeling towards their attackers so that soon their fleet was in total confusion while two of their ships took to their heels and headed for the mouth of the Yalu. One of them rammed a consort in her flight.

Towards dusk Ito drew off for lack of ammunition leaving one Chinese ironclad and three cruisers sunk or sinking while a fourth cruiser ran herself aground. Both the battleships were on fire but both managed to survive. The Japanese were not without their casualties. Apart from the *Hiyai* and the *Akagi*, Ito's flagship, *Matsushima*, lost one man in four from her crew and was so badly damaged that the admiral had to be transferred to another ship. *Matsushima*'s heavy loss was largely due to Ito's determination to close to 'decisive range'. Had he been content to batter the enemy from 1,500 yards he would have achieved the same result with very little loss. In the event the range became so short that the Chinese 12-inch guns were able to make hits with nine shells (and one fragmented ricochet) out of the 199 rounds fired.

The Battle of the Yalu River settled the war and the Treaty of Shimonoseki established Korea as a nominally independent state while China agreed to pay Japan an indemnity of 25,000,000 dollars and to cede to her a strip of Manchuria which included the Liaotung peninsula with the port of Ryojun. These terms were regarded as

The Chinese battleship *Chen Yuen* moored alongside her sister ship *Ting Yuen*

184

being unduly harsh and pressure from France, Germany, and Russia forced Japan to hand back her Manchurian gains. To add insult to injury Russia then leased the regained territory from China and established a powerful naval base, her only all-the-year-round port outside the Black Sea, at Ryojun which she renamed Port Arthur. The Japanese were not unnaturally angry and made up their mind to rectify what they saw as an injustice. Their military expenditure, which was running at an annual rate of £3,500,000 in 1893, rose to £23,000,000 by 1900 and a large proportion of this money was devoted to buying a modern battle fleet from overseas. By 1904 they felt themselves ready for war.

Aiming to take Port Arthur, their first requirement was to transport large numbers of troops, eventually 300,000, and their equipment across the Straits of Korea and through the Yellow Sea. This could only be done with command of the sea and, on paper, there was little to choose between the two navies. The Japanese had 12 battleships while the Russians had only 7 backed up by 3 armoured cruisers, precursors of battle cruisers, which, if they carried nothing heavier than 8-inch guns, could far outpace the Japanese capital ships and were as large. The Japanese had 27 cruisers to the Russians' 8, but 6 of these were very much more powerful than their opponents' and the great part of Japan's cruiser strength had to be absorbed in convoy duties. The Japanese had fewer destroyers, 19 against 25, but had 85 torpedo boats to 17.

In addition to their narrow margin of strength the Japanese had two advantages. They intended to be the aggressors and could strike with their fleet concentrated while the Russians would be divided since their three armoured cruisers were based at Vladivostock, 1,100 miles from the main battle squadron at Port Arthur. The other advantage was fortuitous – the Russians refused to take the Japanese threat seriously. Although peace in the Far East had been precarious for months, they took no steps to reinforce their Pacific fleet even though ships sent to strengthen it from the Baltic must take many weeks to arrive. They were, in fact, absurdly over-confident. In the autumn of 1903 the General Staff enquired of the Admiralty how long it would take the Japanese to land troops in western Korea (where they already had a garrison) or elsewhere on the eastern shore of the Yellow Sea. On 10 October Rear-Admiral Witgeft, Chief of Naval Staff, replied:

So long as our fleet is not destroyed, the operations named are absolutely impossible. In my opinion our fleet cannot be beaten by the Japanese either in the Yellow Sea or in the Gulf of Korea.

Negotiations between Japan and Russia were still in progress when, on 8 February 1904, the Japanese tried a trick that was to stand them in good stead thirty-seven years later. Their main battlefleet arrived off Port Arthur to find the Russians unalerted and with their battle squadron lying fully illuminated in the roadstead. Admiral Togo sent in his torpedo boats which succeeded in damaging and sending aground two of the largest battleships and a cruiser. It was not the triumph Togo had planned as the net-cutting device on the torpedoes was not as effective as had been hoped and next morning the Japanese fleet came within range of the port and indulged in an abortive long-range bombardment of it and the shore batteries. Almost simultaneously a cruiser squadron escorting troop transports off the Korean coast engaged a Russian heavy cruiser and a gunboat and damaged both so severely that they were scuttled by their crews.

Togo made three attempts, all unsuccessful, to obstruct the harbour with blockships and did everything he could to tempt the Russian ships to sea but the Russian admirals lacked the will or the confidence to risk a battle preferring to stay in Port Arthur and be bombarded. This attitude changed briefly when the command passed to Rear-Admiral Makaroff who put some spirit into the fleet and initiated a series of sorties. Unfortunately his flagship, *Petro-pavlovsk*, struck a mine and sank, drowning the enterprising admiral. Only one more sortie was made and this led to an indecisive exchange of fire between the battleships. The Russians abandoned the action when the steering on one of their battleships failed but it was noticeable that, of the rounds fired from the heavy guns, the Japanese scored hits with 6 per cent of their rounds while the Russian score was only 1 per cent. By this time it was August and the Russian ships never attempted to leave Port Arthur again instead landing many guns and seamen to help with the land defences.

Port Arthur fell in January 1905 (see Chapter 12) and at that time a large squadron from the Russian Baltic fleet was lying off the Madagascan coast. St Petersburg had decided to send reinforcements to the Pacific at the end of April 1904 but it was not until 18 October that the force, under Vice-Admiral Rozhdestvensky, sailed from Libau (Liepaja). The fact that they sailed at all was entirely due to the energy of the admiral in wrestling with the incompetence, inertia, and corruption in the Baltic shipyards. It was not the squadron that Rozhdestvensky would have wished to take to sea. The backbone was excellent, four modern battleships and four modern cruisers, but the Admiralty had also insisted that he take with him four ageing ironclads, two of which were fit only for coast defence in a tideless sea, and a number of obsolete cruisers, one of which had only recently been converted from a full-rigged ship. He had, however, successfully resisted pressure to take an additional squadron composed of even more unsuitable ships. For light forces he had eight destroyers, tiny craft of only 350 tons which were quite unfitted for a voyage half round the world. With a number of transports, repair ships, a hospital ship, and a water condensing vessel, Rozhdestvensky's command amounted to forty-two ships.

To get this miscellaneous collection to the Far East would require at least 500,000 tons of coal. Russia had no coaling stations on the route and Britain, who had plenty, refused to assist. Russia's ally, France, would not make coal available but agreed to turn a blind eye if Rozhdestvensky made use of some colonial anchorages away from the main trade routes. The Russians therefore made a contract with the German Hamburg-Amerika line to provide sixty colliers which would refuel the ships at sea, every sack of coal being manhandled from ship to ship.

The voyage started badly. Even in the North Sea many officers became obsessed with the notion that Japanese torpedo boats were lying in wait for them and on 22 October they opened fire on a group of British fishing boats on the Dogger Bank. Three boats were hit, one of them being sunk with the loss of two lives, and for a moment it seemed that an Anglo-Russian war was imminent.

After that things went better and at the New Year the whole fleet was assembled off Nossi Bé in a huge inlet in the coast of Madagascar. The lighter ships had gone through the Suez canal while the heavy units had circumnavigated Africa, steaming 8,000 miles in fifty-four days, an achievement reflecting the highest credit on the admiral. The strain on Rozhdestvensky had been intolerable and by the time the fleet reached Madagascar he was on the verge of a nervous breakdown and was suffering intervals when he was incapable of exercising command. His mental condition was not improved by an order which reached him from St Petersburg informing him that all the obsolete craft which he had refused to take were on their way to join him and instructing him to wait for them. His instinct was to disobey and, with all his ships, he vanished into the vastness of the Indian Ocean. He did not reappear until he reached Singapore but, soon after, he was delayed and on 9 May 1905 he was joined off French Indo-China by a squadron which included a very elderly battleship, three coast defence ships known as 'flat-irons', and another cruiser built for sail. These slowed down his original ships, added nothing to their strength, and greatly complicated the coaling situation.

Since the fall of Port Arthur there was no practicable mission which the fleet could fulfil but St Petersburg ruled that they were to re-establish Russian control of the Yellow Sea. Rozhdestvensky offered to resign in protest against this hare-brained scheme but was sharply told to carry out his orders. Despairingly he ordered the fleet to sail for Vladivostock.

Admiral Togo had had plenty of time since the fall of Port Arthur to overhaul his ships and had assembled them at Masampo, at the southern tip of Korea. His fleet included four battleships comparable to Rozhdestvensky's best, and an overwhelming superiority in cruisers of all types, in destroyers, and in torpedo boats. To the south of his position, screening the approaches to the Tsushima strait which separates Japan from Korea, he stationed a line of armed merchant cruisers.

At 2.30 am on 29 May 1905 the Russian fleet was plodding northwards at 6 knots when it was sighted by the *Siano Maru*, one of Togo's AMCs, near the island of Tsushima. The visibility was poor and the *Siano Maru* was able to turn away and escape, reporting her find to Togo by the new-fangled wireless. The Russians were steaming in three columns with the transports and hospital ship in the centre. The original squadron, led by Rozhdestvensky in *Suvarov*, was on the right and the obsolete reinforcements formed the left column

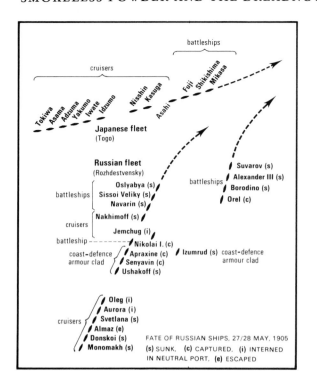

FATE OF RUSSIAN SHIPS, 27/28 MAY, 1905
(s) SUNK. (c) CAPTURED. (i) INTERNED
IN NEUTRAL PORT. (e) ESCAPED

ABOVE LEFT: The Battle of Tsushima

ABOVE RIGHT: The Japanese battle line before Tsushima. In the foreground is a Maxim gun for defence against torpedo boats

which was held somewhat back. The admiral's only reaction to the knowledge that they had been sighted was to call in the three cruisers that had been scouting in front of the fleet and to tell the left column to take station astern of his own. It seems that he had fatalistically accepted the fact that he must be defeated.

Three Japanese cruisers were seen on the port beam at 10.00 am but Rozhdestvensky affected to ignore them and, when one of the other battleships opened fire on them, signalled that ammunition was to be conserved. The Japanese battle squadron, eight heavy ships, was sighted at noon steaming from right to left across the head of the Russian column. The Russian admiral's reaction was to turn the head of his line two points to port but almost immediately ordered the original course to be resumed. This change of orders considerably disordered the Russian line with several ships bunching and others having to reverse their engines to avoid collisions. It was Rozhdestvensky's last attempt to control the course of the action.

Meanwhile Togo, having crossed the Russian 'T', turned parallel to them on a reverse course before putting his squadron through a turn of 180 degrees and continuing on a parallel course, opening fire at a range of 4 miles. He despatched his light cruisers against the rear of the Russian columns. For twenty minutes the Russians fired with creditable accuracy, the 'flat-irons' doing some fine shooting but, once the Japanese layers got the range, their opponents lost range and line and scored no more hits with their heavy guns. The battle became a massacre. At an early stage *Suvarov* was struck in the conning tower and her admiral slightly wounded. No orders were

sent to the rest of the fleet and, after an hour and a half of firing *Suvarov* was put out of control with a hit on her steering and Rozhdestvensky disabled by a second wound. With the flagship swerving out of line and burning, the Russian fleet fell into complete chaos. Things were made worse by the fact that the second-in-command had died on the previous day and, rather than call attention to what might be considered as a bad omen, Rozhdestvensky had ordered the news of his death to be suppressed. Thus the third-in-command did not know that he was now the senior officer with what remained of the fleet.

Of all the Russian fleet only one light cruiser and two of the tiny destroyers reached Vladivostok. The Japanese lost two torpedo boats and only 450 men killed and wounded. The unfortunate Rozhdestvensky, who was transferred unconscious to a destroyer before *Suvarov* was sunk, was taken prisoner and nursed back to health in a Japanese hospital. Few commanders in history have been more decisively defeated but few deserve more sympathy and admiration for the way in which he sailed his fleet half-way round the world despite almost insuperable difficulties. In doing so he destroyed his health and, while his fatalistic acceptance of inevitable defeat may have affected his conduct of the battle, nothing could have changed the outcome. It was a battle between an ill-assorted fleet, manned largely by reservists whose only training was in sail and who were exhausted by their long voyage, and a highly-trained Japanese fleet, exhilarated by victory and based on their home ports.

Tsushima was the first fleet action between ironclads and the only one to be fought to a finish. It was also the first in which the ships were directed by their admirals by wireless. The Japanese casualties would have been even lighter had Togo, like Ito before him, not been an advocate of 'decisive ranges'. For much of the action the heavy guns were firing at only 3,000 yards, scarcely a quarter of the maximum effective range of Togo's British-built 12-inch weapons.

The torpedo proved a sad disappointment. They were freely used by both sides but with little result. Four large Russian ships were sunk by torpedoes but in each case the victim was disabled and stationary. The Japanese fired 370 torpedoes but scored only 17 hits, four of them on the same stationary ship. This figure excludes the two Japanese torpedo boats which were almost certainly sunk in error by their own consorts.

CHALLENGES TO BRITISH SUPREMACY

Having adopted the Two Power Standard, Britain's shipyards were busy. Between 1893 and 1904 she launched an average of 7 battle-ships and 7 armoured cruisers each year for her own use and a considerable number of each for other countries – Japan, Chile, Greece, Turkey, Argentina, and Brazil – whose naval ambitions were not matched by their construction capabilities. The 15,585 ton Royal Sovereign class (1891–2) was followed by 9 Majestics, each 10 feet longer than their predecessors but displacing only 14,900 tons thanks

to their lighter steel armour. These came into service in 1894–6 and
were followed by 6 of the Canopus class (1897–9), 8 Formidables
(1898–1902), and 6 19-knot Duncans (1901). The 8 ships of the King
Edward VII class (1903–5) were the largest battleships so far, displacing 16,350 tons, but they were overtaken, even before they were
completed, by two 16,500 ton ships of the Lord Nelson class (1906).
Powerful as all the ships were, the improvements from class to class
were only marginal. The Lord Nelsons were only 60 feet longer than
the Royal Sovereigns and only the Duncans could manage one knot
more than *Royal Sovereign* herself, which was fractionally faster than
the rest of her class. The main armament on all was four heavy guns
mounted in two turrets, the 12-inch guns of the later classes comparing almost exactly with the 13.5-inch guns of the earlier since they
had a higher muzzle velocity. All carried a very considerable
secondary armament, the Lord Nelsons having ten 9.2-inch guns in
turrets on the beam and twenty-four 12-pounders.

In the aftermath of Tsushima all the naval powers were building
comparable ships. In 1906 the Germans were completing five of the
Braunschweig class (12,997 tons, 398 feet overall, and four 11-inch
guns) and were working on five Deutschlands of 13,040 tons and the
same armament. Japan had just received two Kashimas, built in
England and comparable to the King Edwards although a knot faster.
The latest French battleships, *Patrie* and *République*, were each
14,635 tons, 439 feet long and armed with four 12-inch guns. The
latest Russian, *Slava*, was slightly smaller, 13,516 tons, but with the
same armament mounted in the same way. The United States was
commissioning five of the Georgia class. These were larger than
most, 14,998 tons, but their heavy armament was, once again, four
12-inch guns in pairs in turrets fore and aft. They had a strikingly
numerous secondary armament of eight 8-inch and twelve 6-inch
guns. Several powers were planning more heavily-armed battleships.
The Japanese, who had developed their own shipyards, were
designing the *Satsuma* and the *Aki*, which were to carry twelve
10-inch as well as the standard four 12-inch guns, and in America
plans were afoot for two ships of the Michigan class which were to

have eight 12-inch guns. In the event none of the designs put to sea until 1909 (the *Aki* not until 1911) and before that Britain had changed the rules of the game and made every one of them obsolete.

On 3 October 1906, a year and three days after her keel had been laid at Portsmouth, the sea trials began of a revolutionary battleship. It is not true, as is often asserted, that HMS *Dreadnought* could have sunk single-handed any other battle fleet in the world. There is no doubt that, properly handled, she could have dealt with any two, probably three, battleships afloat. She cost £1,813,100, twice the price of the *Majestic* of ten years earlier, but she carried ten 12-inch guns, each capable of throwing an 850-lb. missile to a range of 18,500 yards. She was driven by turbines, their first application to a capital ship, and their 23,000 horsepower gave her a speed of almost 23 knots. She was 527 feet long and displaced 17,900 tons.

Dreadnought, the brainchild of Admiral Sir John Fisher and Sir Philip Watts, put the naval building race back to the starting line but gave Britain a useful lead. Every other power had to go back to the drawing-board and begin to design ships which could compete with her. It was not until 1909 that Germany succeeded in producing her first Dreadnought-type ships, *Nassau* and *Westfalen*, each mounting twelve 11-inch guns. They were larger than *Dreadnought* but, since their engines only developed 20,000 horsepower, they were two knots slower. By that time Britain had built seven modified Dreadnoughts and in the following year she commissioned the first Super-dreadnought, HMS *Orion*, displacing 22,500 tons and with a main armament of ten 13.5-inch guns.

One feature of the original *Dreadnought* which was not repeated in her successors was the almost total absence of secondary armament. Apart from her heavy guns (and five torpedo tubes) she mounted only twenty-seven 12-pounders, guns large enough only to engage the lightest of torpedo craft. The thinking behind this deprivation was that the range of the new high velocity guns was so great that their fire could no longer be directed individually from the turrets and must be controlled centrally from a level many feet above the guns. The existence of guns of different calibre, such as the 12- and 9.2-inch in *Lord Nelson*, would make the controllers' work impossibly complicated. This thinking, however, had ignored the increasing threat from destroyers and the later Dreadnoughts were equipped with sixteen or twenty 4-inch guns, a practice continued with the Super-dreadnoughts until the Iron Duke class (1912–13) which had twelve 6-inch guns.

A further modification was in the disposition of the turrets. In *Dreadnought* all the turrets were on the same level and two were mounted on either side of the superstructure so that only eight of the ten guns could fire on either broadside. HMS *Neptune*, a modified Dreadnought laid down in 1909, was the first ship to have one turret raised so that it could fire over another, but the Super-dreadnought *Orion* was the first to have such stepped turrets fore and aft and all her turrets mounted on the centre line. Even so she had one turret astern of the funnels where it could only fire to the beam and it was

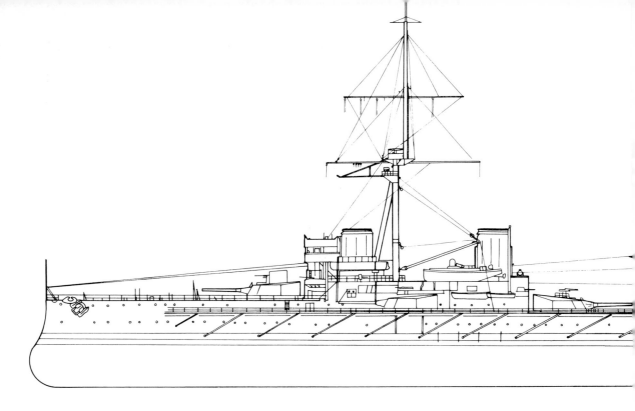

The capital ship revolution

HMS *Dreadnought* (ABOVE), with her 'all big-gun' armament of ten 12-inch guns, not only made all foreign pre-Dreadnoughts – such as the French-designed Russian *Tsarevitch* (TOP RIGHT) with her four 12-inch and twelve 6-inch guns – obsolete, but meant that the Royal Navy also had to build swiftly to maintain its supremacy. Four new classes totalling nine improved Dreadnoughts were built in 1906-9, all – like HMS *Vanguard* of the St Vincent class (CENTRE RIGHT) – with ten 12-inch guns in a similar offset-centre-turrets arrangement. When Germany adopted the 12-inch gun in 1909, the

Royal Navy replied with 'super-Dreadnoughts' – like HMS *Iron Duke* (BELOW) – with ten 13.5-inch guns all arranged to fire on both sides. Admiral Fisher and his staff knew that Dreadnoughts with their 21-knot designed speed would need to be accompanied by faster scouting cruisers, so another revolutionary class was developed at the same time. The 'battlecruiser' was designed to achieve 25 knots with as much armour and as many 12-inch guns as possible. The first of these, HMS *Invincible* (BOTTOM RIGHT) was completed in 1907 with eight 12-inch guns – thus also outgunning all other foreign battleships.

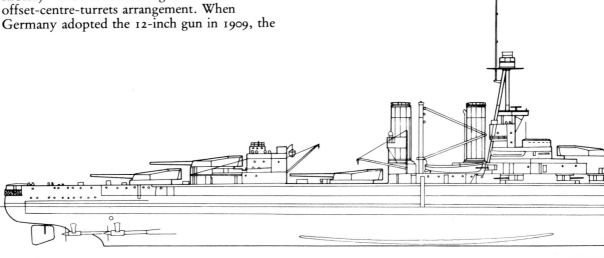

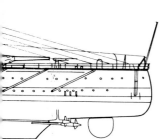

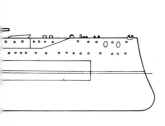

The launching of the armoured cruiser *Fürst Bismarck* at Kiel in 1897

the *Queen Elizabeth*, laid down in 1913 and the first of a class of five, which had all her 15-inch guns mounted so that each could fire throughout an angle of 180 degrees. She was 645 feet long and displaced 27,500 tons but her most revolutionary feature was her oil-driven engines which developed 75,000 horsepower and gave her a speed of 24 knots.

Although as late as June 1903 the war plan for the Home Fleet gave as its first task the prevention of a junction between the French and Russian fleets, it was clear from the turn of the century that if Britain was to fight a naval war her principal enemy would be Germany. The last serious scare of war with France occurred in 1898–9 with the Fashoda crisis and after 1901 relations between the two countries moved steadily towards the Entente of 1904. By that time Russia, even before the final disaster at Tsushima, was no longer a formidable naval power and Japan was Britain's ally. There was little likelihood of war with the United States – still building a formidable fleet under the influence of Captain Mahan, and the not inconsiderable Italian fleet was more likely to be an ally than an opponent.

The position between Britain and Germany was quite different. From 1898 onwards the Kaiser had taken the naval bit firmly between his teeth. In that year the first Navy Law envisaged a fleet of nineteen battleships and thirty-two cruisers large and small. Two years later the Navy Law laid down that:

In order to protect German trade and commerce under existing conditions, only one thing will suffice, namely that Germany must possess a battlefleet of such a strength that, even for the most powerful adversary, a war would involve such risks as to make that Power's supremacy doubtful.

The law postulated that by 1917 Germany should have a fleet of thirty-four battleships with appropriate supporting vessels. Defending the bill in the Reichstag, the Chancellor, von Bülow, insisted that 'our fleet must be built with our eyes on English policy'. When the Reichstag refused to meet the entire cost of this grandiose programme, it was the cruiser programme that was postponed leaving the battleship target unaltered.

Britain could hardly be indifferent to what appeared to be an open challenge to her maritime supremacy coming from a country which was already the predominant land power in Europe and which seemed to have little need for a sea-going fleet. With strong public support the government determined to outbuild the Germans and, in March 1903, decided that the main battle fleet base should be at Rosyth. This was a clear indication that she expected the next war to be fought in the North Sea rather than the English Channel. Work on the new fleet base was started in 1905 but was still incomplete in 1914.

In 1905 Britain had fifty-three battleships to the Germans' twenty and when in the following year *Dreadnought* made all these ships

SMS *Preussen*, one of Germany's last pre-Dreadnought battleships passing through the Kiel Canal

obsolete Britain retained her lead although it was a smaller one. Instead of the Two Power Standard she was, since war with France, Russia, or the United States seemed improbable, prepared to settle for a ratio of 8:5, although she based her interpretation of the proportion only on ships in home waters. By mid-1912 she had seventeen Dreadnoughts against Germany's eleven.

Germany was also faced with another problem. The Kiel canal was essential to her war deployment. Without it part of her fleet could be penned up in the Baltic while the rest could be destroyed at leisure in the North Sea. It had been opened in 1896 but the advent of the *Dreadnought* made it useless for the fleet. *Pommern*, one of the last of Germany's old-style battleships, had a beam of 73 feet and could just pass through, but *Posen*, one of the first of her Dreadnoughts, was 89 feet wide and the entire 61 miles of the canal had to be widened before she could use it. The work was not complete until the summer of 1914. By that time Britain had twenty-nine Dreadnoughts and Super-dreadnoughts with sixteen being built while Germany had only twenty-two with six in preparation.

Potentially the submarine was as significant as the battleship. Here France took the lead. With her eyes still fixed on fighting a *guerre de course* against British commerce, she started work on building an underwater fleet as early as 1886. These were electrically driven both on the surface and under it, a factor which greatly limited their range and in Sweden the ingenious Nordenfeldt was experimenting with boats driven by steam on the surface, the reserve steam being used to drive them under water as long as it lasted, after which electric engines were used.

In America J. P. Holland, a Fenian who hoped to use submarines against the British, invented a horizontal rudder which made a controlled dive possible and the US navy ordered one of his boats in 1893. Seven years later a Holland submarine was commissioned into

USS *Holland*, the US navy's first submarine in dry dock in 1901

One of the Royal Navy's first Holland submarines in Portsmouth Harbour in 1901

the American navy being driven by petrol on the surface at up to 8 knots and by electricity (5 knots) when submerged. It carried a crew of five and was unsuitable for use in anything but the calmest water. Nevertheless in 1901 the British bought five Holland submarines and added a periscope to each since, in the US model the only visibility was through the scuttles in the conning tower. The French, however, were well in the lead and in 1899 commissioned the *Gustave Zédé*, a sea-going submarine capable of 8 knots at a depth of 60 feet.

By 1906 the French had 84 boats in commission while Britain had 52, Russia 27, Japan 13, and Italy and USA a dozen each. Only Germany, thanks to the implacable opposition of Admiral Tirpitz, lagged behind with only one incomplete submarine. The main source of submerged power through the two World Wars, the diesel engine, was invented in Germany in 1905 but the first order for one came from France in 1907. Most fortunately for Britain, Germany had only twenty-seven serviceable U-boats when war broke out in 1914 compared with thirty-seven in the Royal Navy and thirty-six in the French. It was, however, a U-boat which first demonstrated unequivocally the danger which submarines represented to surface ships. Soon after dawn on 22 September 1914 a U-boat torpedoed and sank three British cruisers, *Aboukir, Cressy,* and *Hogue,* off the Dutch coast.

In fact a smaller but more significant victory had already been won by the Russian navy. In August two Russian cruisers attacked the German light cruiser *Magdeburg* in the Gulf of Finland. She was driven ashore on the island of Odensholm and destroyed but, from the floating body of a German seaman, the victors recovered the German naval code book which, with rare good sense, they forwarded to the Admiralty in London.

CHAPTER ELEVEN

Colonial Campaigns

A PART FROM A contingent which marched to Peking in 1900 to relieve the beleaguered legations, the German army saw no active service between the end of the Franco-Prussian War in 1871 and the outbreak of the First World War in 1914. While a lack of experience of active service must be a disadvantage to any army, there were dangers in evolving tactical doctrines from lessons learned in theatres where the conditions of war were totally different from those relevant to fighting in Europe. Most colonial wars were conducted against enemies lacking formal discipline and lacking modern weapons but with abundant numbers and courage. Such fighting frequently ranged over great distances poorly served by roads and scarcely at all by railways. They posed gigantic supply problems and, although the problems were the same as those which might arise in Flanders or Poland, the solutions might be very different.

Nor were the lessons learned in one colonial campaign necessarily applicable to another. The Italians were to learn the truth of this in a disastrous way in the 1890s. As early as 1869 they had purchased the small and inconvenient anchorage of Assab on the western coast of the Red Sea as a staging post for their ships using the Suez canal. In 1889 they annexed the province of Erythrea (which formed the northern part of what was later known as Eritrea) and the natural harbour of Massawa. This they did with the active support of Britain, anxious to check the spread of French influence on the route to India. The status of Erythrea was uncertain but the Turks had a shadowy claim to it which they had neither the means nor the will to enforce. On the other hand the Ethiopians laid claim to all the land between the White Nile and the Red Sea but the Erythreans, being predominately Muslim, were far from anxious to be the vassals of the Copts of Ethiopia. The Ethiopians were in no condition to press their claim, being in their usual state of internecine warfare. Italy had supported the strongest of the Ethiopian chieftains, Ras Menelik, the ruler of the area around what is now Addis Ababa, and it was largely with Italian arms that he established himself as Emperor of Ethiopia. Being busy subduing the great plateau which forms the heartland of his empire, Menelik raised no objection to the occupation of Erythrea.

A British observation balloon being used at Ladysmith during the Boer War

The early Italian troubles were to the north where they extended their colony to include Kassala, now in the Sudan and then dominated by the followers of the Mahdi. In a series of minor campaigns against the Dervishes the Italians, using locally recruited troops (Ascari) with Italian officers, established a clear superiority culminating in the Battle of Agordat (21 December 1893). Against an enemy armed with little more than spears and shields, the Italians deployed their men, apart from some reserves, in a single rank, shoulder to shoulder, thus producing the maximum of fire effect with the minimum expenditure of ammunition.

Menelik, meantime, was beginning to resent the Italian assumption that Ethiopia was under their protection and this resentment was carefully fostered by the French who, in 1893, made him a present of 100,000 Lebel rifles with 2,000,000 rounds of ammunition. By this time he had consolidated his position in his own empire and turned his attention to fomenting trouble among the tribes in and around Erythrea. The governor of the colony, General Oreste Baratieri, who had been one of Garibaldi's Thousand, decided to establish a defensible southern boundary to Erythrea, a line hitherto left vague, on the line of hills running east and west from Adigrat to Adowa so that he could contain the threat from Menelik. This was a sound military precaution and might well have gone unremarked had not Italy's expansionist Prime Minister, Francesco Crispi, persuaded him to mark the border much further south. The resulting expansion included the entire province of Tigré which, if it had not in the past been notably loyal, was incontestably Ethiopian. In November 1895 Menelik declared war on Italy.

The war began badly for the Italians. They had sent a small force, 2,150 men (of whom 700 were Erythrean irregulars) with four guns, to the south on the 'English road', the road built by Napier in 1868 (see p. 157) and still the only track up to the highlands. They halted on a group of hills known as Amba Alagi and, although Baratieri had given their commander discretion to retire, the orders had become mangled in transmission by telegraph and he believed himself bound to hold his ground. On 7 December the force was attacked by 30,000 Ethiopians armed with Lebels and supported by mountain guns. In a large-scale replica of Majuba, the Ascari fought bravely but were massacred, with their officers, almost to a man.

There followed a pause for the rainy season during which Crispi's government sent out some reinforcements and obtained a note of credit for £750,000 (compared to the £9,000,000 required by Napier in 1868). Baratieri, who had only 6,000 men including a single Italian battalion, abandoned Tigré and concentrated his strength near Adigrat. By some error a single Ascari battalion was left at Makale, 60 miles to the south, where it was invested by the 30,000 men who had been victorious at Amba Alagi. Believing his prime task to be the defence of the colony, the governor rightly left them to their fate but when, having come to the end of the water supply, Makale surrendered on 18 January, Baratieri was vilified in Italy with Crispi being particularly bitter.

At the end of the rainy season Menelik advanced on Adowa with 80,000 men armed with rifles, 20,000 irregular spearmen, and 42 guns. Baratieri, who had received reinforcements, mostly volunteers, from Italy, proposed that peace negotiations should be opened or, if that should be impracticable, a slow withdrawal. He believed that Menelik's army would disintegrate either from its own internal stresses or from lack of food since it had no commissariat and could not live for long on the infertile countryside. Safe in Rome, Crispi, a Sicilian of Albanian descent, replied that the only peace terms he would consider were a considerable expansion of Erythrea and a closely-controlled protectorate over the whole of Ethiopia. On the subject of a withdrawal his messages were increasingly insulting and ended with the announcement that he had decided to appoint a new governor.

Stung by accusations of cowardice and urged on by his four brigade commanders, Baratieri decided to attack before his successor arrived. Had he waited another week he would have had no enemy, for the Ethiopians were at the end of their food and Menelik was praying daily for an Italian attack.

Baratieri's available force consisted of 17,700 men, of whom 10,596 were Italians, and 56 field guns. Before setting out he issued a set of tactical instructions which included:

4. The bayonet is to be used on every possible occasion.
7. In the firing line a close formation is to be employed.

These were the methods that he had used successfully against the Dervishes with their spears. They were suicidal against an enemy armed as well as his own men.

With the troops divided into four columns, Baratieri decided to emulate Wolseley's success at Tel-el-Kebir by making a night approach followed by a dawn attack on Menelik's position near Adowa on 1 March 1896. Unfortunately the rugged landscape he had to traverse bore no relation to the flat hard sand beside the Nile and chaos supervened. The leading column lost its way and blundered into the Ethiopian position. It was destroyed and the remaining brigades, attacked on the march, were successively outflanked and infiltrated. Both Italians and Ascari fought with the greatest gallantry but they were overwhelmed. They lost 7,560 killed and 1,428 wounded. The number of prisoners taken may have been as high as 4,000 but only 1,759 ever returned from captivity. It was only the disintegration of Menelik's army which allowed Italy to keep Erythrea.

Baratieri was brought before a court-martial and grudgingly acquitted of all criminal acts. The only faults that can be attributed to him were bowing to political pressure and, like most of his contemporaries, failing to appreciate the killing power of the magazine rifle. His personal bravery and the persistence with which he had repeatedly organised stragglers into a rearguard to cover the retreat of his survivors and the wounded, more than expiated any mistakes he made.

The Omdurman campaign

Two years after Adowa the British were fighting shoulder to shoulder in the Sudan. One of the principal reasons for the campaign was the desire to take the pressure off the Italians in Erythrea, where the Dervishes, taking advantage of the colony's precarious situation, were pressing in on Kassala. The British government gave out that the object was to stamp out slavery in the Sudan and the public was content to regard the expedition as a well-merited revenge for the deaths of General Gordon and Hicks Pasha when the Mahdist rising had swept over the territory in the early 1880s. Ostensibly the operation was controlled by the Egyptians and the command was entrusted to Sir Herbert Kitchener who, although only a colonel in the Royal Engineers, was Sirdar (commander-in-chief) of the Egyptian army which, since Tel-el-Kebir, had been wholly reformed and trained by the British.

Kitchener was faced by a daunting problem but it was one of logistics rather than fighting. The Khalifa, who had succeeded to the leadership of the Dervishes on the death of the Mahdi in 1885, had a huge army but its armament was not impressive although it had some artillery and a number of western rifles, including 10,000 Remington repeaters. There was little doubt that it could be defeated if it could be brought to battle but it was not going to be easy to reach it. Cairo was, inevitably, the administrative base and from there it was 755 miles by rail and river to Wadi Halfa on the Egyptian-Sudanese border. From Wadi Halfa to Khartoum, the Khalifa's capital, is more than 450 miles as the crow flies – but most of the direct route lay across singularly inhospitable desert. Alternatively the army could follow the course of the Nile, long stretches of which were sometimes or always unnavigable. This would make the advance from the frontier more than 700 miles. The traditional supply system for crossing the desert relied on camels but a camel carries a load of only 300lb. of which it eats 10lb. a day on a 20 mile journey. Since each camel would need to return to the advance supply base (and eat while it did so) its effective load would be only 200lb. over 100 miles. Thus 15,000 camels would be required to transport supplies for a month over 100 miles for each 10,000 men. It was clearly going to be impossible to assemble enough camels to transport supplies for 25,000 men and 2,500 horses over 450 miles.

As a distinguished engineer officer the Sirdar was exactly the right man for this task. He attempted no strategic or tactical subtlety but set about the operation with the greatest deliberation, scarcely concerning himself about how long he took. His method was to push forward a small covering force, supplied by camel, and then build the railway behind them. As soon as that stretch of line was complete, he would build up a new advance supply depot and repeat the process.

His greatest triumph was the construction of a railway line across 230 waterless miles of the Nubian desert from Wadi Halfa to Abu Hamed. Every railway expert whom Kitchener consulted assured him that the project was impossible so he entrusted the task to eight Royal Engineer subalterns led by a Canadian, Lieutenant Edouard

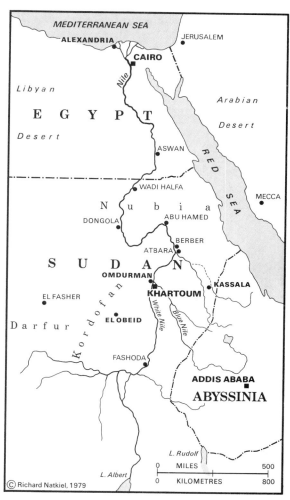

© Richard Natkiel, 1979

ABOVE: Colonel Sir Herbert Kitchener while Sirdar of the Egyptian army

RIGHT: The theatre of operations in the Sudan

Girouard. For a labour force Girouard employed 2,000 Egyptian conscripts who had first to be taught the skills of platelaying. Every item they required had to be obtained, at best, from Cairo or Alexandria, and many essentials, including 15 locomotives and 200 waggons, had to come from England. Even the smallest item of stores was irreplaceable and on one occasion when a vital nut was mislaid in transit from Wadi Halfa a squadron of cavalry was detached to search the track until, miraculously, they found it.

The first steps towards the line were taken in January 1897 but intensive work could not start until May. Abu Hamed was reached on 1 November, thus cutting out the huge, and largely unnavigable, westward loop of the Nile. By 3 July 1898 a further 155 miles had been added, extending the line from Wadi Halfa to the point where the Atbara river joins the Nile.

There was then a pause while stores and men were accumulated at this new southern railhead. Among the stores were a large number of barges and some gunboats, most of which were brought to Atbara in sections and assembled. From there the Nile, which is navigable to Khartoum except for the sixth cataract, was to be the main supply artery for the army and throughout August the troops and their supplies were ferried up river to Wadi Hamid, 70 miles from the capital.

The final advance started on 26 August. The army consisted of 25,800 men (of whom 17,600 were from the Egyptian army) with 44 guns (including 2 40-pounders) and 20 Maxims. The artillery was supplemented by 36 guns and 24 Maxims mounted on the gunboats. Despite the reliance on river transport the army was accompanied by a very large number of animals – 3,524 camels, 2,469 horses, 896 mules, and 229 donkeys. Twenty-seven days' rations were taken for all, each soldier carrying rations for two days, five more were carried in boats under regimental arrangements and the remainder in sailing barges. As a colonel, who was later to command a corps at Mons and Le Cateau, described the advance:

We moved in battle array, namely echelon of brigades, right refused, left resting as near the river as swamps and thorny shrub would allow, each brigade in attack formation (battalions in line each with two companies in reserve) moving in fours, advancing from the flank of companies – the last time, probably, any army will move in the presence of an enemy in the close order of the Peninsular and Crimean days.

Each afternoon the column halted and bivouacked for the night 'in a hollow oblong formed of battalions in double company column and a zariba (hedge of camel thorn) was made all around'.

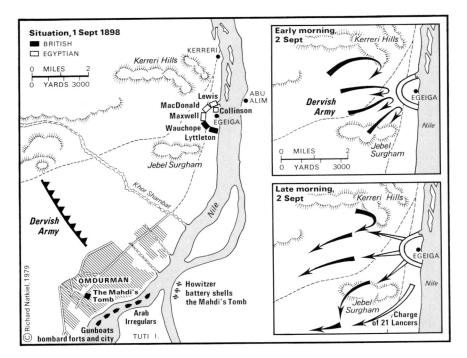

The Battle of Omdurman

On 1 September the army reached Egeiga, a village 7 miles from Omdurman. Here it was possible to encamp in a semi-circle with both flanks secured on the Nile and covered by the gunboats. The orders were 'either to make a zariba or, where the ground was soft, to make a small shelter trench' which should be capable of holding men in two ranks. In the event the two British brigades 'cut and built around their front a good stout thorny zariba' while the three forward Egyptian brigades covered their sectors with double lines of trenches.

Kitchener's intention was to bombard Omdurman and to assault with the bayonet when the walls were breached. It would have been a costly attempt and the Khalifa made it unnecessary. On the morning of 2 September he deployed his army on the glaring reddish amphitheatre of hills which encircles Egeiga and tried to assault the bivouac on all its faces. He had some 50,000 men of whom more than half had rifles while the remainder relied on swords and spears. They advanced in well ordered masses which earned the admiration of the Sirdar's army.

It was a suicidal move. The 12-pounders of the field artillery opened on them with shrapnel as soon as they came over the crests at a range of 2,800 yards and soon afterwards, on Kitchener's particular orders, the Grenadier Guards started firing section volleys with the sights of their Lee Metfords set at 2,700 yards. A war correspondent remarked, 'Occasionally they caught and slew a group but at that period it was difficult to make out, even through good field glasses, whether the infantry fire was really effective.'

The Dervish attack was not checked despite the combined fire of the artillery, the gunboats, and the infantry. It was noted that the rifle fire became really effective at 900 yards but still the enemy came on with quite extraordinary courage, many of them reaching a dip in the ground about 400 yards from the defenders. Beyond that point all attempts to advance were shot down. An officer noted that 'within three hundred yards of the British and within two hundred yards of the Egyptians, scarcely a Dervish could live', a revealing comment on the relative effectiveness of the magazine Lee Metfords of the British and the single-loading Martini Henrys of the Egyptians.

The assault had been broken within two hours and Kitchener decided to prevent the Dervishes from regaining Omdurman. Since there was no hope of intercepting them with infantry, he sent out the only cavalry he had immediately available, the four squadrons of the 21st Lancers who included among their 400 men Lieutenant Winston Churchill, 4th Hussars.

Churchill's graphic account of the Lancers' charge is well known. A brother officer put the affair in less dramatic terms:

The regiment was wheeled into line. When 300 yards off we started to charge and were met with a heavy musketry fire from the enemy. At first it was ill-directed but very soon casualties appeared in our ranks from it. Instead of a few Dervishes we tumbled upon over 500 hidden in a fold in the ground. They were in a Kohr, or nullah, into which we had to drop, and they lined it twenty deep in places. Our weight, however, carried us through. The Dervishes when we struck them bunched together, showing no fear of cavalry. There was half a minute's hacking, cutting, spearing and shooting in all directions; then we cleared them and rallied on the far side. Halting about 300 yards off, men were dismounted and we opened a sharp fire from our carbines, driving them westward in ten minutes.

The 21st lost 5 officers, 65 men, and 119 horses in this charge and it is difficult to see what they achieved. The battle was already won and the Dervish army was streaming away to the west of Omdurman. Only a small contingent returned to the city and made a short and ineffective stand there. Eleven thousand eight hundred Dervish bodies were counted on the battlefield. The Anglo-Egyptian casualties amounted to 482 killed and wounded of whom 150 were British. The Khalifa's army never rallied and Khartoum was taken without resistance.

The Omdurman campaign was tactically insignificant but it was a magnificent logistic achievement, showing how far the British administrative machine had improved since the Crimean débâcle of 1854. Despite the vast length of the lines of communication, which ran through country as inhospitable as any in the world, the supply of rations, ammunition, and reinforcements never failed or looked like failing. Only one item which might have been invaluable was not provided – barbed wire. The Khalifa's only serious chance of defeating Kitchener's army once they had reached the heart of the Sudan lay in a night attack when the superiority of the Anglo-Egyptian arms would have been nullified by darkness and this would have been impossible had the bivouac been surrounded with wire. This addition to the already overweighted armoury of the defence had been invented for agricultural purposes in the United States. The first patent had been taken out by Lucien Smith in 1867 and a further patent for its manufacture on a large scale was granted to Joseph E. Gideon in 1874. A British patent was taken out two years later. Barbed wire was used at this time in Egypt where, according to Churchill, it had formed part of the defences of Fort Sarras, near Wadi Halfa, but the Sirdar seems to have decided that its weight and bulk would be too much to bring forward from his railhead since his transport was already very heavily laden. It was, in fact, used on active service in the same year as Omdurman when Colonel Theodore Roosevelt employed it to protect the camp of his Rough Riders in the Spanish-American War.

THE AMERICAN ADVENTURE IN CUBA

The Spanish-American War contributed little to military science except a lesson on how things should not be done. The American aim was to acquire some colonial coaling stations, as Mahan had recommended, but the war was put forward as a crusade to rescue Cuba from Spanish oppression although no explanation was given as to why so many Cubans volunteered to fight for their oppressors. To do the American government justice, it was most reluctant to go to

One of the issues of the New York Journal which helped to whip up American enthusiasm for war against Spain

0,000 REWARD.—WHO DESTROYED·THE MAINE?—$50,000 REWARD.

The Journal will give $50,000 for information, furnished to it exclusively, that will convict the person or persons who sank the Maine.

EDITION FOR GREATER NEW YORK.

NEW YORK JOURNAL
AND ADVERTISER.

The Journal will give $50,000 for information, furnished to it exclusively, that will convict the person or persons who sank the Maine.

Copyright, 1898, by W. R. Hearst—NEW YORK, THURSDAY, FEBRUARY 17, 1898.—16 PAGES.   PRICE ONE CENT In Greater New York Elsewhere TWO CENTS

STRUCTION OF THE WAR SHIP MAINE WAS THE WORK OF AN ENEMY

$50,000!

0,000 REWARD!
r the Detection of the Perpetrator of the Maine Outrage!

New York Journal hereby offers a reward of $50,000 for information, FURNISHED TO IT EXCLU-V, which shall lead to the detection and conviction of the person or government criminally responsible for the explosion resulted in the destruction, at Havana, of the United States Maine and the loss of 258 lives of American sailors.

$50,000 CASH offered for the above information is with Wells, Fargo & Co.

No one be barred, be he the humble but misguided woman eking miserable dollars by acting as a spy, or the attache of a govt secret service, plotting, by any devilish means, to revenge fancied insults or cripple menacing countries.

er has been cabled to Europe and will be made public in tal of the Continent and in London this morning.

urnal believes that any man who can be bought to commit n also be bought to betray his comrades, FOR THE ETRATOR OF THIS OUTRAGE HAD MPLICES.

W. R. HEARST.

Assistant Secretary Roosevelt Convinced the Explosion of the War Ship Was Not an Accident.

The Journal Offers $50,000 Reward for the Conviction of the Criminals Who Sent 258 American Sailors to Their Death. Naval Officers Unanimous That the Ship Was Destroyed on Purpose.

$50,000!

$50,000 REWARD!
For the Detection of the Perpetrator of the Maine Outrage!

The New York Journal hereby offers a reward of $50,000 CASH for information, FURNISHED TO IT EXCLU-SIVELY, which shall lead to the detection and conviction of the person, persons or government criminally responsible for the explosion which resulted in the destruction, at Havana, of the United States war ship Maine and the loss of 258 lives of American sailors.

The $50,000 CASH offered for the above information is on deposit with Wells, Fargo & Co.

No one is barred, be he the humble, but misguided, woman eking out a few miserable dollars by acting as a spy, or the attache of a government secret service, plotting, by any devilish means, to revenge fancied insults or cripple menacing countries.

This offer has been cabled to Europe and will be made public in every capital of the Continent and in London this morning.

The Journal believes that any man who can be bought to commit murder can also be bought to betray his comrades. FOR THE PERPETRATOR OF THIS OUTRAGE HAD ACCOMPLICES.

W. R. HEARST.

DER MAGAZINE

NAVAL OFFICERS THINK THE MAINE WAS DESTROYED BY A SPANISH MINE.

George Eugene Bryson, the Journal's special correspondent at Havana, cables that it is the secret opinion of many Spaniards in the Cuban capital that the Maine was destroyed and 258 of her men killed by means of a submarine mine, or fixed torpedo. This is the opinion of several American naval authorities. The Spaniards, it is believed, arranged to have the Maine anchored over one of the harbor mines. Wires connected the mine with a ... magazine, and it is thought the explosion was caused by sending an electric current through the wire. If this can be proven, the brutal nature of the Spaniards will be shown by the fact that they waited to spring the mine ... after all the men had retired for the night. The Maltese cross in the picture shows where the mine may have been fired.

A Mine or a Sunken Torpedo Believed to Have Been the Weapon Used Against the American Man-of-War---Offic and Men Tell Thrilling Stories of Being Blown Into the Air Amid a Mass of Shattered Steel and Exploding Shells---Survivors Brought to Key West Scout the Idea of Accident---Spanish Officials Pro-test Too Much---Our Cabinet Orders a Searching Inquiry---Journal Sends Divers to Havana to Report Upon the Condition of the Wreck. Was the Vessel Anchored Over a Mine?

BY CAPTAIN E. L. ZALINSKI, U. S. A.

(Captain Zalinski is the inventor of the famous dynamite gun, which would be the principal factor in our coast defence in case of war.)

Assistant Secretary of the Navy Theodore Roosevelt says he is convinced that the destruction of the Maine in Havana Harbor was not an accide The Journal offers a reward of $50,000 for exclusive evidence that will convict the person, persons or Government criminally responsible for the of the American battle ship and the death of 258 of its crew.

The suspicion that the Maine was deliberately blown up grows stronger every hour. Not a single fact to the contrary has been produced.

Captain Sigsbee, of the Maine, and Consul-General Lee both urge that public opinion be suspended until they have completed their investigati taking the course of tactful men who are convinced that there has been treachery.

Washington reports very late that Captain Sigsbee had feared some such event as a hidden mine. The English cipher code was used all day yesterd officers in cabling instead of the usual American code.

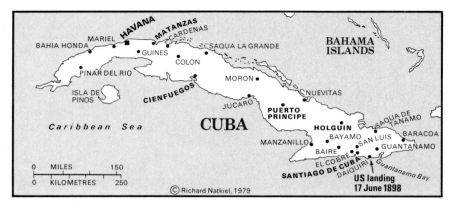

 map labels:

MARIEL · HAVANA · MATANZAS · CARDENAS
BAHIA HONDA · GUINES · SAQUA LA GRANDE · BAHAMA ISLANDS
PINAR DEL RIO · COLON
ISLA DE PINOS · CIENFUEGOS · MORON · NUEVITAS
JUCARO · PUERTO PRINCIPE
Caribbean Sea · CUBA · HOLGUIN · SAQUA DE TANAMO
MANZANILLO · BAYAMO · SAN LUIS · BARACOA
BAIRE · GUANTANAMO
EL COBRE · DAIQUIRI · Guantanamo Bay
SANTIAGO DE CUBA · US landing 17 June 1898

0 MILES 150
0 KILOMETRES 250
© Richard Natkiel, 1979

LEFT: The American attack on Cuba

war but was driven to it by a sustained newspaper campaign with William Randolph Hearst's *New York Journal* leading the pack and imitating the role played by *The Times* before the Crimean War. The immediate *casus belli* was an explosion which sank USS *Maine* in Havana harbour on 15 February 1898. The cause of the explosion has never been established but of all the explanations put forward that favoured by the newspapers – Spanish sabotage – is the most improbable. Nevertheless it sufficed, and on 22 April Cuba was blockaded. Congress voted a state of war three days later. Within a week the US navy was able to announce a great victory when Admiral George Dewey destroyed the Spanish Pacific Fleet at Cavite in Manila harbour. It was a force greatly inferior to his own and the only American casualty was an engineer officer who died of heat stroke.

It was a much more serious undertaking to send an expedition to Cuba to assist insurgents who were ineffective, disunited, and more troublesome to their allies than to the Spaniards. There were 80,000 regular Spanish troops on the islands and they could count on being supported by at least as many local levies. The entire US army was only 28,000 strong and had been neglected for years. The Quartermaster Corps consisted of only fifty-seven men, and the infantry were still using black powder although even the Spaniards had smokeless. State militias were called out and volunteers enlisted by the thousand but, apart from lack of training, there were problems of every kind. Some states refused to put their militias under federal control and many of the volunteers would not serve under regular officers.

Despite fearful administrative problems, 17,000 men were landed at Daiquiri on 17 June under the command of General William Shafter who, as the press were delighted to point out, weighed one-seventh of a ton. It was typical of the way the war was being conducted that no one had seen fit to tell the general that the US marines had already established a beachhead some distance away at Guantanamo Bay. It was fortunate that the Spanish command, which was sluggish in the extreme, decided not to oppose Shafter's landing as even a small force could have driven the invaders back into the sea as they shambled ashore to be faced with logistic chaos of Crimean

BELOW: Bringing up the
guns during the advance
on Santiago de Cuba

proportions – to say nothing of serious outbreaks of yellow fever, malaria, dysentery, and typhoid with which the medical services were quite inadequate to cope.

Shafter's aim was to capture Santiago de Cuba where a considerable squadron of Spanish warships, all of them obsolete and ill-found, was being blockaded by the US Atlantic Fleet, commanded by two admirals who were at loggerheads. He decided to capture the city on 1 July and, having given his orders, retired to bed with fever and heat stroke. His plan was complicated and impractical, aiming to capture two objectives, the village of El Caney and the hill of San Juan as a first step to seizing the city itself. Despite advice to the contrary, he insisted that both assaulting divisions should advance on a single, inadequate forest track, deploying when they reached the open. Naturally there was extreme congestion and the troops came under heavy shell fire, made more accurate since the defenders had an excellent aiming point formed by an observation balloon which was raised in the centre of the milling battalions. Fortunately the regimental and battalion commanders decided to ignore their detailed orders and stormed their objectives out of hand.

The city still held out and Shafter, unwilling to embark on another attack, settled down to persuading the Spaniards to surrender without further fighting while his army endured disease and an irregular supply of unpalatable rations with such equanimity as they could muster. During this period the Spanish squadron, on unequivocal orders from Madrid, put to sea in a gallant but hopeless attempt to escape from the blockade. Every Spanish ship was sunk amid scenes of unparalleled ill-will between the American admirals. Santiago surrendered on 17 July but before an armistice was agreed in August the Americans made a bloodless conquest of Puerto Rico, and landed an expedition in the Philippines which had considerably more trouble with the inhabitants than with the Spaniards. At the peace treaty of Paris which concluded the hostilities Spain ceded Cuba, Puerto Rico, Guam, and the Philippines for a payment of $20 million.

During the course of the war the United States annexed Hawaii, hitherto independent, and at its close acquired the Philippines, Puerto Rico, and Guam from Spain, a reasonable reward for under-taking a war against colonialism. The war had reflected little credit on the commanders on either side but much on the stoical courage of the American soldiers and the Spanish sailors. The proprietors of American newspapers greatly increased their circulations and regularly revealed American plans in advance. Outside the newspaper world the only person who derived advantage from the war was Theodore Roosevelt who resigned office as Assistant Secretary to the Navy to raise and command a volunteer cavalry unit known as the Rough Riders. His bravery and his skill in handling the press made him such a reputation that he had little difficulty in being elected Governor of New York on his return. From there he became Vice-President in 1901 and, when McKinley was assassinated in the same year, he stepped into the Presidency.

BRITAIN AGAINST THE BOERS

On 12 October 1899 the South African Republic (the Transvaal) and the Orange Free State declared war on Great Britain and set her a problem to which none of her past experience of war suggested a solution. Her soldiers had learned to deal with the vast but poorly armed masses of the Khalifa's army and with the cunning marksmen of the North-West Frontier of India. They were well-enough trained to give a good account of themselves in Europe, should the need arise, but they had learned nothing that would enable them to cope with the Boers of the two republics, and it is probable that no other European army could have tackled the problem any more efficiently than they did.

The regular army of the two republics consisted of no more than 1,000 trained artillerymen backed by about twice as many mounted police. Their strength lay in some 40,000 burghers who had a liability to serve in times of emergency and to bring their own horses, rifles, ammunition, and rations. They elected their own officers but were not bound to obey their orders. The weaknesses of such a military system are obvious but they were largely offset by the determined independence of the Boers and by their marksmanship, which they had developed from their youth since they depended largely on the shooting of game for their food. They were also helped by the terrain of their country, especially the huge tracts of rolling country, plentifully supplied with good defensive positions which could only be approached by a long open slope on which assailants offered excellent targets. In these conditions the Boers had, in a long series of campaigns against indigenous tribes, evolved an effective tactical system. As a German military observer wrote:

[each man] had learned to study the country, to avail himself of its cover in order to get within effective range of his adversary, and only to fire when success was certain, but to fly quickly from danger. This system of fighting was not conducive to the carrying out of a costly attack, and on religious grounds he held defence to be more justifiable; he did not pursue but contented himself with victory, nor did he lightly risk his life; but he would quit a dangerous position without damage to his moral strength and, instead of holding out to the last, would occupy a new one.

The two republics were well armed, having imported 43,000 of the newest pattern of the German 0.27-inch Mauser rifles and sufficient ammunition to give 2,000 rounds a man. The Mauser was at least equal in performance to the long model 0.303-inch Lee Enfield and had one considerable advantage. Both magazines held ten rounds, but the Lee Enfield magazine had to be loaded with single rounds, while the Mauser used a clip holding five rounds. Having had some experience of the effects of shrapnel at Majuba (see p. 158), the Transvaal had equipped itself with some artillery. Apart from some heavy pieces, originally used for arming the forts at Pretoria and later used as siege guns, they had acquired 19 3-inch, quick-firing field guns (from Creusot, Krupp, and Vickers-Maxim), 24 1.45-inch pom-poms, and 31 Maxim machine-guns. The 3-inch guns all outranged the 15-pounders of the British field artillery which had a maximum range of 6,000 yards while their shrapnel fuses were graduated only up to 3,360. Since this was the Boers' first experience of using artillery they used them conventionally in batteries in the early engagements but found that this hampered the mobility of their forces. Thereafter they used them as single guns, usually at extreme range, so that they could easily be withdrawn before they ran the risk of capture or even before they came within range of the British guns. They employed them, in fact, in very much the same way that the ordinary burgher used his rifle.

Skilful and determined as the Boers were, their only hope lay in a swift victory, a *fait accompli* that would convince the British that any riposte would not be worth the trouble and expense involved. To do this they would have to make an immediate invasion of Cape Colony where, in the country districts, there was a majority of Boers who would rise to support them. They had an excellent opportunity to do this since their own mobilisation was practically immediate while the British garrison in the whole of South Africa was only 14,750 men exclusive of a reinforcement of 5,600 men from India who began to arrive in Natal four days before war was declared. The Boers thus had a numerical advantage of two to one – but this could not last. A field force of 47,000 men was mobilised in Britain as soon as war broke out and, in the long run, the wealth and manpower of Britain and her empire must prove overwhelming.

The Boers squandered their advantage. It was extremely difficult to come to any decision in the high command of the two republics and as a result they devoted themselves to a multiplicity of irrelevant operations. The main Transvaal force, 18,000 men with fourteen guns, set out on an invasion of Natal, where there was no hope of raising a rebellion. Eight thousand men sallied out westward in attempts to seize Kimberley and Mafeking, towns much coveted by the Boers but with no strategic value. Only 2,000 men were available on the southern frontier of the Orange Free State for an invasion of Cape Colony, where they raised only 2,359 supporters.

In this situation the British could only lose the war by a total collapse of morale, but winning it was a most formidable under-taking. Geography was against them. The Orange Free State drove a huge wedge into the British-held territory, splitting the war into two separate halves while leaving it open for the enemy to switch troops from one to the other. In the western theatre all British operations had to be based on the ports of Cape Town, Port Elizabeth, and East London. These three were connected to each other by railway but only in the most devious fashion. The rail link between Cape Town and Port Elizabeth ran through De Aar (500 miles from Cape Town; 339 from Port Elizabeth) and thence to Middelburg, a stretch of line within easy reach of the Free State border. The eastern theatre, in Natal, was wholly detached. Its administrative base was Durban which was connected to Cape Town only by a sea voyage of 1,000 miles.

President Kruger and
Louis Botha lead out a
commando

The logistic problems caused by the huge geographical scale of
the war were, on the whole, satisfactorily solved but there was no
answer to the tactical problem. No contemporary army had
discovered a way of attacking good positions defended by modern
rifles without incurring casualties on a scale which, especially in
Britain, would have been unacceptable. In South Africa the
difficulties were heightened by the extreme mobility of the Boers
which meant that, even if a successful attack was delivered, the
enemy would have slipped away and established himself in another
equally strong position.

In any case the tactics with which the British started the war were
more suitable for their Sudanese campaign than for their present task.
The standard attack procedure called for an advance in column to
within 800 yards of the enemy before deploying. At that point one
section (a quarter of the company's strength), or possibly two, from
each company were to advance as rapidly as possible to within
effective range and then cover the advance of the remainder by firing
volleys. The remainder were to advance by rushes of 30 or 40 yards
until they were 300 yards from their objective when they were to halt
and fix bayonets. Three more short rushes, during which they were
to fire five of the ten rounds in the magazine, would bring them to
200 yards from the enemy and this distance was, after a short pause,

to be covered in a single breathless charge.

This clumsy and mechanical system might have stood some chance of success if the artillery could have smothered the enemy positions with shrapnel but since the Boer guns outranged the 15-pounders (and even more the 12-pounders of the horse artillery) there was little that the British gunners could do to assist, the more so since all their training was based on firing only at 'effective ranges', between 1,500 and 3,000 yards. It should be remembered that all field guns had a flat trajectory so that, except where there was time to build earthworks round the guns, they had to be deployed in the open. Some gunner officers maintained that the only way to counteract the shortness of their range was for the guns to be brought to 'decisive ranges', 1,000 yards or less. This manoeuvre had proved effective against Dervish spearmen but resulted, in South Africa, in the gunners being picked off by rifle fire.

EARLY DISASTERS FOR THE BRITISH

The only way in which the British could have achieved a quick victory would have been by the deployment of enormous numbers of mounted troops, but even if all the thirty-one regular cavalry regiments had been sent to South Africa (and twenty-eight of them eventually were) they would not have been enough. True to their traditions the cavalrymen had clung to their swords and lances, remembered von Bredow's success, and resolutely declined to take seriously their role of mounted infantry. Even when they attempted it the carbine they were issued with was so far outclassed by the Boers' Mausers as to be useless. To make matters worse on 21 October 1899, in one of the first engagements of the war, Elandslaaghte, a squadron of lancers and one of dragoon guards got in amongst some flying Boers and massacred them. It was a dramatic moment and convinced all true cavalrymen that the day of the *arme blanche* was not over. The Boers were even more impressed and took care never to be caught in the same situation again. Later in the war lances were withdrawn and infantry rifles issued to all cavalrymen.

The tasks that should have been performed by dragoons were delegated to infantrymen. Lieutenant-Colonel (later Field Marshal) William Robertson recalled that on the ship that took him to the Cape there was an infantry battalion which:

was met on reaching port by a staff officer with orders to detach one company that evening to De Aar, where it would find horses and saddlery and thereupon become a mounted infantry company. Three weeks later this same company, with others equally untrained, was sent forward to meet the enemy . . . Many of the men crossed a horse that day for the first time in their lives.

The business of providing enough horses for the army was one of enormous size and complexity since South Africa was notoriously the grave of horses not born and bred in the country. The Army Remount Depot was only geared to the business of providing the usual number of horses required by the army in Britain, 2,500 a year, while there was a registered reserve of 14,000 more. During the war they provided 518,794 for South Africa alone. Of these 13,144 died on the voyage out and 347,007 were 'expended during the campaign'.

Another branch of the service that suffered from a shortage of essential stores was the field telegraph section. They sailed for the Cape with 80 miles of cable. Before the end of the war they had laid 18,236 miles of line.

It was inevitable that, in view of the Boer superiority in numbers, mobility, and skill-at-arms, things should go badly for the British in the early stages. In fact both sides started with unrealistic beliefs in a speedy victory, the Boers with their memories of Majuba, the British because they refused to admit that a handful of farmers could with-stand large numbers of regular troops accustomed to victory. Thus when Lieutenant-General Sir Redvers Buller VC reached Cape Town ahead of his Army Corps (three divisions of infantry and two cavalry brigades) his orders were to march from Cape Colony to Bloemfontein, capital of the Orange Free State and 750 miles from Cape Town, and thence to Pretoria, 1,014 miles from Cape Town. Meantime the Boers in the Transvaal were to be held in check by the reinforcements from India which had arrived previously.

On his arrival, on 19 October, the situation looked very different. The force in Natal, although it had won two small but expensive victories, had been outmanoeuvred and its commander, Sir George White VC, had decided to allow himself and his 12,000 men to be invested in Ladysmith. This was the right decision, although he would have done better to send out his four regular cavalry regiments, but it left Buller with the obligation to give priority to relieving him since all that stood between the Boers and Durban was a single British battalion and a handful of locally-raised troops. This was not the whole of Buller's problem. Commandos from the Free State were threatening the rail link between De Aar and Middelburg and, to the north-west Mafeking and Kimberley were under siege, and from the latter the immensely influential Cecil Rhodes was sending a stream of importunate demands to be relieved. In the whole of Cape Colony there were only four and a half battalions and a single regiment of cavalry.

Over-confident in the capabilities of regular soldiers, Buller tried to solve all his problems at once. He divided his Army Corps into three, sending units to the various fronts as they landed rather than keeping them within the brigades and divisions into which they had been formed. Two infantry brigades under Lord Methuen were detailed to relieve Kimberley. The southern frontier of the Free State and the safety of the vital transverse railway was entrusted to a single brigade of infantry and the bulk of the cavalry. Four brigades and two cavalry regiments were shipped round to Natal where, after some hesitation, Buller joined them, having first dispersed his staff into various administrative posts.

The result was known as Black Week. The British were defeated three times between 10 and 15 December. In each case an attempt was made to storm a well-established Boer position across open

country. Given the range and the accuracy of Boer rifle fire this was an impossibility in daylight but the first defeat was the result of an attempted night attack and set a most unwelcome precedent. Attempting to surprise a Free State force at Stormberg by a night march, General Gatacre's force of 3,000 men was misled by its guides and was discovered at daylight in column of fours within 400 yards of the enemy. Before they could be extricated Gatacre had lost 700 men of whom nearly 600 were prisoners. Next day Methuen tried to seize a long, rocky ridge near Maggersfontein after a night march. On this occasion it was a thunderstorm which upset the timing and the Highland brigade was caught in the open, in extended order, within 150 yards of the Boer trenches. Nine hundred and forty-eight casualties were suffered before the retreat of the Highlanders could be secured.

The most crushing disaster occurred in Natal. Buller aimed to cross the Tugela river, 120 yards wide but fordable in places, and then advance the 12 miles beyond to Ladysmith. The ground to the south was open and gently rolling. To the north there were successive ranges of high hills through which the railway, which crossed the river near Colenso village, wound its way through a steep-sided valley. After considering the shortest route up the railway line on 12 December, he cabled to London that 'after a close reconnaissance by telescope I came to the conclusion that a direct

British troops marching across the veldt with a waggon train in the background assault would be too costly'. Instead he decided to cross the Tugela 17 miles upstream at Potgeister's Drift where there was more cover for the approach to the river. This resolve did not outlast the receipt of the news from Stormberg and Maggersfontein and, on 14 December, he sent a second cable:

A flank march of 45 miles with an enormous waggon train across the front of an active and successful enemy seems to me too great a risk when it involves uncovering the communications of the only effective force we have in the field. I am therefore advancing today to attack Colenso and try to force the direct road. I fully believe I shall be successful, though I fear at heavy cost.

Even assuming that this decision was correct, it seems, with the benefit of hindsight that Buller's plan for seizing the crossing at Colenso contained a flaw which would have been obvious to a newly-commissioned subaltern. By the village the Tugela turns sharply northward to avoid a dominating hill, Hlangwane, which is on the south, British, bank. The Boers had put a garrison on Hlangwane but the men there thought their position was so dangerous that they evacuated it, without orders, on 13 December. Twenty-four hours later it was reoccupied, on the direct orders of President Kruger, by volunteers. Buller, however, refused to see that possession of Hlangwane would make Colenso untenable. In his view, 'Its possession did not in any way assist the crossing . . . to take it would have been a stiff fight in any case, but if I took it and then failed at Colenso, I should have to evacuate it.' Although he had four infantry brigades in hand he sent only 1,000 mounted colonials against the hill in what could only be a demonstration.

A signal lamp and heliograph in operation near Bloemfontein

The plan he did adopt was to send forward two columns – each consisting of one infantry brigade with another in support. The

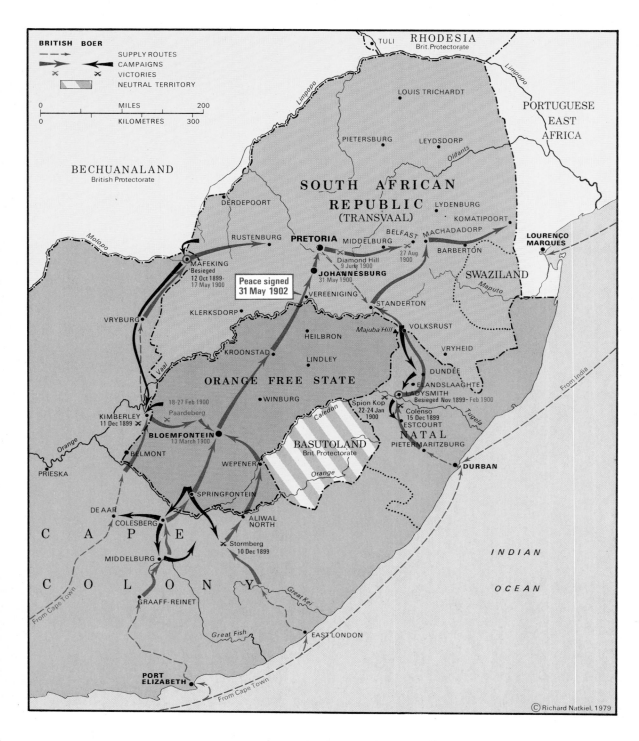

BRITISH BOER
→ - - → ━━→ SUPPLY ROUTES
━━▶ ◀━━ CAMPAIGNS
✕ ✕ VICTORIES
▨ NEUTRAL TERRITORY

MILES 200
0
KILOMETRES 300
0

RHODESIA
Brit. Protectorate
TULI

PORTUGUESE
EAST
AFRICA

BECHUANALAND
British Protectorate

Limpopo

LOUIS TRICHARDT

DERDEPOORT

PIETERSBURG
LEYDSDORP
Olifants

SOUTH AFRICAN
REPUBLIC
(TRANSVAAL)

LYDENBURG
KOMATIPOORT

RUSTENBURG
PRETORIA
MIDDELBURG
BELFAST
MACHADADORP
LOURENÇO
MARQUES

MAFEKING
Besieged
12 Oct 1899-
17 May 1900

Diamond Hill
9 June 1900
27 Aug
1900
BARBERTON

Peace signed
31 May 1902

JOHANNESBURG
31 May 1900

SWAZILAND
Maputo

VRYBURG

KLERKSDORP
VEREENIGING
STANDERTON

Molopo

Vaal

KROONSTAD

HEILBRON
Majuba Hill
VOLKSRUST

LINDLEY
VRYHEID

ORANGE FREE STATE
DUNDEE

18-27 Feb 1900
Paardeberg
WINBURG
Spion Kop
22-24 Jan
1900
ELANDSLAAGHTE
LADYSMITH
Besieged Nov 1899- Feb 1900

KIMBERLEY
11 Dec 1899

BLOEMFONTEIN
13 March 1900

Caledon
Colenso
15 Dec 1899
ESTCOURT
From India

BELMONT

Orange
WEPENER
BASUTOLAND
Brit. Protectorate
NATAL
PIETERMARITZBURG

PRIESKA

Orange

SPRINGFONTEIN
DURBAN

DE AAR
COLESBERG

ALIWAL
NORTH

C A P E

Stormberg
10 Dec 1899

MIDDELBURG

C O L O N Y

INDIAN

OCEAN

Great Kei

GRAAFF-REINET

From Cape Town

Great Fish
EAST LONDON

PORT
ELIZABETH
From Cape Town

© Richard Natkiel, 1979

ABOVE: South-east Africa, showing the major engagements of the Boer War

OPPOSITE ABOVE: The charge of the 21st Lancers at the Battle of Omdurman

OPPOSITE BELOW: Royal Horse Artillery crossing a river under fire during the Boer War

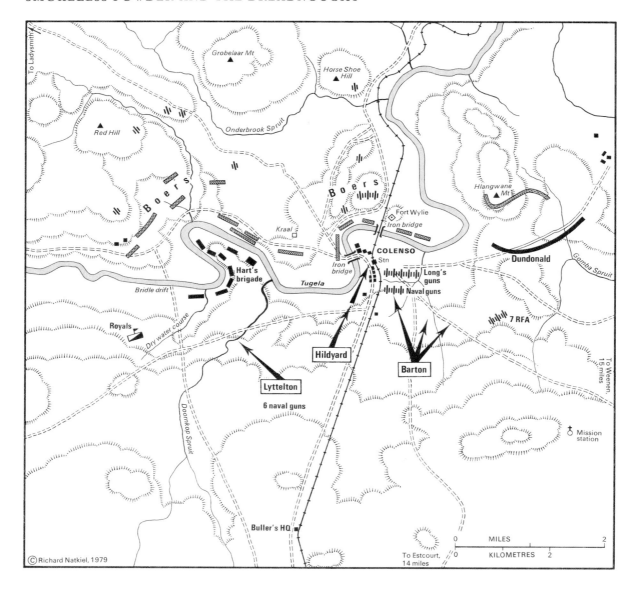

The following labels appear on the map:

To Ladysmith

Grobelaar Mt

Horse Shoe Hill

Red Hill

Onderbrook Spruit

Boers

Boers

Hlangwane Mt

Fort Wylie

Iron bridge

Kraal

COLENSO

Stn

Dundondald

Gomba Spruit

Iron bridge

Hart's brigade

Tugela

Long's guns

Bridle drift

Naval guns

Royals

Dry water course

7 RFA

To Weenen, 15 miles

Hildyard

Lyttelton

6 naval guns

Barton

Doornkop Spruit

Mission station

Buller's HQ

MILES

0   2

KILOMETRES

0   2

To Estcourt, 14 miles

© Richard Natkiel, 1979

The Battle of Colenso

right-hand attack aimed at the railway bridge, the left at a ford 2½ miles to the west. Having secured the river crossings, the columns were to push on and capture the kopjes beyond.

Although he was employing 16,000 men with forty-four guns (two of them naval 4.7-inch pieces) against 5,000 Boers with twelve guns under Louis Botha, Buller's plan had little chance of success since it combined a maximum dispersion of force with long exposed approach marches. The commander of the leading brigade in the left column, Major-General A. F. Hart, was a convinced advocate of the virtues of close order and, after his Kaffir guide had decamped when the first Boer shell was fired, he led his battalions into a projecting loop of the river where they could be fired into from three sides. This

A 4.7-inch naval gun in action at Colenso

persuaded him to allow them to extend to three-pace intervals. Two field batteries which went to his support found the Boer guns beyond their range.

The right-hand attack fared better since the leading brigade commander, Major-General J. H. T. Hildyard, sent his men forward by half-companies with the men in single rank at six to eight paces interval so that they got to within 350 yards of the bridge with few casualties. Any advantage that might have ensued was then dissipated by the Commander, Royal Artillery, Colonel C. J. Long. Having been at Omdurman he was an ardent disciple of the 'decisive range' school and was determined to demonstrate the rightness of his views. With twelve 15-pounders he trotted forward and unlimbered them 1,250 yards from the enemy riflemen. The gunners went into action with a precision that would have earned high praise on the parade ground at Woolwich and for a short time their fire was effective enough to allow the infantry to reach Colenso village. Nevertheless the Boer reply was devastating and before long many of the gunners were down and their ammunition exhausted. Long was wounded and orders were given for the survivors to withdraw to a sheltering fold in the ground while they waited for more shells to be brought forward.

The sight of the twelve guns standing deserted in the open in their smartly dressed line riveted Buller's attention. He forgot about crossing the Tugela and devoted all his energies to organising attempts to recover them. Four Victoria Crosses and eighteen Distinguished Conduct Medals were won but only two of the

15-pounders were brought back. Ten were left for the Boers to capture when, at 11.00 am, Buller sadly gave the order to return to camp. The morning's fighting had cost him 1,127 casualties, 523 of them in Hart's brigade. The Boers lost six killed and twenty-two wounded apart from one burgher who was drowned in the river.

The disasters of Black Week made Britain realise that beating the Boers was not to be an easy task that could be left to professional soldiers. Field Marshal Sir Frederick Roberts, whose son had been awarded a posthumous VC for trying to rescue the guns at Colenso, was made commander-in-chief in South Africa with Kitchener as his chief of staff. Before the war was over 448,435 men saw service in South Africa, of whom 52,000 came from South Africa itself, and 31,000 from other overseas countries of the empire. Even with this gigantic force it took three years and 21,942 British deaths, 13,000 of them from disease, to subdue the two republics, the last year being occupied by a particularly frustrating guerrilla war.

THE LESSONS OF THE BOER WAR

Throughout the campaign the mobility and flexibility of the Boers posed an insoluble problem. Only once did the British succeed in outmanoeuvring them. In February 1900 Major-General Sir John French, having relieved Kimberley, made a remarkable march round the rear of Cronje's camp at Paardeberg with 1,100 cavalry. He then managed to impose enough delay on the Boers to allow the infantry and artillery to come up and force them to surrender with 4,000 men and two guns. During the rest of the war all the tactical successes were on the Boer side and the eventual British victory was the result of grinding persistence with overwhelming strength.

The lessons learned in South Africa bore little relation to war in Europe. The phenomenon of a small but highly-mobile force manoeuvring at will in a vast area was not to be seen again until the desert campaigns of 1940–3. Nevertheless the army was able to rectify a large number of faults before it had to fight another major war. Not the least was the lack of experience of the British generals in handling large bodies of men. This was due to the fact that, apart from a tract of Salisbury Plain which had been bought in 1897 for artillery practice, there were no areas in the United Kingdom where as much as a brigade could be exercised except Aldershot and the Curragh. As a result Field Marshal Roberts had to report that 'during the eleven months I was commanding in South Africa I got rid of five generals of division for incompetency, six brigadiers of cavalry and eleven out of seventeen commanding officers of cavalry regiments, besides some half a dozen infantry colonels'.

The artillery was thoroughly overhauled and the artillery component of each infantry division settled at fifty-four 18-pounders, eighteen 4.5-inch howitzers, and four 60-pounders. When it was seen that the 18-pounders were provided with rifle-proof shields for the gun crew, there was an outcry in the press alleging that such protection was not in accordance with the best traditions of the Royal Artillery.

The .303-inch SMLE showing the magazine and bolt-action loading mechanism

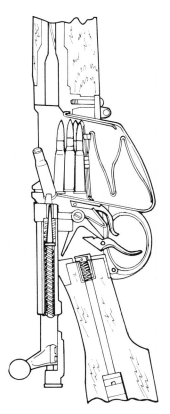

In 1902 the long model Lee Enfield was superseded by the short, the SMLE, which was to remain the British rifle until 1954. Issued to both infantry and cavalry it was loaded with a clip and was one of the greatest hand-held weapons of all time. Its rapid fire rate of up to twenty-five rounds a minute was to astonish Britain's enemies in 1914. By that time the cavalry had been persuaded that it was not beneath their dignity to fight on their feet and, having at last been issued with a practical weapon, their musketry almost rivalled that of the infantry. Every regiment of cavalry and battalion of infantry was equipped with two Maxim-guns, which were not replaced by the famous Vickers machine-gun until 1915.

Infantry training manuals were rewritten to lay stress on the principle of fire and movement, that part of any attacking force should be employed to keep the enemies' heads down by aimed individual fire while the remainder worked their way forward by short rushes until they reached assaulting distance. It was still suggested that the final charge should be made from 200 yards but it was now a matter on which commanders were allowed discretion, and it was emphasised that no attack should be made until fire superiority had been established. This was a great advance on the rigid rules laid down at the opening of the Boer War and, if it did not give the full answer to the problem of attacking entrenched rifles over open ground, it was at least as practicable a solution as any devised by any other army.

The best feature of all that emerged was the new spirit outlined by Lord Roberts (as he became) in the foreword to a training pamphlet issued in 1902:

Success in war cannot be expected unless all ranks have been trained in peace to use their wits. Generals and Commanding Officers are therefore not only to encourage their subordinates in doing so by affording them constant opportunities of acting on their own responsibilities, but they must also check all practices which interfere with the free exercise of their judgment, and will break down by every means in their power the paralysing habit of an unreasonable and mechanical adherence to the letter of orders and to routine.

This was a great step forward in the revolution which had been set in motion a century earlier by John Moore, Kenneth Mackenzie, and Coote Manningham at Shorncliffe, a revolution in the conception of discipline which was to spread to every army in the world. It was, when technology restored mobility to the battlefield, to change every aspect of soldiering but, in the early years of the twentieth century, it could not break the tyranny imposed by the rifle, the shrapnel shell, and the spade.

CHAPTER TWELVE

Approach to Armageddon

THE POWER OF THE DEFENCE, already made overwhelming by the rifle and the machine-gun, received a new accession of strength when the French army introduced the 75-mm. field gun in 1896–7. This 16-pounder weapon had both fixed ammunition (i.e. rounds which contained both the propellant charge and the projectile in one package like a rifle cartridge) and an efficient hydraulic system for absorbing the shock of recoil. Fixed ammunition meant that loading was a simple and speedy business while recoil absorption ensured that the carriage did not run back on firing so that relaying was much quicker. Thus the *soixante-quinze* could fire twenty or more rounds a minute, a rate inconceivable for earlier guns. The French example was quickly followed by the other powers. All these quick-firers used only shrapnel since their flat trajectory made it difficult to design a percussion fuse which would make shells burst on impact. Nevertheless they added another gigantic hazard to the task of infantry committed to a frontal attack. The difficulties they now had to encounter were vividly demonstrated in the land fighting of the Russo-Japanese War.

The peacetime strength of the Russian army was more than 1,000,000 men and calling up the reserves would raise it to 3,500,000. The Japanese standing army amounted to 270,000 men and mobilisation would triple its strength but, once Admiral Togo had seized command of the Yellow Sea, the Japanese had a clear numerical advantage. The Russians had 148,000 men in Manchuria, of whom 41,000 formed the garrison of Port Arthur, but this substantial force had only the most tenuous lifeline connecting it to its homeland – its source of reinforcements and munitions. It had to depend on the Trans-Siberian railway, a ramshackle, single-track affair more than 5,000 miles long. It was short of rolling stock and locomotives, and there were not enough double-tracked sections where trains going in opposite directions could pass each other. The railway's main coal stocks were at the unfortified port of Dairen (Luta), more than 20 miles from Port Arthur. In this long rail link there was a gap of 100 miles represented by the waters of Lake Baikal. From May to October this had to be crossed by ferry. During

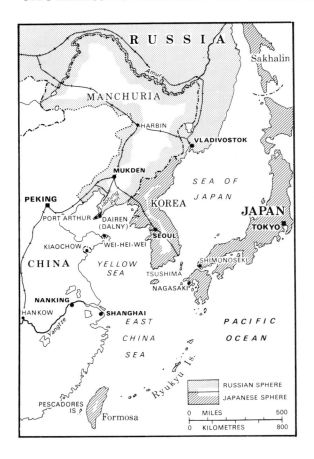

LEFT: The theatre of
operations during the
Russo-Japanese war

PREVIOUS PAGE: French
troops on manoeuvres in
1911

the winter the lake meant a week's march and all supplies had to be
hauled across by sledge and, since the ice was unreliable, there was
no guarantee that heavy items would reach the far side. Even
supposing that the railway was in full working order, which was
seldom the case, it took a month to move a battalion from Moscow
to Mukden (Shenyang).

In the five months following the first naval attack on Port Arthur
(see p. 185) the Japanese had landed four corps on the mainland. These
had pinned the Russian field army under Kuropatkin to the vicinity
of Mukden, while pushing back a detachment of it, principally two
East Siberian Rifle divisions, in the direction of Port Arthur. The
Russian commander there, General Stössel, was an officer of little
talent but of unyielding obstinacy in minor matters. Such was his
determination that when orders arrived from Moscow for him to
hand over his command to the brave and inspiring General Smirnoff,
he succeeded in suppressing all copies of the message and continuing
his incompetent direction of the defence.

Kuropatkin, knowing that Port Arthur was likely to be able to
withstand a long siege, was anxious to build up his strength for a
relief attempt but he was overruled and forced to attack with only
28,000 men. He was halted at Te-li-su and thereafter devoted his

ABOVE: Japanese 11-inch howitzers in action against Port Arthur

main energies to protecting his base at Mukden and to securing his communications, which were extremely vulnerable to Japanese cavalry raids and to the attacks of Japanese-inspired guerrillas.

Meanwhile one Japanese corps under General Nogi was endeavouring to take Port Arthur. The defences were incomplete when the war broke out and, thanks to differences of opinion between Stössel and Smirnoff, had made little progress in the period between the February naval attack and Nogi's arrival in front of the place in July. In particular they had not been extended to include a group of hills to the north-west, one of which, known as '203-metre hill', gave clear observation down to the Russian fleet and shore installations in the harbour. Although Stössel had insisted on sending large quantities of stores forward to stock improbable delaying positions on the approaches, there was plenty of ammunition and the food stocks, if unappetising, were adequate for many months.

It was not until the beginning of December that the Japanese finally succeeded in taking Hill 203 and from that time the defences and the fleet were under constant and well-directed artillery fire, much of it from 11-inch howitzers which threw an explosive charge of 39¾lb. compared to the bursting charge of 13oz. used by the 24-pounder siege guns at Sebastopol half a century earlier. Nevertheless at the end of the year a council of war decided that Port Arthur could and should continue to resist. Stössel had other ideas. He opened secret negotiations and, to the delight, not unmixed with surprise, of the Japanese surrendered the town on 2 January 1905. Some 33,000 soldiers became prisoners-of-war and the Japanese also acquired four battleships and thirty-six smaller vessels, all more or less damaged.

Despite Stössel's pusillanimity, the Japanese paid a shocking price for their victory. Nogi's force had never been more than 90,000 men under command but he had lost 57,780 men in action and, at the end, had a sick list of 33,000. Probably the high rate of battle casualties was largely due to the sanguine attitude of General Nogi who, in the early days of the siege, persistently attacked fortified and entrenched positions in formations more suitable for open country. He was ably seconded by the patriotic fervour with which the Japanese soldiers went into the assault, a fervour lethally matched by the dour bravery with which the Russians defended their positions. It was not until he began to treat his attacks as siege operations by sapping forward toward the fortifications and attempting, with mixed success, to drive mines under the defences, that he made any substantial progress. Even then his progress was slow and his casualties high. The final attack which captured the improvised defences on Hill 203 took six days and cost 11,000 killed and wounded, the Russians losing only 1,200.

Such casualties showed that, despite the reckless bravery of the Japanese, there was no future in making frontal attacks against entrenched positions obstinately defended by magazine rifles and machine-guns supported by a powerful and well-handled artillery, though the losses were greatly increased by the Japanese practice of

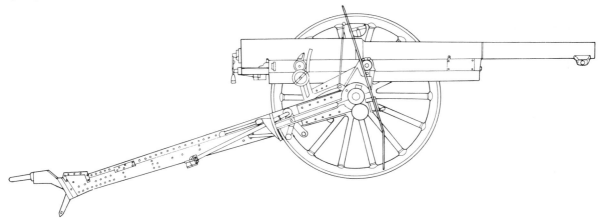

attacking in close formations and taking their colours into battle with them. Even by night they found it difficult, if not impossible, to cross open ground since the Russians made excellent use of electric searchlights to show the defenders their targets. The Russians used barbed wire, although they did not have as much of it as they required, and both sides reverted to the use of grenades, a weapon which had fallen into disfavour in the middle of the eighteenth century.

Had the Russians been freed from the dead hand of Stössel the defence could have been prolonged for many weeks. They still had 8,000,000 rounds for small arms and 200,000 shells while their food supplies could have been spun out for a long time. It is probable that had Smirnoff been in command Hill 203 would not have been lost but it must be open to question whether a longer defence would have convinced the Japanese that the prize was not worth the price that was being exacted from them in blood.

To other nations the lesson of Port Arthur was that attacks on fortified positions would, in future, be impossibly expensive. Many theorists turned back to Jomini and the 'strategy of the indirect approach' but other developments were conspiring to make every approach a direct one. Ever since Prussia had become a great military power the size of armies had been growing and every major power, except Britain and the United States, raised their armies by conscription. The population explosion of the nineteenth century meant that the yield of every country's annual intake of conscripts raised armies to sizes never previously contemplated. By the end of the Franco-Prussian War the German army had raised 850,000 men. This was the size of the German peacetime army (including officers, NCOs, one-year volunteers, and supernumerary recruits) in August 1914. Germany's mobilisation strength of trained men was 4,300,000. France should have been able to mobilise 567,000 men in 1870. In 1914 she had 856,000 men with the colours and a mobilisation strength (including troops in the colonies) of 3,683,000.

The common frontier between France and Germany was only 160 miles long so that the French would be able to defend it with 23,000 men to the mile, thirteen to the yard, a defensive strength which, properly dug in, would be unassailable. Even if, as the French were

Typical of the new rapid-fire artillery was the French 75-mm howitzer which had a range of 13,700 yards and a rate of fire of fifteen rounds per minute

French infantry in training in 1911; advancing in 'close lines of companies elbow to elbow'

most reluctant to believe, the Germans attacked the whole length of the Belgian frontier, the French would be able to deploy a defensive strength which would be impregnable on the whole front from the North Sea to the Swiss frontier even if they received no help from the Belgian field army of 117,000 men. The growth of armies meant that there was no position in western Europe that could not be held in impenetrable strength and with its flanks secured on impassable objects. Where there are no flanks there can be no indirect approach.

In 1914 neither of the main antagonists would accept the contention that any war between them must become a stalemate and the situation was complicated by the economists who asserted, with their customary bland omniscience, that no state could support the cost of a war for more than a few months. Both France and Germany convinced themselves of the necessity of a quick victory but they came to opposing conclusions as to how this must be achieved.

The French answer was the *attaque brusqué* on the grandest scale. Abandoning the experience of all armies since the introduction of the rifle (to say nothing of the machine-gun and their own *soixante-quinze*) they decided to give up loose formations and to send their infantry forward in 'close lines of companies marching elbow to elbow'. Their contention was that, regardless of casualties, only thus could fire power be built up and morale sustained.

The Germans put their faith in step by step attacks, each mounted only after intense artillery preparation. They paid lip service to open formations and, while their men were less tightly packed than the French, the British, with their South African experience, believed, when they had them in their sights, that the Germans were advancing shoulder to shoulder.

Thus neither side made preparations for the 'siege warfare in open country' that was to follow, although, almost coincidentally, the Germans found themselves better equipped for it than their enemies. While the French decided to deliver their suicidal assaults on the common frontier, the Germans, seeking an open flank, planned to swing their main thrust through neutral Belgium. To do so they had to overcome the powerful fortresses of Liège and Namur and, with

The coming of mobility

The nineteenth century brought a measure of mobility to the battlefield. The railway could be used, where it existed, to bring forward troops and stores to a railhead but as late as the Russo-Japanese war the Russian railhead at Mukden (RIGHT) had to discharge its stores into horse-drawn vehicles to get them to the troops. Developments in the air were first useful in extending vision. The balloons of the Air Battalion, Royal Engineers, (shown exercising at Frensham Ponds) (BELOW RIGHT) gave artillery observation officers the opportunity to see where their longer range shells were falling while the Bristol Boxkite (BELOW LEFT) allowed a commander to observe enemy movements further away than light cavalry could hope to penetrate. The early aeroplanes were, however, unsuitable for aerial combat and most of the pilot's attention had to be devoted to keeping his frail craft in the air

this in mind, they made a close study of siege work, paying particular attention to the Japanese experience at Port Arthur. In consequence they equipped themselves, on a limited scale, with such aids to siege warfare as trench mortars, hand-grenades, periscopes, flares, and searchlights. They also, alone among the European armies, acquired very heavy artillery, including 21-cm. howitzers, 30.5-cm. mortars (which were made in Austria), and, biggest of all, 42-cm. (16-inch) howitzers which fired a shell weighing a ton to a range of six miles. Thus, when the war settled down to prolonged trench fighting, the Germans had at least some of the weapons that were needed while their opponents were having to do with makeshifts, such as heavy naval guns on makeshift carriages, until better pieces could be designed and manufactured. Similarly when the first German hand-grenade was hurled at the British on 27 September 1914, the only reply they could make was a slab of gun cotton with a length of fuse attached. The British army had hand-grenades but they were so complicated and so expensive (they cost £1 1s. 3d. each) that it had not been thought worthwhile to bring them to war.

THE REVOLUTION IN MOBILITY

Away from the railways, the armies of 1914 were still restricted to the pace of the horse for the movement of field guns and supplies in the forward areas, but the development which was to increase tactical mobility on the battlefield was already under way. In 1885 Karl Benz of Mannheim had produced the first practicable 'horseless carriage' using the internal combustion engine. Naturally the first military application of the invention was to load-carrying and in March 1897 the Austro-Hungarian army took delivery of a 5-ton Daimler truck, the first self-propelled military vehicle in the world. In the same year the German army borrowed a 2-ton truck for tests and put in orders for another and a smaller version in the following year. On their grand manoeuvres of 1899 they used motor cycles for despatch carrying and some motor cycles were used by Britain in the South African war.

The return of mobility: Maxim guns loaded on motor vehicles (ABOVE) and signallers with a motor cycle (BELOW)

Soon all armies were using petrol-driven trucks. Britain formed her first Mechanical Transport Company, Army Service Corps, in 1902 and in 1914 all the warring armies used trucks to move stores from railhead to divisional depots from whence they were forwarded by horse-drawn vehicles. The mobilisation strength was achieved in most armies by a subsidy scheme whereby a civilian lorry owner received a payment on condition that he undertook to make his vehicle (which had to conform to certain standards) available to the army on the outbreak of war. The British system, which was typical of most, made a payment of £110 for each truck. £30 was paid on registration and the remainder in instalments at six-month intervals.

The movement of artillery received early attention. The British had used steam tractors in South Africa and, in fact, the Royal Engineers had acquired their first tractor as early as 1868, but the first use of the internal combustion engine to moving guns seems to have been when the Germans brought out a field gun *portée* (i.e. carried

on the back of a truck from which it is run down on ramps before firing) in 1910, the French following suit in 1911. As early as 1906 the French had produced a light vehicle mounting a Hotchkiss machine-gun pointing to the rear and about the same time the Germans produced a prototype armoured car with two machine-guns.

The advantages of motor cars for commanders were appreciated from an early stage. The Germans ordered their first staff car in 1900 and in 1902 Sir John French, commanding at Aldershot, was issued with 'a motor car . . . in order to facilitate the inspection of work in progress in your district, and also in order that this class of vehicle may be tried as to its suitability for aiding, by its capacities of rapid locomotion, the command of troops in the field'.

All these types of vehicle increased the mobility of armies but only, except under favourable circumstances, on roads or tracks. To play a full part on the battlefield the internal combustion engine needed a cross-country capability so that it could take to the fields, cross ditches, and, although this was little considered at the time, make its way through mud. The French set about achieving this by giving some of their vehicles six wheels and mounting the additional axle centrally. A truck of this design was produced for trials in 1903, having chain drive on the centre axle and steering on front and rear wheels. Vehicles of this kind took part in their army manoeuvres from 1907 onwards. The final answer was to be caterpillar tracks and here the British were the leaders. In 1907 a standard wheeled truck was equipped with tracks for army use and two years later the Royal Artillery acquired a number of 'Little Caterpillars' for moving the new 60-pounder guns. It is said that an Australian, L. E. Mole, put forward a design for an armoured tracked vehicle for fighting purposes in 1912.

The invention of the internal combustion engine was also to bring about another drastic change in the conditions of war. Men had been trying to fly for centuries and as early as 1785 Pierre Blanchard had crossed the English Channel in a balloon. In the same year a British officer, John Money, made two flights in a balloon during one of which he was blown out into the North Sea and spent seven hours up to his neck in water before being rescued. This did not prevent him from becoming an ardent advocate of the balloon for observation, a purpose for which the French used one at the Battle of Fleurus in 1794. They had also been employed at Solferino and in the American Civil War. In 1884 the balloon section of the Royal Engineers had attempted to assist in anti-guerrilla operations in Bechuanaland only to find that the base they had chosen was already so far above sea-level that the balloons would scarcely rise any higher. They were of more service directing artillery fire in the Boer War.

The extensive use of the air had to await the development of some compact and relatively non-flammable source of motive power. Steam, which had produced such a revolution in land and sea travel, was unsuitable since it had to be produced by fire, a dangerous element when juxtaposed with the hydrogen which kept balloons

The armies of 1914

By 1914 most armies had appreciated that they would lose fewer soldiers if their uniforms allowed them to merge into the landscape. The Prussian part of the Imperial army still, however, wore the ugly *pickelhaube* presumably in an attempt to impress their opponents. It was an absurd headgear since although heavy, it gave no protection to the head. The private, 157th Infantry (4th Silesian) Regiment (BELOW LEFT) is otherwise dressed in a practical fashion. The front and rear views of a British infantryman (BELOW CENTRE) show the 1907 pattern web equipment without the pack. In his pouches he can carry 150 rounds of ammunition (fifteen in each of ten pouches). His chest was left

unencumbered until, after 1915, he had to wear an anti-gas respirator. His cap is more practicable and more comfortable than the *pickelhaube* but affords equally little protection against shrapnel. The trooper, 4th Dragoon Guards (OPPOSITE ABOVE RIGHT), is dressed almost identically to the infantryman except that he has his ammunition in a bandolier. Although he has a sword, his principal weapon is an infantry-style rifle and bayonet for dismounted action. His German equivalent would have also carried a lance and some regiments still affected Uhlan-style *czapka*. From motives of economy French dragoons were still wearing brass helmets of grecian design and their infantry had red trousers. Some British regiments also kept distinctive headgear (OPPOSITE ABOVE LEFT). The divisional organisation (BOTTOM RIGHT) had increased enormously in complexity over the century

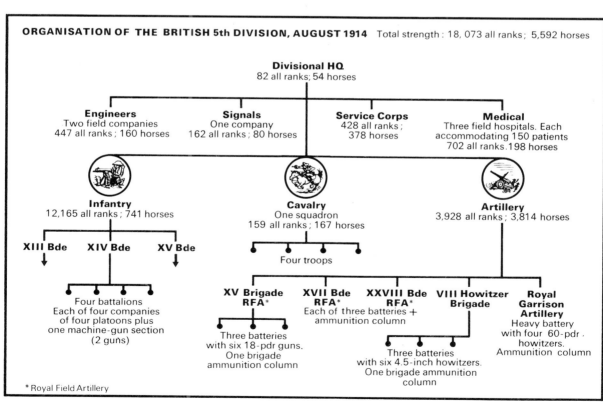

ORGANISATION OF THE BRITISH 5th DIVISION, AUGUST 1914 Total strength: 18, 073 all ranks; 5,592 horses

Divisional HQ
82 all ranks; 54 horses

Engineers
Two field companies
447 all ranks; 160 horses

Signals
One company
162 all ranks; 80 horses

Service Corps
428 all ranks;
378 horses

Medical
Three field hospitals. Each
accommodating 150 patients
702 all ranks. 198 horses

Infantry
12,165 all ranks; 741 horses

Cavalry
One squadron
159 all ranks; 167 horses

Artillery
3,928 all ranks; 3,814 horses

XIII Bde **XIV Bde** **XV Bde**

Four troops

Four battalions
Each of four companies
of four platoons plus
one machine-gun section
(2 guns)

**XV Brigade
RFA***

**XVII Bde
RFA***

**XXVIII Bde
RFA***
Each of three batteries +
ammunition column

**VIII Howitzer
Brigade**

**Royal
Garrison
Artillery**
Heavy battery
with four 60-pdr.
howitzers.
Ammunition column

Three batteries
with six 18-pdr guns.
One brigade
ammunition column

Three batteries
with six 4.5-inch howitzers.
One brigade ammunition
column

* Royal Field Artillery

aloft. The Austrians produced a gas-driven airship, capable of 3 m.p.h., in 1872 but in the same year the French flew one which travelled rather faster powered by human muscles. Twelve years later they commissioned *La France*, an electric-driven airship 162 feet long but the batteries were so heavy that the range was very short. The first experiments with petrol-powered flights were made by the Germans but their first aircraft caught fire in the air and crashed, killing its crew of two, while their second had to make a hasty descent and was torn to pieces by a derisive crowd. It was not until 2 July 1900 that Count Zeppelin made a successful flight of 3½ miles in a 400-foot airship. Seven years later, with his third machine, he made a flight of 211 miles in eight hours, an achievement which induced the German army to invest in his craft. Nevertheless seven of the first ten Zeppelins were wrecked or burnt.

Meanwhile the heavier-than-air flying machine had been born. On 17 December 1903 the Wright brothers made four short flights at Kitty Hawk, North Carolina. Flying into a 25 m.p.h. wind, the longest of these flights covered 852 feet and 'the landing was due to a slight error of judgment on the part of the operator'. The American, British, and French governments all refused to buy Wright aircraft until 1908, by which time flights of as long as an hour were possible in them, but the French were making their own experiments. They were several years behind the Wright brothers and their first flight, 80 yards, was not made until 1906 but they soon outstripped all competitors. In July 1909 Blériot flew the Channel in forty minutes and in the following month Henri Farman stayed in the air for three hours.

Building on this success, the French set about establishing a force of military aeroplanes and, in a creditably short time, devised means of using them for deep reconnaissance in front of, and in co-operation with, their cavalry. The Germans at this time were devoting all their attention to airships while the British remained undecided. An official report in 1912 echoed very closely their attitude to the introduction of steam at sea (see p. 57):

Up to the end of the year 1911 the policy of the government with regard to all branches of aerial navigation was based on a desire to keep in touch with the movement rather than hasten its development. It was felt that we stood to gain nothing by forcing on a means of warfare which tended to reduce the value of our insular position and the protection of our sea-power.

Nevertheless an Air Battalion, Royal Engineers, was established in that year with two companies, one for lighter and one for heavier-than-air craft.

There was much to be said for this open-minded attitude in the contemporary state of development. The military value of all types of aircraft was seen to lie wholly in reconnaissance and, while there were frequent and serious accidents to both types, the airship, with its ability to hover in the sky, seemed to have many advantages. Lord Roberts spoke for many when he said that as aeroplanes 'to sustain

British military aviation on review; various types in use with the army and navy at Hendon in 1912

themselves in the air, necessarily have to move at a very high speed, say from 30 to 40 miles an hour, I doubt whether a reconnaissance of value can be made at that speed'. Airships had a much longer range, an important factor especially in reconnaissance at sea, and their greater load-carrying capability made it possible for them to carry cameras and wireless telegraphy equipment enabling them to report quickly on their findings. It was not until the war of 1914 had been in progress for some weeks that W/T became a practicable proposition for aeroplanes, indeed, in the early models the noise of the engine made it impossible for the pilot to communicate even with his own observer.

The disadvantage of airships was their extreme vulnerability to the weather and the enemy, the first being the more serious hazard. It was almost impossible to land an airship safely in a high wind until the mooring mast was invented in 1919. Aeroplanes were, of course, equally exposed to weather hazards but they were cheaper and carried a smaller crew. Damage from enemy action was not considered a serious possibility. Since no high-angle artillery existed, all nations believed that their aircraft would be safe from enemy fire if they kept to a height of more than 3,000 feet. Air-to-air combat was an

Two maps showing the kaleidoscopic changes in the Balkans as the Ottoman empire was gradually squeezed out between 1878 (LEFT) and 1913 (RIGHT)

even less serious risk. An aeroplane could only fire to the front if it was a 'pusher' (i.e. had its propeller behind the pilot) and pushers were so slow that aerial combat could only be a tentative and inconclusive business. Some 'tractor' aircraft (i.e. with the propeller in front of the pilot) mounted light machine-guns pointing to the rear and sides but it was difficult to take seriously the risks of aeroplanes fighting back to back. Airships, on the other hand could mount heavy machine-guns and although their hydrogen containers were potentially vulnerable, they proved surprisingly difficult to ignite until the arrival, during the 1914 war, of tracer and incendiary bullets.

Despite the airship's advantages, opinion swung rapidly in favour of the aeroplane, due largely to a series of lighter-than-air disasters, although the German Parseval factory continued, up to the war, to sell non-rigid airships to the armies of Austria, Italy, Japan, and

Russia and to the British navy. The Germans, while maintaining a force of Zeppelins, gave priority to aeroplanes and found themselves in a strong position since the large engines developed for their airships were much more powerful than any aero engines available to the French and the British (who were almost wholly dependent on French engines).

Naturally there was some opposition to the new-fangled flying machines in all countries and the unreliability of the early types gave some justification to the conservatives. Not all their comments need to be taken at their face value, such as Lieutenant-General Sir James Grierson's remark to King George V: 'I think, Sir, that these aeroplanes are going to spoil war. When they come over I can only tell my men to cover their heads with hay and make a noise like a mushroom.' In fact Grierson made very intelligent and successful use of the seven biplanes allocated to his force in the manoeuvres of 1912 and became a strong advocate of the Royal Flying Corps which was formed out of the Air Battalion in that year.

It was the cavalry who had the most to lose from the advent of the flying machine. Their role in shock action was long since dead, if not buried. Their neglected function as dragoons could now be done by lorry-borne infantry and now their only remaining role, deep reconnaissance, was being pre-empted by the aeroplane.

CAMPAIGNS IN THE BALKANS

Bismarck remarked that 'the next European war will come from some damned silly incident in the Balkans' and, if the assassination at Sarajevo was no more than the spark which set off the final explosion, at least the dress rehearsal for the war was held in the Balkans. The Turks had barely recovered from a humiliating defeat at the hands of the Italians on the south shore of the Mediterranean when they were set upon by an uneasy alliance of Bulgaria, Greece, and Serbia which aimed to dispossess them of Macedonia. The first move was made on 8 October 1912 by the Montenegrins who invaded that age-old trouble spot the Sanjak of Novipazar. The Turks immediately mobilised and, for the first time in their history, the operation, which had been planned by German advisers, went with great smoothness. By the time that the three allies declared war there were 130,000 Turkish troops in Macedonia equipped with the latest Krupp guns, field telephones, steel pontoons, and all the latest paraphernalia of war, including a few aeroplanes manned by French pilots. Unfortunately none of these devices could be used since the Turks could not maintain them and even the artillery, which had done so well at Plevna, proved a disappointment since the long ranges of modern guns required skills in range finding and fuse setting which were beyond the capabilities of the gunners. The Turkish commissariat was as incompetent as ever and the only rations issued during the war came from 400 waggons of grain which the Serbs were importing through Salonica and which were impounded *en route*.

All three invading armies fought their way deep into Macedonia. The Turks, misjudging the plans of their opponents, launched an offensive against the Serbs north of Üsküb (Skoplje) and on 23 October they were within sight of breaking through at Kumanova. The Serbian defence was greatly outnumbered but entrenched rifles and well-directed artillery just managed to hold the line and, reinforced during the night, their counterattack drove the Turks back in a retreat that degenerated into a rout. On the previous day the Greeks, with a numerical advantage of three to one, had defeated the Turkish flank guard at Sarandaplron in the shadow of Mount Olympus, and on 9 November they took Salonica, beating the Bulgarians into the town by a short head.

There was little more fighting. The Bulgars seized Adrianople and threatened Constantinople, only to be halted by long-prepared and well-sited earthworks. The Serbs devoted most of their strength to capturing Durazzo (Durrës) in Albania, their long-coveted outlet to

Bulgarian machine-guns dug in during the second Balkan war. Note the range finder in the centre

the sea, of which they were later deprived by Austrian diplomatic pressure. The Greeks won a notable success at Yenidje-Vadar (Janitza), where they broke through a seemingly impregnable position while inflicting more casualties than they suffered. The striking feature of these battles was that, except for the Turkish repulse at Kumanova, all the victories went to the attackers, a reversal of all recent experience which was probably explained by a collapse of Turkish morale. It was noticeable that at Yenidje-Vadar, the Turkish troops, usually the dourest of defensive fighters, had had no rations for four days and could glean nothing from the barren countryside.

These successes for the offensive were repeated in the following year when, after peace with Turkey had been made, the Bulgars turned on their former allies in an attempt to grab a larger share of the spoils. They made a series of surprise (but not unexpected) attacks on the Greeks and Serbs who promptly went over to the offensive and, joined by the Romanians and Turks, defeated the Bulgarians every time they attacked them. Again it was largely the collapse of the defenders' confidence which was responsible for the victories but the fact that rifle fire and modern artillery did not succeed in halting assaulting infantry must have influenced those who, a year later, were planning offensive operations on a far wider scale in France and Flanders.

At sea the Balkan wars were not instructive. In 1912 the Turks had, on paper, a vastly superior fleet with four battleships and two cruisers against four Greek cruisers. The Turks, nevertheless, were most reluctant to emerge from the Dardanelles and when they did so were induced to turn tail by a single salvo from the four 9.2-inch guns of the brand-new Italian-built Greek cruiser *Giorgios Averoff*. This was not perhaps surprising since none of the Turkish battleships had been built since 1891 and the earliest of them dated from 1869.

EPILOGUE

Mons

War Office
August 1914.

To:— Field Marshal Sir John French, G.C.B., G.C.V.O., K.C.V.O.

    Owing to the infringement of the neutrality of Belgium by Germany . . . His Majesty's Government has decided, at the request of the French Government, to send an expeditionary force to France and to entrust the command of the troops to yourself . . .

    It must be recognised from the outset that the numerical strength of the British Force and its contingent reinforcements is strictly limited and, with this consideration kept steadily in view, it will be obvious that the greatest care must be exercised towards a minimum of loss or wastage.

    Therefore, while every effort must be made to coincide with the plans and wishes of our Ally, the gravest consideration will devolve on you as to participation in forward movements where large bodies of French troops are not engaged and where your Force may be unduly exposed to attack. Should a contingency of this sort be contemplated, I look to you to inform me fully and give me time to communicate to you any decision which His Majesty's Government may come to in the matter. In this connection I wish you distinctly to understand that your command is an entirely independent one,

243

*and that you will not in any case come under the
orders of any Allied General . . .*

*The high courage and discipline of your troops
should, and certainly will, have fair and full
opportunity of display during the campaign, but
officers may well be reminded that in this their first
experience of European warfare, a greater measure of
caution must be employed than under former
conditions of hostilities against an untrained
adversary . . .*

*Kitchener,
Secretary of State*

In 1815 Wellington had been given his commission as 'Commander of Our Forces serving on the Continent of Europe' and left to fight the war in his own way. Sir John French was instructed to indulge in no independent operations without first giving the cabinet an opportunity of discussing the pros and cons of his plan. Few things illustrate the technological advance made between Waterloo and Mons better than the British government's assumption that they would be able to control the movements of the British Expeditionary Force at the end of a telephone. One thing appeared not to have changed. The implied suspicion of Britain's main ally ('forward movements where large bodies of French troops are not engaged') suggests that the cabinet trusted the French little more in 1914 than they had in 1815.

At least the movement of the army across the Channel was very different from that of a century earlier. In 1815 regiments, battalions, and batteries had been scraped together, as best they could be found, and shipped piecemeal to Ostend. In 1914 the move of two Army Corps, each larger than Wellington's entire British contingent, was conducted with clockwork smoothness, no easy task since each of the four infantry divisions required eighty railway trains and in all 1,800 special trains were run in five days to get the expeditionary force and its stores to the embarkation ports.

There were, however, similarities. There were still far too few experienced staff officers. The decision to form the force into two Army Corps, each of two divisions, was taken at the last moment to conform with French practice. In peacetime only one corps staff existed but only in skeletal form while in the infantry divisions there were, until mobilisation, only two of the six staff officers called for in the War Establishment. When war was declared all the remaining appointments had to be filled with inexperienced newcomers and French's own staff was only gathered by taking tried men from the War Office.

Once railhead in France had been reached the problems and pace of moving cavalry, infantry, and artillery remained much as they had been but one small section of the force was entirely new. Four

PREVIOUS PAGE: British artillery during the retreat from Mons

squadrons of the Royal Flying Corps went to France. Flying from their peace stations at Montrose, Netheravon, Eastchurch, and Gosport to an assembly area in Kent, the motley collection of types of aircraft – B.Es, Bleriots, Avros, Henri Farmans – flew the Straits of Dover, two planes being wrecked and two damaged on the crossing. By 16 August they had reached their concentration area at Maubeuge having lost two more planes on the way. Their second-line transport was horse-drawn, waggons requisitioned from tradesmen and the speed of mobilisation had not given time for them to be repainted. In the early days of the campaign it was a comfort to the pilots of 5 Squadron to be able to identify their base by a scarlet van with 'The World's Appetiser' painted in gold on its sides.

There was no week-long journey by carriage across Europe for Sir John French. He left his temporary headquarters in the Metropole Hotel, Northumberland Avenue, on 14 August and reached Amiens that evening. His army had started embarking on 12 August, the troops taking ship from Southampton, Dublin, Cork, and Belfast; stores and supplies sailed from Newhaven while motor transport was embarked at Avonmouth and Liverpool (where frozen meat was also loaded aboard). By 20 August the entire force was assembled around Maubeuge with headquarters at Le Cateau.

The task of supplying this assembly of 100,000 men and 40,000 horses could now be tackled in a way very different from the self-help methods forced upon Wellington's commissaries. As the Quartermaster General described it:

'Bases' are established at selected overseas ports and there large depots of food, stores, men, animals, etc., are formed, and from these the supplies are sent up by rail to a 'regulating station'. From this place trains, each carrying the right proportion of each kind of article required, are despatched to 'railheads', i.e. the stations nearest to the front-line troops to which it is feasible to work the railway. Each railhead may serve one or more army corps according to circumstances, and at it the supplies are loaded on convoys of motor lorries called 'supply columns'. Each column then conveys the supplies of its division, or other formation to which it belongs, to previously selected rendezvous called 'refilling points', where they are met at the appointed hour by horsed waggons of the 'regimental train'. These, having been loaded with their proper quota of supplies, carry them to the units to which they belong. The distances travelled by the 'supply columns' may be as much as forty miles between railhead and 'refilling point', and the horsed waggons may cover six or seven miles each way.

If the mechanics of supply were more impressive than they had been in 1815, the fog of war lay quite as thickly on the battlefield. This was largely the fault of the French whose war plan laid down that: 'From a careful study of information obtained it is probable that a greater part of the German forces will be concentrated on the common frontier . . . Whatever the circumstances, it is the Commander-in-Chief's intention to advance, all forces united, to attack the German armies.'

The fact was that four of Germany's seven western armies, 940,000 of their 1,485,000 men, were not on the common frontier but were wheeling through Belgium but the French were so obsessed by their ill-fated offensive towards Strasbourg that they paid no attention to events in the north. They even neglected to establish contact with the Belgians. On 17 August, the day on which the Germans took Liège, Sir John French reported that the French had a cavalry corps north of the Sambre between Charleroi and Namur. This, he added, 'is the nearest French force to the Belgian army, and I do not know if and where they have established contact with them, nor do the French'.

Nor was Sir John helped by the sub-chief (and effective head) of his general staff. Major-General (later Field Marshal) Henry Wilson had such faith in his French allies that he refused to believe that the Germans were employing any significant forces north of the Meuse. It was on his inspiration that on 21 August the BEF started moving to a line near Mons with the intention of taking the offensive.

It was the aeroplanes that gave the first indication of the avalanche that was rolling across Belgium. The RFC's first reconnaissance flight was made on 19 August by two machines, a Bleriot and a B.E.8. Both lost their way but one saw a small body of cavalry heading south-east from Gembloux towards Namur. On the following day another aircraft, this time one carrying an observer, spotted two enemy forces of all arms. One was marching through Wavre, the other was a few miles to the north and both were heading south-west, towards Mons. 21 August saw the RFC fly three machines despite rain and mist. Large German forces were seen, with burning villages, in the vicinity of Charleroi and a cavalry division was observed to be in a large wood south of Nivelles, within 25 miles of Mons. On the same day British cavalry outposts saw German patrols approaching Mons on the north bank of the canal. The enemy soon withdrew and were taken to be the advance scouts of a larger force.

The first shots fired by the British in the war of 1914 were discharged by a patrol of the Fourth Dragoon Guards on the road between Mons and Soignies in the early morning of 22 August. Later that day a squadron of the same regiment charged some German horsemen. Since their enemy were armed with lances they reported that they had engaged uhlans but in fact all German cavalry were armed with the lance at this time and this particular unit were cuirassiers. The British squadron commander, echoing his predecessors who had fought Napoleon's lancers in Spain, noted: 'The uhlans were hampered by their long lances and a good many threw them away.'

The Dragoon Guards' charge was a success, several cuirassiers were killed with the sword and the rest forced into a hasty retreat. The Fourth pursued until brought up short by rifle fire from a cyclist battalion. They then dismounted and engaged the cyclists until withdrawn by their brigadier. That day the RFC flew twelve reconnaissance missions and, partly from aerial observation and partly from information gathered when two of the planes landed for petrol, confirmed the cavalry's view that heavy German forces, including cavalry, infantry, and artillery, were closing on Mons. The airmen added that more Germans were marching in a direction that would take them wide of the British left, an area held only by elderly French territorials and a cavalry corps. Sir John French was still determined to attack but this information, coupled with disquieting news from the French Fifth Army on his right, persuaded him that the army should halt on the following day to await more news. The Second Corps held the line of the Mons canal with the First on their right, swung back to try and keep touch with French First Army.

If the BEF knew little of the German's movements and tried to fit what they did know into a preconceived estimate of the enemy's intentions, the Germans were equally in the dark and disinclined to believe that the British were on their front. On 20 August the Supreme Command's information was that:

Disembarkation of the English at Boulogne and their employment from the direction of Lille must be reckoned with. The opinion here, however, is that large disembarkations have not yet taken place.

Their first definite indication of a British presence in France came on 22 August when a two-seater aircraft was shot down over German-occupied Belgium, the RFC's first battle casualties. General von Kluck, commanding First Army, believed that if the British appeared at all they would come from the direction of Tournai. He expected to find nothing but cavalry around Mons.

At British headquarters optimism was still in the ascendant. On 23 August Henry Wilson wrote in his diary:

During the afternoon I made a careful calculation and I came to the conclusion that we only had one corps and one cavalry division (possibly two corps) opposite us. I persuaded Murray [chief-of-staff] and Sir John that this was so, with a result that I was allowed to draft orders for an attack tomorrow, by Cavalry Division, 19th Brigade and 2nd Corps, to the north east, pivoted on Mons.

Wilson, comfortably isolated at Le Cateau, was drafting his orders 25 miles from Mons where Second Corps had been under fire of increasing ferocity since 9.00 am that morning. When the German field guns opened on the defenders of the canal line, one soldier recalled that: 'We didn't expect anything like the smashing blow that struck us. All at once, so it seemed, the sky began to rain down (shrapnel) bullets and shells.' Three hours earlier Sir John French had visited Second Corps headquarters and 'told us that little more than one, or at most two, enemy corps, with perhaps a cavalry division, were facing the BEF. Sir John was in excellent form and told us to be prepared to move forward or to fight where we were.' The Field Marshal then set out for Valenciennes, 8 miles behind his extreme left flank and did not reappear at his headquarters at Le Cateau until the middle of the afternoon, by which time his army had been closely engaged for six or seven hours.

The fact was that six German divisions, the equivalent of three corps, supported by cavalry were attacking two British divisions spread out over a front of 21 miles. The action developed from the (British) right to the left as the Germans in their wheeling movement came up to the British line. It was obvious that they did not expect to meet serious opposition. One Scottish soldier wrote:

They advanced in companies of quite 150 men in files five deep . . . We could steady our rifles on the trench and take deliberate aim. The first company were simply blasted away to Heaven by a volley at 700 yards and, in their insane formation, every bullet was bound to find two billets. The other companies kept advancing very slowly, using their dead comrades as cover, but they had absolutely no chance.

Except on the extreme right of Second Corps' front the British were protected by the canal, 64 feet wide, but even their outposts on the north bank were able to defend themselves by the weight and accuracy of their rifle fire. The Duke of Cornwall's Light Infantry had two companies across the canal some 8 miles west of Mons and the Germans did not start to attack them until late afternoon. According to their War Diary:

At about 4.45 pm the enemy began moving along the road southward from Ville Pommeroeuil towards the canal. He presented an extraordinary appearance, mounted men preceded by jägers all in close order, marching slowly and deliberately forward in one solid mass and occupying the entire roadway . . . The only fire that could be brought to bear was from the breastwork [across the road and holding only ten men]. The O.C. Post waited until the head of the advancing enemy reached the level crossing, the range of which was known to be exactly 750 yards. Then with combined sights at 750 and 800 yards fire was opened. The number of rifles was all too few, but every shot must have taken effect. The result upon the enemy was miraculous. In a moment the road was clear except for a few skirmishers at the level crossing who opened fire at so long a range as to be absolutely harmless.

Only on the extreme right of the Corps' front where there was no protection from the canal and where a whole division was attacking two battalions did the Germans make even the smallest advance and that at a savage cost in casualties. The German official account leaves no doubt of their view of the encounter:

Well entrenched and completely hidden, the enemy opened a murderous fire . . . casualties increased, the rushes became shorter and finally the whole advance stopped. With bloody losses the attack gradually came to an end.

In the British lines the troops were fascinated to hear the German bugles sounding 'Cease Fire' and, as darkness fell, men of the

Brandenburg Grenadiers could be heard singing *Deutschland über Alles.*

The Battle of Mons had shown what well-trained rifle fire could do even when backed by a numerically inferior artillery. But the BEF was soon to find itself with both flanks in the air and retreat was inevitable. It continued until, south of the Marne, the Germans themselves offered an open flank, but when the allies counterattacked they found that there was no way to break through a well-defended front. The First Battle of Ypres was the last desperate effort to find an open flank, to exploit the indirect approach, but when the 'Race to the Sea' finished in a dead heat, and the trench lines were established from the sea to the Alps, there was nothing left but frontal attacks foredoomed to failure in face of the rifle, the machine-gun, the quick-firing artillery, barbed wire, and the spade. The war could then only be won by attrition and it was appropriate that it was the countrymen of Ulysses S. Grant who should be the men to add sufficient numbers to the western alliance to grind the German army into defeat.

Selected Bibliography

Archibald, *The Wooden Fighting Ship of the Royal Navy* (1968)

Archibald, *The Metal Fighting Ship of the Royal Navy* (1971)

C. Brackenbury, *European Armaments in 1867* (1867)

E. P. Brenton, *The Naval History of Great Britain* (vol ii, 1837)

Bernard Brodie, *Sea Power in the Machine Age* (1941)

B. Burleigh, *The Khartoum Campaign* (1899)

Cambridge New Modern History (vol ix, 1965; vol x, 1960; vol xi, 1962)

Winston S. Churchill, *The River War* (2 vols, 1899)

G. S. Clarke, *Fortification* (1907)

Reginald Custance, *The Ship of the Line in Battle* (1912)

John Fortescue, *History of the British Army* (vols x–xiii, 1920–30)

John French (Earl Ypres), *1914* (1919)

Frank Friedel, *The Splendid Little War* (1958)

Michael Glover, *Rorke's Drift* (1975)

Reginald Hargreaves, *Red Sun Rising: The Siege of Port Arthur* (1962)

Frank A. Haskell, *The Battle of Gettysburg* (Ed. Bruce Caton) (1957)

G. F. R. Henderson, *The Science of War* (Ed. N. Malcom) (1905)

F. W. V. Herbert, *The Defence of Plevna* (2nd Edn.) (1911)

Christopher Hibbert, *The Destruction of Lord Raglan* (1961)

Alistair Horne, *The Fall of Paris* (1965)

Richard Hough, *The Fleet that had to die* (1958)

Michael Howard, *The Franco-Prussian War* (1961)

H. M. Hozier, *The Seven Weeks War* (1872)

Allan Keller, *The Spanish American War* (1969)

G. B. Laurie, *The French Conquest of Algeria* (1909)

Arthur J. Marder, *British Naval Policy 1880–95* (1941)

Frederick Maurice, *The Russo-Turkish War 1877* (1905)

Major Miller, *A Study of the Italian Campaign in 1859* (1860)

R. F. H. Nalder, *Royal Corps of Signals* (1958)

'An Officer', *The Sudan Campaign 1896–99* (1899)

U. Pericoli & M. Glover, *1815: The Armies at Waterloo* (1973)

Edwin A. Pratt, *The Rise of Rail Power in War & Conquest* (1915)

Walter Raleigh, *The War in the Air* (vol i, 1922)

William Robertson, *From Private to Field Marshal* (1921)

Albert Seaton, *The Crimean War: A Russian Chronicle* (1977)

Horace Smith-Dorrien, *Memories of Forty Eight Years Service* (1925)

John Terraine, *Mons* (1960)

H. W. Wilson, *Ironclads in Action* (2 vols, 1896)

C. M. Woodhouse, *The Battle of Navarino* (1965)

E. L. Woodward, *Great Britain and the German Navy* (1935)

Acknowledgments

BCA Picture Library: p. 164.
Bildarchiv Preussischer Kulturbesitz: pp. 126, 127 (both), 129, 130, 132, 140–1, 146, 147 (bottom).
Bulloz: pp. 36, 40, 42–3, 44, 147 (top).
Bundesarchiv: p. 194.
John Brichieri-Colombi: p. 82 (both).
Cooper-Bridgeman Library: p. 2.
Mary Evans Picture Library: pp. 30–1 (both), 82–3, 87 (top), 116, 133, 162, 163.
Giraudon/Paris Bibliotheque Nationale: pp. 43 (bottom), 145.
Giraudon/Paris Musee de l'Armee: pp. 46, 230–1.
Michael Holford/The Scots Guards: p. 72.
Imperial War Museum: pp. 235, 242.
Keystone Press Agency: p. 148.
Leeds City Art Gallery: p. 26 (bottom left).
Marius Bar: p. 64.
MARS: pp. 148 (top), 150.
MARS/ECP Armées, France: p. 122.
MARS/Fujifotos: pp. 188, 226.
MARS/National Army Museum: pp. 47, 74 (left), 93, 94, 157, 216, 219 (bottom), 221.
MARS/National Portrait Gallery: p. 203.
MARS/RAF Museum: p. 231.
MARS/Science Museum: p. 197.
MARS/US Navy: pp. 180, 190, 196.
MARS/US Signal Corps: p. 209 (both).
MARS/Roger Viollet: p. 213.
Mansell Collection: pp. 77, 91, 92.
E. J. Martin: pp. 52, 173.
J. G. Moore: pp. 25, 182–3, 183 (bottom), 207.
J. G. Moore/RAF Museum: p. 230.
J. G. Moore/US Navy: p. 69.
National Archives: pp. 105, 108, 109, 110 (both), 118 (left and right), 119, Endpapers.
National Army Museum: pp. 8, 10, 13, 15, 18, 20, 23 (both), 30 (top), 31 (top), 48, 49, 86, 87 (bottom), 159, 160, 198, 219, 232.
National Portrait Gallery: p. 90.
Peter Newark's Western Americana: pp. 6, 67 (both), 102, 106 (top left), 106 (bottom left), 107 (bottom), 111, 116–7.
Popperfoto: pp. 62, 166, 169, 171 (both), 175 (top), 193, 195.
Radio Times Hulton Picture Library: pp. 55, 99, 100, 125, 141, 153, 155, 168, 217, 224.
Real Photographs: p. 193.
W. P. Trotter Collection: pp. 57, 60, 70–1, 174 (top), 176, 177, 184, 193 (top).

Line artwork: John Batchelor
Map artwork: Richard Natkiel
Figure artwork: Richard Scollins

Index

Numerals in italic refer to captions